# Birdir

# Kent

C000253221

# Birding in Kent

DON TAYLOR

PICA PRESS
SUSSEX

© Don Taylor
Pica Press (an imprint of Helm Information Ltd.),
The Banks, Mountfield,
Nr. Robertsbridge,
East Sussex, TN32 5JY

ISBN 1-873403-53-4

A CIP catalogue record for this book is available from the British Library.

All rights reserved. No reproduction, copy or transmission of this publication may be made without written permission.

No paragraph of this publication may be reproduced, copied or transmitted save with written permission in accordance with the provisions of the Copyright Act 1956 (as amended), or under the terms of any licence permitting limited copying issued by the Copyright Licensing Agency, 7 Ridgmount Street, London WC1 7AE.

Any person who does any unauthorised act in relation to this publication may be liable to criminal prosecution and civil claims for damages.

Front cover: Dungeness landscape depicting three species of birds originally described from Kent, Sandwich Tern, Kentish Plover and Dartford Warbler. Painted by David Boys.

Back cover: White-throated Needletail *Hirundapus caudacutus* at Wierton Hill Reservoir on 26 May 1991. Photographed by Don Taylor.

Computer graphics and typesetting by Fluke Art, Bexhill-on-Sea, East Sussex.
Printed and bound by Hartnolls Limited, Bodmin, Cornwall.

# CONTENTS

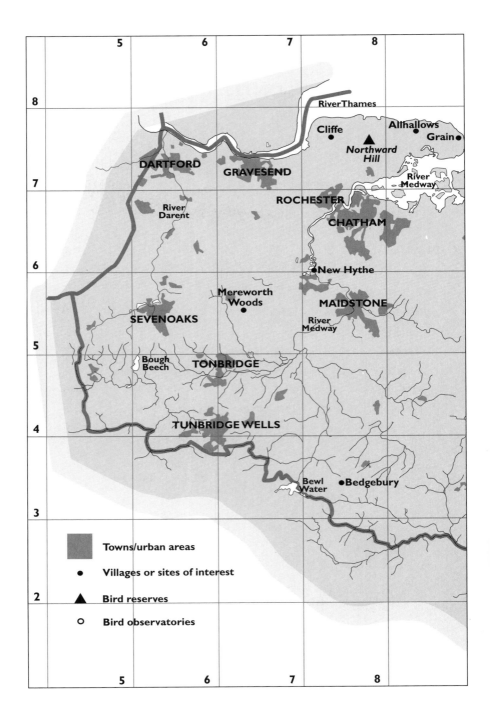

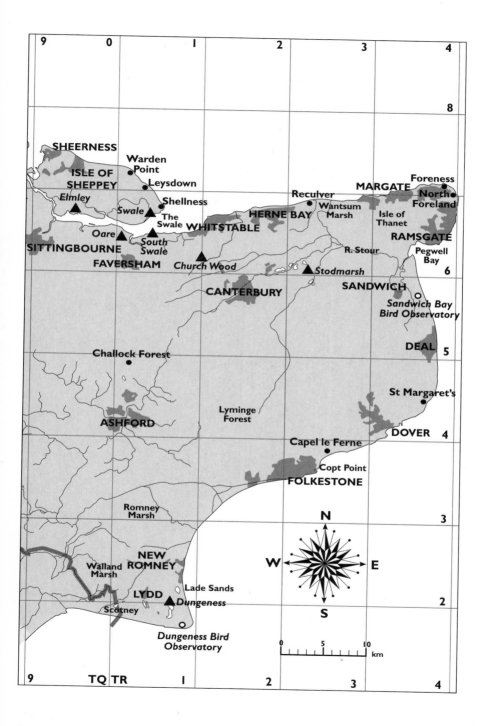

*To the late Peter Stoodley for his
friendship, support and encouragement*

# Foreword

When I was a teenage birdwatcher, living in landlocked Birmingham, I was in the habit of seeking out books about estuaries and coastlines, and promising myself that one day I'd go and check out some of these places myself. One of the books that made a very big impression on me was called *The Birds of the North Kent Marshes*. It told me of as yet unseen birds and unfamiliar landscapes, and I was enthralled. Thus, when I moved to London in the early sixties, I set out to explore Kent. And not just the northern marshes. As it happened, I had been in the county once during my schoooldays. I'd spent a week at Dungeness Bird Observatory, where I just about survived Bert Axell's almost paramilitary regime. It was an experience that – in terms of early mornings, discipline and spartan accommodation – should have qualified me for a Duke of Edinburgh's Award! To be fair though, I saw some good birds and discovered how fanatical birdwatchers, especially ringers, can be.

Anyway, my Kent explorations since then have generally been a little more relaxing. They have also been immensely enjoyable and, over the years, have left me with many memorable images. Some have been individual birds I went down specially to 'tick off', like the Stodmarsh Glossy Ibis, or the Sheppey Rock Thrush. Others have been happy surprises – a Broad-billed Sandpiper pitching down in front of a hide at Elmley and lit up by a glorious evening sun; or the trip of a dozen Dotterel that delighted me and the late Peter Grant and, most of all, the bloke we were visiting for Sunday lunch who'd never seen the species before. The birds were in fact in a field next to his house, right in the middle of the county, not at one of the 'traditional sites'. Perhaps that incident sums up one of the continuing delights of Kent. There are definitely good spots still to be discovered. That is pretty amazing considering how heavily watched the region is these days.

It is surely the variety of the habitats and special places that ultimately makes Kent so inexhaustibly rewarding for birdwatching, and indeed nature study in general; the woods and their butterflies, the dunes and their orchids, the marshes and their dragonflies – all these as well as the birds. Actually, when it comes down to it, it is simply a terrific county to be out and about in.

This book is a testimony to Don Taylor's expertise, thoroughness and, above all, enthusiasm. I doubt that you will find a more complete compendium of what makes a birdwatcher's particular region so special to him, or a better example of how to make the most of it. After reading this book, I am personally left with two wishes. One is that I can get to Kent even more often in the future – no matter what state the M2 is in! The other is that young birdwatchers might read this and be inspired to explore for themselves, just as I was many years ago.

Bill Oddie

# Introduction

This book, like *Birdwatching in Kent* (1985), describes different ways of enjoying birdwatching in Kent, together with detailed information on the birds and the habitats in which they occur. The inspiration for both books came from my own enjoyment of birding and my considerable involvement, through the Kent Ornithological Society, with the study of birds in this county. My enthusiasm remains unabated and I hope that this book will suggest a variety of ways in which others will be able to share the pleasures of birdwatching in Kent.

Due to its close geographical relationship to the Continent, its lengthy coastline and wide variety of natural and man-made habitats, Kent attracts a considerable number of different species. The major habitat types are described in the book as well as some of their typical birds.

Interest in birdwatching continues to increase and I am convinced that it is not just because new technology has accelerated the speed of communication about desirable rarities and where they may be found, but because you can select your own individual level of interest. For some, this means an appreciation of garden birds, and occasional days out, for which I will suggest some itineraries. Others find particular satisfaction in studying one small area regularly; my experiences of my own patch are described in the book. Visits to bird observatories give an opportunity to witness bird migration, or to assist with bird ringing. Some like to concentrate on watching seabird movements and are happy to sit for hours, in all weathers conditions, gazing out to sea. Others like the challenge of listing, building annual, county or life lists of species identified; I will describe a single day during which I saw more than 140 species, and a year when I managed to see over 240 species in Kent. I will also make suggestions for regular birdwatching trips during a calendar year.

## Organisations

A concern for the welfare of our birds may lead to an interest in the conservation of habitat, and to membership of the Kent Trust for Nature Conservation. Again, there are different levels at which you can become involved in this worthy organisation.

The Kent Ornithological Society, which was founded in 1951 to study and record all aspects of the avifauna of Kent, plays a major role in conservation by producing the facts – the numbers and distribution of birds throughout the county. Anyone interested in contributing records, or getting involved with surveys and census work, will find much scope for this by joining the Society. In return, there is the opportunity to share the interest with others, while receiving regular Newsletters and Annual Reports. The *Birds of Kent*, published by the Kent Ornithological Society in 1981, with a second edition in 1984, is an essential reference for serious birdwatchers living in the county. A new *Birds of Kent* is now in production which will include the results of the latest Breeding Bird Survey, as well as a thorough analysis of the records for the twenty-year period 1977-96.

The Royal Society for the Protection of Birds has various local groups operating in Kent. They meet regularly, and among other activities raise money for the purchase of items like hides on their reserves. In Kent there are four RSPB reserves, at Dungeness, Northward Hill, Church Wood and Elmley, with hopes of another at Cliffe in the future. The RSPB also manages Tudeley Woods and Nor Marsh.

The British Trust for Ornithology organises bird censuses throughout the United Kingdom. Bird population study is absolutely vital in establishing the true numbers of our British species, and is the sort of thing in which individuals can assist. The BTO is always on the look out for volunteers. Typical surveys for which they need help are the Breeding Bird Survey (BBS), the Waterbird Breeding Survey (WBS) and the Common Bird Census

(CBC). The BTO also has overall responsibility for bird ringing in the United Kingdom. The addresses of all these organisations may be found in Appendix IV.

## Numbers of Species

Recording the number of different species seen during specific periods of time, or for different areas, is one of the challenges that many birdwatchers enjoy. By the end of 1994 the total number of species on the Kent list had risen to 390, of which 352 have been seen during the last ten years. These are all included in the Systematic List. On average a total of 275 species is recorded each year, the highest number being 285 in 1994.

It is fascinating to see the influence that the increased interest in birdwatching has had on the Kent species list. There are other factors, of course, notably the establishment of the two observatories, at Dungeness and Sandwich Bay, and the natural expansion of species' ranges, such as the Collared Dove, and Savi's and Cetti's Warblers, which have colonised Kent and other parts of Britain in recent decades. During 1900-1954, just 28 species were added to the county list – one species every two years. In the 40 years since then, the additions have averaged over two species per year. Exceptionally, there were ten new species in 1984 and six in 1989.

## Additional New Species

In *Birdwatching in Kent*, I suggested that three North American gulls were likely to occur soon. Two of them, Ring-billed and Bonaparte's, have done so. I am sure it will not be long before Franklin's Gull joins them. As for other new species, it is tempting to suggest another American warbler – the Blackpoll Warbler in December 1994 at Bewl Water was just over the county boundary. However, in addition to Franklin's Gull, the following could well comprise a top ten candidate list. A Little Crake is really overdue, while some wader species are great travellers – what about a Killdeer from North America, or maybe a White-tailed Plover from further east? Another eastern thrush, like Eye-browed, can certainly be expected, while possible passerines include Citrine Wagtail, Lanceolated Warbler and Pine Bunting. A Ross's Gull, probably easier to identify than the previous three, would be greatly appreciated by many. Finally, one of the next additions to the British list may well be Audouin's Gull, which is increasing its range; so why not find the first one in Kent?

## Identification and Equipment

The ability to identify birds is one of the pleasures that is essential to the enjoyment of birdwatching. It is a skill which produces new challenges all the time. In its most sophisticated form, it is an exacting art, but it is possible to set your sights at any level. The fascinating discussion regarding identification by character or 'jizz' and the 'new approach to identification' continues (Hume 1990, Grant & Mullarney 1989). Each has its place, while aspects of both techniques can be crucial for correct identification of certain more difficult species.

You will of course need a good pair of binoculars and a reliable field guide. There is such a varied choice of optical aids available that I would recommend seeking advice from experienced observers. Try out several different binoculars before committing yourself. Some of the optical companies set up exhibitions of their products from time to time, where you can test them in the field, for example at bird fairs, at Dungeness and at Bough Beech. A number of the birdwatching magazines periodically test and review optical equipment, including telescopes as well as binoculars.

The best field guide at present is unquestionably *Birds of Europe with North Africa and the Middle East* by Lars Jonsson (Helm). Less expensive, but good value is *Birds of Britain and Europe* by Brunn, Delin and Svensson (Hamlyn) and *Birds of Britain and Europe* by Heinzel, Fitter and Parslow (Collins), the latest editions of which are vastly superior to earlier ones. I would also recommend *The RSPB Book of British Birds* by Holden and Sharrock (Macmillan), which is an attractive identification guide just covering the 272 most common species found in the British Isles, if that is where your main interest lies. An extremely good pocket guide for use in the field is *The Mitchell Beazley Birdwatcher's Pocket Guide* by Peter Hayman. One other book that I strongly recommend is *The Macmillan Field Guide to Bird Identification* by Harris, Tucker and Vinicombe. It is much more than an identification guide – it is a problem solver, suitable for all birdwatchers whether experienced or not. It concentrates on separating 'confusion species', with each plate comparing those birds which have strong similarities, such as Chiffchaff and Willow Warbler. Have a good look at a range of field guides and seek advice from experienced observers. Acquiring field skills is the vital factor and birding with someone who has these skills can save many frustrating hours. Joining the KOS or one of the local RSPB groups and going on their field meetings is a good way to get started. Try to get to know the common species first, in all plumage stages, and learn their various calls and songs. A wide selection of tape recordings is now available and listening to sounds on a cassette tape or CD is a good way to learn. *All the Bird Songs of Europe* by Jean C. Roché is the most comprehensive compilation. The ear is an invaluable aid, not only in identification but also for locating birds. Get into the habit of using a notebook in the field rather than relying on your memory. Try to record precisely what you see, as you see it. Simple outline sketches can help to show the distribution of plumage colour, but it is more useful to know the names of the different feather tracts so that you can relate the colours to them. So much can be of value when trying to identify a bird, not just plumage and bare part colours, but size, shape, general proportions, behaviour, manner of feeding or flight, as well as calls or song. When you have completed your description, add notes about the habitat and weather, your optical aids and distance from the bird. As your knowledge increases, you will begin to learn what characteristics separate similar species.

## Acknowledgements

Finally, I take this opportunity to thank all those who have given me encouragement and support for this project. In particular, the Kent Ornithological Society who gave me permission to use their records, and Bob Bland, whose frequent visits to Boughton Park and Wierton Hill Farm helped to provide more complete data for the chapter on a local area study. Thanks are due to David Boys for his delightful vignettes and original cover design. I am also greatly indebted to Trish Pringle, June Stoodley, David Davenport, Andrew Henderson and David Tomlinson for their helpful comments on the original draft. Finally, thanks to Christopher Helm and Nigel Redman of Pica Press, and Julie Reynolds and Marc Dando of Fluke Art for their expertise in the editing and production of this book.

Cormorants

# Kent Habitats

This county is blessed with a wide range of habitats, both natural and man-made. In this chapter and in the systematic list a number of specific localities where you are most likely to find particular species are mentioned. I also strongly recommend exploring other areas of similar habitat. Once you are familiar with a habitat and the species it attracts, it is often more satisfying to find your own birds elsewhere. This also takes the pressure off frequently watched sites.

Kent County Council produces an excellent series of countryside publications. Its pamphlet *Kent Countryside and Coast* describes over 80 sites to visit, from country parks to nature reserves, and many are good for birds. Again, once you have identified species with habitat, it will pay to search for other sites, if you have the time. Records, particularly on a regular basis from less well-known sites, will be useful to the Kent Ornithological Society to aid conservation.

Natural sites like Dungeness and managed reserves such as Elmley are unique, but one of the pleasures that I derive from birdwatching is that it encourages me to explore areas relatively undisturbed by other humans. There are still such areas in Kent, despite the ever increasing population and expanding road and rail networks. A more encouraging aspect of land use is the way that a few farmers are taking positive strides to conserve and improve habitats for wildlife, alongside their essential commercial crops. I find the idea of a 'conservation crop' an attractive one and hope that many more farmers will adopt this practice, making use of subsidies available from the European Union.

Although I find great pleasure in the peace and quiet of the countryside, sharing a hide on a reserve does provide an opportunity to gain from the experience of others. As with all things, a degree of compromise is required.

The large scale 1:50,000 Landranger Ordnance Survey maps are invaluable for discovering new areas and locating footpaths, and the even larger 1:25,000 Pathfinder Series is excellent when you wish to concentrate on smaller areas, within one or two 10 kilometre squares.

In the following paragraphs, I describe a number of habitat types and mention the species that are commonly associated with them.

## Chalk Downland

The North Downs, stretching the length of the county, from Westerham in the west to Dover in the east, provide a rich and varied habitat for a number of species. Some open grassland remains, but much of the escarpment, which is too steep to plough, is now covered with thorn, yew, ash and beech woodland. The combination of grassland and mature trees attracts species such as Green Woodpecker, while the open scrub is much favoured by Linnets and Yellowhammers. Of particular interest are the mature beech woods. Here, in the winter months, the beech mast attracts a few Bramblings with the Chaffinches. Hawfinches also find beech, ash and in particular hornbeam, much to their liking and a few pairs breed regularly in areas where these trees predominate. Most members of the tit family can be expected, including Coal Tit amongst the yews and Marsh Tit in the deciduous woodland. A few pairs of Long-eared Owls probably breed regularly, but nocturnal visits are needed; hearing the adults calling will establish their presence. However, you may be fortunate enough, during daylight hours on summer walks, to hear the distinctively mournful calls of the young. Regular observation will produce several raptor species. Common Kestrel and Sparrowhawk can be anticipated throughout the year, although both become secretive during the breeding season. Common Buzzards are seen occasionally and in the winter months Hen Harrier, and even Merlin, occur from time to time.

## Woodland and Parkland

The variety of woodland habitat in the county provides suitable sites for nesting, feeding and roosting for a wide range of species . Some mature woodlands near river valleys or marshes attract breeding Grey Herons, as they have done at Chilham, for example, for hundreds of years. The heronry at Northward Hill, which may hold over 200 pairs, is the largest in Britain. When will the first Little Egrets breed there, I wonder? Rookeries are widespread in all sorts of woodland, where the commonest breeding species are Wren, Robin, Blackcap and Chiffchaff, along with Willow Warbler where young stands are present.

Some species have more specialised requirements. The relatively scarce Common Redstart prefers mixed woodland and parkland, with old timber to provide nest holes, while the Wood Warbler, which has also declined as a breeding species, favours sessile oak, mixed with birch and bracken. Common Nightingale breeds quite commonly, with higher concentrations in the woods around Canterbury, but it requires dense undergrowth to provide sufficient ground cover for nesting. Sweet chestnut coppice and young conifer plantations provide suitable breeding habitat for Tree Pipits, Woodcock and a few pairs of Nightjars. Following the great storm in 1987, the numbers of Nightjars increased, as large areas of forestry plantation were first decimated, then cleared and replanted. Grasshopper Warblers, which were once attracted to young conifer plantations, have declined in recent years, but a few pairs of Golden Orioles occasionally breed in copses of sweet chestnut.

Dense conifer plantations attract Goldcrests and Coal Tits, and occasionally a few pairs of Common Crossbills. The Firecrest, too, has recently colonised this habitat, favouring mature Douglas Fir and Norway Spruce. The pinetum at Bedgebury is renowned for attracting finches to roost, including good numbers of Hawfinches, Bramblings and Siskins.

Hobbies and Sparrowhawks now breed in increasing numbers. The persecution of the Sparrowhawk and some of the larger raptors has declined and perhaps the Common Buzzard may start breeding in the county soon. The range has expanded into Sussex in recent years and much of our woodland seems suitable, particularly along the North Downs.

Few woodland walks are complete without hearing or seeing a Great Spotted Woodpecker, or watching a Nuthatch pecking at an acorn, which it has wedged in a cleft, or almost running over the bark as it hunts for insects.

One important aspect linked with the parkland and public open spaces in this county, is the presence of small lakes, often created by damming streams. As Kent has virtually no natural lakes, these man-made waters provide an important habitat for waterfowl. The Canada Goose is now widespread in Kent. Large flocks frequent Mote Park and the Leeds Castle grounds, often flighting between the two. During the breeding season, many disperse to small ponds scattered over the neighbouring farmland to nest and raise their broods. Moorhens, Coots, Little and Great Crested Grebes are usually present too, along with Mallard and Tufted Duck, the numbers of which increase during the winter months. The colourful Mandarin Duck is slowly spreading: it requires old trees with holes for nesting. Visits from less common wildfowl, such as Eurasian Wigeon, Gadwall, Common Pochard and Goldeneye can occur, particularly during cold spells. The muddy fringes may attract migrant waders during the spring and autumn, and in the more boggy, reed-fringed areas Water Rail, Common Snipe and even Jack Snipe may be found in the winter.

The typical short grassland is much favoured by Green Woodpeckers, often to be seen on playing fields, pecking for ants. Both the Great Spotted and Lesser Spotted Woodpeckers may also be found, particularly where there is dead wood, while the thin, high-pitched song and calls of Common Treecreeper and the piping call of the Nuthatch are frequently heard. The deer-grazed pasture and ancient oaks of Knole Park still attract nesting Common Redstarts.

# Wealden Farmland and Hedgerows

Throughout the year the Lapwing was once a common sight on the pasture and arable land of the weald. It has declined as a breeding species, but in the autumn and winter months large flocks can still be seen, unless the ground becomes snow-covered. They then disperse to milder climes and flocks can often be seen flying south-west. The Golden Plover, too, favours certain meadows, particularly those below the greensand ridge between Sutton Valence and Boughton Monchelsea, near Rabbit's Cross. Here, wintering flocks of up to 500 can be seen, and similar numbers may occur on the return passage during March and early April, when attractive summer plumaged birds are a bonus. Of the gulls, Black-headed is the species most frequently seen following the plough and feeding, though a few Common Gulls also occur. Both Grey and Red-legged Partridges are to be expected, though their numbers, too, have declined in recent years. Flocks of hungry Rooks frequently blacken the fields while they search for leatherjackets.

Hedgerows provide invaluable cover for many birds. They are the motorways of the natural world – routes for the wildlife of the countryside. Thrushes, warblers and finches of various species find the variety of bushes and trees to their liking for nesting and feeding. The more mature hedges, with occasional trees, attract such species as Lesser Whitethroat, while those with broad bases provide cover for Grey Partridge and Yellowhammer to nest. As you walk along hedgerows during the winter months, you are likely to come across such species as Long-tailed Tits, Bullfinches and Magpies. Little Owls may be seen perched on a fence post or a low branch; their angry-looking yellow eyes will often be focused on you, and if you choose to try, you'll have difficulty outstaring the owl.

# Rivers and Wetlands

The many tributaries and the main rivers of the Darent, Medway and Stour attract such resident species as Grey Wagtail and Common Kingfisher, and in the winter months the alders, which are often associated with damp areas, are much favoured by Siskins.

The excavation of gravel along the Medway Valley below Aylesford has increased the attraction of this area, not only for wintering wildfowl, but also for common breeding species such as Meadow Pipit and Yellow Wagtail. However, the Stour Valley, partly as a result of man's intervention, now provides diverse breeding sites for a great variety of species. Extensive reedbeds are scarce in Kent and those at Westbere and Stodmarsh are renowned for the attractive and successful Bearded Tit. Whether Cetti's Warbler will return to breed remains questionable, since their demise as a result of the cold winters of the eighties. More hopefully, again with man's intervention, it is possible that Common Bitterns may once more boom before nesting. In parts of Stodmarsh NNR, English Nature has undertaken to produce the breeding habitat that this fascinating species requires. In another area a flood has been created and Garganey, together with freshwater waders such as Wood Sandpiper and Ruff, can certainly be anticipated during spring and autumn. The new hide provides excellent opportunities to see these attractive species.

The drumming of Common Snipe and the song of the Water Rail are additional attractions in the spring, while large numbers of migrant Reed and Sedge Warblers, and their attendant Common Cuckoos, breed commonly. In recent years, Hobby numbers have increased. Up to ten or more can sometimes be seen in the air together during late May and early June, before they disperse to breed. The proximity of the Stour Valley to the coast helps to make it a good site for vagrants, such as Purple Heron and Spotted Crake. Exceptionally, extreme rarities such as Cattle Egret, Whiskered Tern, Pallas's Warbler and Isabelline Shrike have been seen. In the winter months, the number and variety of waterfowl increases. One of the main attractions for many observers is the gathering of Hen Harriers towards dusk, before roosting in the reedbeds. In some winters Stodmarsh is a site much favoured by the scarce Great Grey Shrike, but as this species hunts over an extensive winter territory, it can be difficult to see.

Wetlands generally are on the decline and much of Romney and Walland Marshes is now well drained. However, some conservation-minded farmers are aware of the benefits of returning some of their land to its traditional wet state, which would encourage breeding species such as Garganey and possibly Black-tailed Godwit to return. The number of wintering Bewick's Swans now exceeds 300 on Walland Marsh, providing a magnificent spectacle, together with the roosting Hen Harriers and an occasional Barn Owl. Mute Swans also form large winter flocks, grazing on what pasture remains or moving into the arable fields. Similar habitat exists on the Chislet and Wantsum Marshes, north of the Stour Valley, and on the North Kent Marshes.

## Reservoirs

As there are no natural inland waters, apart from rivers, the development of two reservoirs in the west of the county has provided a most attractive new habitat, particularly as sections of them have been set aside as nature reserves. Sadly, boundary changes now mean that none of Bewl Water remains in Kent. However, at Bough Beech the public vantage points afforded by the causeway provide a good opportunity to see most of the visiting waterfowl and many other regular and rarer visitors. The number of species recorded there, since it was created in 1969, is now over 230.

In the winter months, particularly during severe weather, the Goosander is a regular visitor to Bough Beech and a few Smew may also be seen. Goldeneye and rarer surface feeding duck such as Pintail occur. Exceptionally, divers and rare grebes may visit, but they are more regular during the spring migration period. Mandarin and Ruddy Ducks are scarce visitors throughout the year.

In spring, the overland migration of waders and waterfowl can be well observed at Bough Beech. Brief visits by such species as Common Scoter, Whimbrel, Bar-tailed Godwit and Common Tern often coincide with the main up-Channel passage off Dungeness. A good variety of other species can also be anticipated.

Bough Beech provides breeding sites for Great Crested and Little Grebes, Canada Geese and a few duck species, as well as many passerines. A man-made reedbed on the nature reserve attracts nesting Reed Warblers. For some years, Little Ringed Plover bred here. To prevent predators such as Carrion Crows from taking the eggs, the nests were covered with wire cages, and this proved to be very successful. In 1995, after an absence of a few years, they successfully bred again.

In autumn, the overland passage is again well marked and waders often make longer visits. Terns too may stay for a few days. In good autumns, five species may be seen including the attractive Black Tern. A few flocks of Brent Geese may be seen flying south-west during late October and early November. In recent years it has become a surprisingly good area for seeing raptors. Ospreys occur annually and have been seen visiting the man-made nest platform, erected to encourage them to stay. Will they ever be tempted to breed? Sparrowhawks are resident and Hobbies may be seen throughout the summer months. The Marsh Harrier is an almost annual migrant and rarer species such as Common Buzzard, both Red and Black Kites, and Goshawk have been recorded.

## Gravel Pits

Old gravel workings, particularly those that have become reserves, now provide invaluable refuges for many species, not just waterfowl. Some, in co-operation with the owners, have been worked with the future interests of birds in mind. Those at Sevenoaks and Dungeness are prime examples. Without gravel workings there is no doubt that Little Ringed Plover would still be a scarce migrant. Instead, it is a regular breeding species, albeit in small numbers. Another new breeding species, attracted to the gravel pits of the Dungeness Reserve, is Mediterranean Gull. Roseate Tern has nested occasionally and after nearly 40 years absence Sandwich Tern has returned. Common Gull, a rare breeding species in southern England, also nests there.

In addition to other breeding species such as Great Crested Grebe, Tufted Duck and Common Tern, the gravel pits attract many wintering wildfowl, including Goldeneye, Goosander and Smew. Migrant waders, particularly common species such as Green and Common Sandpipers, are frequent visitors. Some of the shore waders may roost on the pits at high tide, as do many gulls. Regular watching will inevitably produce scarce species as well as extreme rarities. As well as those pits on the reserve, including the ARC pit and the New Diggings, there are others on Dengemarsh and at Scotney, and a little further north at Lade.

Without man's interest in excavating sand, relatively few Sand Martins would be nesting in Kent. Not surprisingly, the breeding distribution of this species closely coincides with the geological map showing the location of greensand in the county.

## Coastline and Estuaries

The long and varied coastline is a haven for many birds. Facing north, east and south, migrants from all three directions can be expected, according to the season and prevailing weather.

Dungeness, the unique shingle spit that juts out into the English Channel, provides an ideal point from which to observe seabird passage in spring and autumn. Southerly winds in summer may bring Manx Shearwaters within sight of the shore.

Although nuclear power stations may have a harmful effect on the environment as a whole, the effect for a few birds has so far been positive. Black Redstart is attracted by these man-made 'cliffs' and a large percentage of the county's small breeding population is associated with them, or similar industrial buildings. The warm water outflows provide a great attraction for feeding gulls and terns. Close to the shore and locally known as the 'Patch', the Dungeness outflow offers an ideal opportunity to study these species, as well as the chance of seeing a rarity such as the Laughing Gull that appeared last summer, or a skua creating havoc amongst the gulls and terns.

The wardens at the bird observatory will usually welcome anyone interested in the activities of this well sited ringing station. They can direct you around the trapping area and tell you what is about. By becoming a 'Friend of Dungeness' you will not only help to finance the work of the observatory, but you will also gain access to the seawatching hide and receive regular Bulletins and the annual *Dungeness Observatory Report*. Although the area, to some eyes, may not be the most scenically attractive, it can be most exciting, particularly when there has been a fall of migrants. Among the large numbers of commoner species one always hopes to find something more unusual. In the autumn, such species as Pied Flycatcher and Common Redstart, and the rarer Wryneck and Icterine Warbler, are regular visitors.

Working north, towards Greatstone, Lade Sands attracts large numbers of feeding gulls and waders when the tide is out, and is an area much favoured by Sanderling. All along this coast in the winter months, flocks of Great Crested Grebes form, while divers can sometimes be seen close to the shore. Folkestone Harbour and Copt Point are also good areas for studying gulls, the latter in particular is the best site in the south-east for seeing numbers of Mediterranean Gulls. Shags too may be seen here, more often in the winter months.

Folkestone Warren provides a sheltered haven for passerine migrants, occasionally attracting rarer species, while in winter the foreshore attracts Purple Sandpipers and Rock Pipits. The chalk cliffs from here northwards attract breeding Fulmars and Kittiwakes, while the extremely successful Herring Gull is now nesting on numerous rooftops. The return of the Peregrine as a breeding species is a more welcome change.

For studying migration, the cliff top between Capel-le-Ferne and Abbot's Cliff is good. In addition to numbers of common passerine migrants, there are almost annual sightings there of rarities such as Alpine Swift as well as migrant raptors.

Stonechats and Black Redstarts are both specialities of the Dover area, the former sometimes breeding on the clifftop gorse and the latter on the old wartime buildings, either on the cliff or around the town.

The sheltered, wooded valley near the lighthouse at St. Margaret's Bay is also an excellent site for observing migrant passerines. Regular observation here is producing a fascinating range of common and rare visitors.

North of Deal there is Sandwich Bay, the site of Kent's second bird observatory. Here too visitors are welcome and membership will help to keep you informed about the birds of this region, as well as various activities organised by the Sandwich Bay Observatory Trust. They have recently created an extensive scrape which has already attracted a variety of migrant waders, including Pectoral Sandpiper and Temminck's Stint, almost before it was completed. The trapping area bushes attract a wide variety of passerine migrants and in the autumn these may include regular visits from such eastern rarities as Yellow-browed and Pallas's Warblers. It is a long walk to the point and back, but it can be most rewarding. In winter, a flock of Snow Buntings is invariably present and occasionally a few Lapland Buntings or a Shore Lark may be seen. At high tide roosting waders can be observed well from close to the point, while offshore a few Common Eider may sometimes be present.

Stonar Lake occasionally attracts the rarer grebes and ducks in winter, while Pegwell Bay, at the mouth of the Stour, is another good area for waders, terns and gulls. In the Pegwell Bay Country Park, a hide is available from which to watch.

The geographical position of Thanet makes it an obvious landfall for Scandinavian migrants in the autumn. Despite being heavily built up, all the small wooded plots, the open areas along the coast from North Foreland to Foreness Point, the golf course and Northdown Park all attract a good variety of migrants. It is also an excellent site for seawatching, while the rocky shoreline and sheltered bays attract internationally important numbers of Turnstone and a wintering flock of Purple Sandpipers.

Westwards, between Minnis Bay and Reculver, there is an open stretch of undeveloped coastline, with the Wantsum Marshes straddling the railway line to the south. Regular observation here has produced a fascinating range of species. The shingle attracts Little Terns in the summer, Snow Buntings and possibly Shore Larks in the winter, while offshore in autumn, seabird movements can often be observed well from Reculver Towers.

West of Whitstable lies one of the most important areas in Britain for waders and wildfowl, the North Kent Marshes: the name given to the combined area formed by the estuaries and surrounding marshland of the Swale, Medway and Thames. During the winter months, the mudflats in the river estuaries attract thousands of waders. At each high tide they need to find suitably undisturbed roosts on which to rest. This provides good opportunites to see the birds well and to estimate their numbers. However, in recent years a system of low tide counts appears to be providing more accurate totals of the birds actually feeding in the estuaries, as many become invisible when roosting on saltmarsh islands and large numbers, particularly Knot and Dunlin, often roost in Essex. The roost sites vary according to the height of the tide, but in the Swale the shingle beach at Shellness, the saltings at Harty Ferry and the Elmley RSPB Reserve are all used regularly. Impressive flocks of waders such as Oystercatcher, Grey Plover, Dunlin, Knot and Bar-tailed Godwit can be seen. In the Medway, some of the important roosts, which are often favoured by Spotted Redshank and Greenshank in the autumn, are on the islands or on private land. Fields adjacent to the estuary are also used on the south Medway, while in the Thames the shingle at Yantlet Creek and the pools at Cliffe provide sanctuary for more waders. Large numbers of Ringed Plovers, in particular, frequently roost at the latter site.

In the summer months, the coastal margins of north Kent attract breeding species such as Common Shelduck, Oystercatcher, Common Redshank and Ringed Plover, with colonies of Black-headed Gulls and Common Terns on isolated tracts of saltmarsh. Avocets are now breeding successfully on the reserves and elsewhere.

All three estuaries are of international importance for wintering wildfowl and waders, regularly holding over one per cent of the north-west European totals of Brent Goose, Common Shelduck, Eurasian Wigeon and Pintail, as well as Ringed Plover, Grey Plover, Knot, Dunlin, Black-tailed Godwit, Bar-tailed Godwit, Common Redshank and Turnstone. A further seven species – Great Crested Grebe, Cormorant, Eurasian Wigeon, Gadwall, Oystercatcher, Avocet and Curlew – are present in nationally important numbers. In the winter months, the estuaries of the Swale and Medway also play host to Red-breasted Mergansers.

Large flocks of White-fronted Geese winter regularly on Sheppey, with smaller numbers at Cooling, while several birds of prey find the marshes equally attractive. Small numbers of Hen Harriers, Short-eared Owls and Merlins have always been regular visitors, while the now regular occurrence of Peregrine and Marsh Harrier on Sheppey is a most exciting recent development. Occasionally Rough-legged Buzzard also winters. English Nature has been responsible for creating the Swale National Nature Reserve, close to Shellness, with hides from which the wildfowl and waders can be observed, while the adjacent Shellness spit is an important nesting site for species such as Ringed Plover and Little Tern. One of the most impressive birdwatching experiences this county can offer must be the sight of thousands of ducks and waders wheeling over Elmley as a Peregrine streaks in, intent on a meal.

Oystercatchers

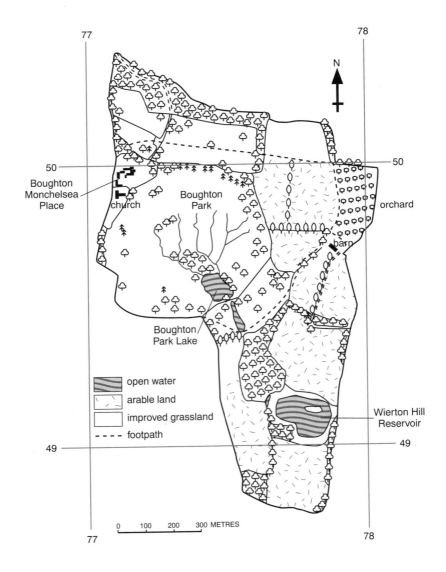

**Boughton Park and Wierton Hill Farm**

# A Local Study: The Birds of Boughton Park and Wierton Hill Farm (1985-94)

For many birdwatchers the study of one small area holds an irresistible attraction. Although some may find sufficient interest in a patch of woodland or farmland, for me an area combining different habitats has a greater appeal. With a more diverse habitat a wider range of species can be expected and studying the interaction of species with their habitat is fascinating.

In *Birdwatching in Kent* (1985) I described the rewards that 12 years of watching at Langley Park Farm had provided. I concluded my local study chapter by saying that I was looking forward to the prospect of finding my new local patch, Boughton Park and Wierton Hill Farm, even more exciting (Taylor 1992). And so it is proving.

Several factors led to the choice of this study area, one of which was the construction of a new reservoir that would undoubtedly provide an attraction for a wide variety of birds. Secondly, as it was situated between my home and place of work, it would encourage daily visits. Finally, I already knew that a pair of Barn Owls was in residence and that the area attracted rarer species. Both Bob Bland – a fellow enthusiast with whom I shared the study of Langley Park Farm – and I had seen a Wryneck there in August 1984, but there have been no sightings of that species since.

By a strange coincidence the Loose stream, which was dammed to create the lake at Langley Park Farm, divides farther down the valley and one tributary disappears under the greensand ridge to emerge as a line of springs in Boughton Park. These streams run into another man-made lake on the southern edge of the park. As a result, I am still watching birds associated with the Loose stream.

The study area is marginally smaller, covering just over 100 hectares from the top of the greensand ridge down to the edge of the Weald. It comprises 27% arable, 25% mixed woodland, 19% parkland and 19% grass, with about two hectares of reservoir and about a hectare of lake and marsh. The range of habitats, particularly following the construction of the irrigation reservoir, is more diverse than at Langley. The splendid views from the ridge, over the study area and out across the Weald are an incentive for frequent visits. The greensand ridge offers another advantage, it tends to attract birds moving east or west on passage.

The area was intensively farmed during the first five years of the study but, with a change of ownership, much of the arable farming during the second half of the study was far less intensive. The opportunity to monitor the changes provided additional interest.

During the early years, the arable fields were used mainly for the intensive production of strawberries and lettuces. The former occasionally attracted finch and pipit flocks in the winter months, as did the lettuce fields when they were not ploughed in the autumn. A new apple orchard was planted in 1986, as were a number of alder windbreaks, which have since matured and now provide winter seed for Siskin and Goldfinch.

Other significant changes that took place include the effect of the great storm on 16th October 1987, which wreaked havoc, tearing down numerous, magnificent, mature trees in the park and also breaking off many poplars. Strong winds in the following January brought down another 40 or so poplars, all weakened by the October winds. Although quite a number of hole nesting species lost traditional sites, the effect on the bird population seems to have been minimal. Some replanting has been carried out in the park, but it will be many years before the wildlife can benefit.

The constant variation in the reservoir water level makes it unsuitable for planting *Phragmites*, but some rhizomes were planted along an adjacent stream in autumn 1987. This eventually created a small reedbed which attracted a pair of Reed Warblers to nest.

A few trees were also planted on an island in the reservoir, together with bramble and other ground-cover plants. Several waterfowl have since found the island attractive for breeding.

The ten years between 1985 and 1994 proved to be fascinating. The bare statistics, impressive though they are, do not tell the whole story; 170 different species of bird were identified (see Appendix II). Of these 88 were seen annually, while a total of 67 species bred, 38 of them in every year. The annual totals ranged from 111 in 1990 to 128 in 1993, with an average of 120 species. Numbers breeding successfully varied from 46 in 1991 to a most impressive 59 in 1993, with a mean of 51 species. The increased frequency of visits was partly responsible for the higher numbers, with the annual number of visits varying from just 277 in 1985 rising to 351 in 1993, with an average of 337 visits per year.

Another important aspect of studying an area is visiting it at different times of the day. Early morning is usually best, when newly arrived migrants are most active and when the majority of species are most vocal. However, late afternoon and dusk visits are also important to learn about roosting behaviour. A few nocturnal visits will be necessary to hear such species as Tawny Owl, as well as night-flying migrants.

Species that are common elsewhere can often be quite rare locally, so they acquire a different status on your own patch. The different seasons, marked by the arrival and departure of migrant species, offer a continually changing pattern. The grubbing of mature hedgerows and changing agricultural practices gives one an insight into the natural balance and an opportunity to assess man's influence. Sometimes the changes can be linked with similar patterns elsewhere in the county, or nationwide, but on occasions they may be purely local. The decline of the Willow Warbler as a breeding species may be the result of changes occurring on its wintering grounds south of the Sahara, rather than any changes in Britain. The *Common Birds Census* data, produced by the British Trust for Ornithology, show a 40% decrease during 1989-92, with a marginal increase in woodland breeding during 1993 (Marchant 1994), followed by slight increases on both woodland and farmland in 1994 (Marchant 1994).

By accumulating records over a period of time, it is possible to note changes based on fact rather than impression, and this helps in understanding them better. Recording species on a monthly basis can produce surprising results. An analysis of the ten-year period shows that the numbers of species recorded in each month are as follows:

|  | J | F | M | A | M | J | J | A | S | O | N | D |
|---|---|---|---|---|---|---|---|---|---|---|---|---|
| Mean | 66 | 69 | 72 | 83 | 78 | 74 | 77 | 84 | 85 | 77 | 71 | 67 |
| Highest | 71 | 74 | 80 | 91 | 87 | 82 | 82 | 91 | 90 | 83 | 75 | 73 |
| 10-year total | 84 | 94 | 101 | 122 | 116 | 101 | 106 | 113 | 117 | 107 | 92 | 88 |

Not surprisingly, the greatest variety occurs during migration in spring and autumn, but it is interesting to note just how many species are recorded during the winter months, while over 100 in June is also impressive. The peak monthly totals of 91 were recorded in April 1989 and August 1987.

Another aspect of the study involves conducting a census each month, when every bird is counted during a single four or five hour visit. An analysis of these figures also makes interesting reading:

|  | J | F | M | A | M | J | J | A | S | O | N | D |
|---|---|---|---|---|---|---|---|---|---|---|---|---|
| Mean | 47 | 46 | 50 | 52 | 56 | 55 | 54 | 55 | 53 | 52 | 50 | 49 |
| Highest | 54 | 50 | 56 | 59 | 61 | 58 | 58 | 63 | 62 | 56 | 60 | 54 |

This shows that totals in excess of 50 can be expected on a daily basis during most months of the year. In 1993 *Birdwatch* magazine initiated Patch Watch UK. This scheme encouraged birdwatchers, on 1 May each year, to spend as many hours as possible on their local patches. We took part and now do this annually. In 1994 we achieved a splendid total of 70 species in a period of 16 hours, the highlights of which are mentioned later.

# January – February

The weather has a considerable influence on the numbers of species one can expect to see, and this is particularly evident during the winter. On the first visit of the year I would be disappointed not to find in excess of 40 species. What is more surprising is that the combined total for January and February is 99 species. Many of the less common species on that list are present or seen flying over during severe wintry conditions, often when the ground is snow-covered. There were several severe spells during the late 1980s, but the winters in the 1990s, with one exception, have been generally milder.

January 1985 experienced 200mm of snow, with very low temperatures for two weeks during which both the lake and the reservoir were frozen over. Eight Common Snipe were seen and 700 Woodpigeons survived on brussel tops that projected through the snow. As a rapid thaw set in, a flock of 38 White-fronted Geese flew north-east, while five Goosander flew south towards the flooded River Beult. Another severe spell in February 1985 attracted a Jack Snipe and a Green Sandpiper, while numbers of Lapwings flew south-west. A similarly severe spell in February–March 1986 concentrated a flock of 21 Bullfinches on seeding dock, while one or two Woodcock were seen, a species that seems to need snow before visiting this site.

In January 1987 400mm of snow fell and a northeastly wind caused considerable drifting. This blocked the access roads. To maintain the frequency of visits, I walked the two-and-a-half kilometres to and from the site. This dramatic change in the weather brought marked changes in the birdlife; a number of species became scarce or absent, while some cold weather movements also occurred.

In contrast, the winter of 1989 was one of the mildest and driest on record and relatively few species were seen, but the open water encouraged a pair of Little Grebes to winter. In mild conditions the following winter up to 500 Fieldfares remained to feed in the orchard.

February 1991 saw the coldest weather since January 1987. Both the lake and reservoir were frozen over for nearly three weeks and there were heavy snowfalls, again blocking the roads. Daily visits were just possible and a record February total of 74 species was recorded, including an exhausted Dunlin at the reservoir, two Jack Snipe, two Woodcock and a flock of Brent Geese flying east. After the thaw, two Shoveler and a Merlin flew over, while the monthly census revealed that both Wrens and Robins had suffered serious losses during the cold spell, their numbers being down by almost 50%.

Although there was no snowfall in January 1993, the open waters remained frozen over for a few days, but much of the month was unsettled, windy and wet, until an exceptionally mild, spring-like spell encouraged considerable bird song and duetting by Little Owls. In these variable conditions the highest January total of 73 species was recorded, most surprisingly with seven different waders, including the only January records of Greenshank and Grey Plover. It is unexpected sightings like these that make me keen not to miss a single day's visit. Anything can turn up.

Some specific winters and their effects on the bird life have been mentioned. The following includes some of the anticipated patterns of events, together with a few of the more unusual, seasonal highlights.

In the winter of 1992 up to nine Little Grebes wintered, following the exceptional breeding success in the previous summer, but usually there are relatively few winter sightings, while there is only one winter record of a Great Crested Grebe, in February 1993. Cormorant numbers increased markedly when the reservoir was used for rearing fish, but the highest count for the first two months is just five. One or two Grey Herons make occasional visits, as do pairs of Mute Swans. A few Greylag Geese and up to 80 Canada Geese are occasionally attracted to the reservoir, or are seen flying over, as a Bean Goose did in February 1987. Lone Common Shelduck have also flown over in two years at this time, while six Eurasian Wigeon visited the lake in February 1994. Gadwall are scarce visitors, but Common Teal now winter regularly and up to 18 have been seen. A few Common Pochard are seen almost annually, but a peak count of 49 in January 1990 was exceptional. There have been up to 42 Tufted Duck, though less than 25 is more usual. To complete this winter wildfowl section, two different Goldeneye were present in January–February 1992.

Two pairs of Common Kestrels are normally resident, but the occurrence of Sparrowhawks has increased during the ten years and three or four different individuals may now winter. The only other raptor that has been seen during these two months, in addition to the Merlin mentioned above, is a lone Common Buzzard, in January 1988.

Sightings of partridges at this time of year are scarce, but a Water Rail can occasionally be seen. Waders have already featured in the earlier highlights and a total of 10 species is quite impressive for January–February. Small flocks of Golden Plover fly over occasionally, with exceptional peaks of 200 in February 1988 and 150 in January 1990. With many hectares of open fields to the south, wintering flocks of Lapwings within the study area are rare. Small flocks fly over at this time, but an exceptional total of 306 flew south on 3 January 1991, before the cold spell set in. Jack Snipe is a rare winter visitor and both Common Snipe and Woodcock have become increasingly scarce, with only one record of the former and none of the latter during 1994. Common Redshank is also a scarce visitor, but there was one at the reservoir in February 1993.

During the winter months there are almost daily local movements of Black-headed Gulls flying between their roost in the Medway estuary and the Weald, where they feed. Totals of several hundreds may be counted, while fewer than 20 Common Gulls are usually involved. There was an interesting exception to this pattern in mid-January 1993, when a well manured field of pasture attracted an astonishing 500 Common and 600 Black-headed Gulls. Small numbers of the three larger gull species also fly over at this time of year and there was a record count of 20 Great Black-backed Gulls flying south on 27 January 1985.

Another unexpected sighting occurred in late February 1988 when an adult Mediterranean Gull was identified as it flew north-west, during a movement of Black-headed and Common Gulls.

Stock Dove and Woodpigeon numbers are influenced by the availability of food, but flocks of Woodpigeons, flying over the area from a roost in woods to the west, have produced the highest winter counts, with 1,500 on 3 January 1994. Flocks of up to 60 Stock Doves are occasionally seen. Up to three pairs of Collared Doves are usually resident.

Three owl species are usually present, but the nocturnal behaviour of the resident Barn Owls is extremely frustrating and sightings of Tawny Owls in the winter months are also scarce. With three or four pairs of resident Little Owls, this diurnal species is seen quite frequently, often staring at you with fierce yellow eyes.

All three woodpecker species are resident and frequent sightings can be expected at this time, when the drumming of Great Spotted Woodpecker often resonates around the park.

Winter stubble will occasionally attract flocks of up to 20 Skylarks, but the peak numbers are related to cold weather movements, when totals of up to 38 have been recorded. Flocks of 40–50 Meadow Pipits occasionally winter, attracted by fields of lettuces and strawberry or raspberry plants in which they find plenty to feed on. A Grey Wagtail makes visits from time to time, more often favouring the fringes of the lake, rather than the reservoir. A flock of up to 70 Pied Wagtails was present in a field of strawberry plants in January–February 1989, but usually there are just occasional sightings of one to three birds.

February 1993 attracted another scarce visitor, a female Stonechat. The occurrence of the larger winter thrushes is dependent on the availability of food. Fieldfares invariably outnumber Redwings, with flocks of several hundreds remaining through the milder winters.

Goldcrests are never common during the winter months, with just one to three on any one day, but their numbers fluctuate considerably, with none at all in January–February 1987 compared with a total of 48 bird/days in the same period in 1989. That gem of a species, the Firecrest, appeared on one winter's day – 21 February 1994.

Careful monitoring of the frequency of occurrence shows that both Marsh and Willow Tits have now become rare visitors (see table on page 36). In the winter months, other tit species sometimes form mixed feeding flocks, which may attract other birds such as Goldcrests and Common Treecreepers. The Nuthatch is another resident, and its piping call is frequently heard from the oaks and beeches.

One of the rarest winter visitors, a Great Grey Shrike, was present on a series of dates between 12 December 1986 and 21 March 1987.

The crow family is well represented, with the nearest rookery less than a kilometre away. However, for much of the year Rooks are only seen flying over. Jays are seen frequently, finding numerous acorns to hide in order to supplement their winter diet. Magpies have increased during the period of study and a winter roost of 16 birds was discovered in February 1993. Though Jackdaws roost elsewhere, up to 100 spend many daylight hours in the park oaks. The numbers of Carrion Crows have also increased, with all the peak monthly counts occurring during 1991–94. Up to 15 have been seen in January and February.

Varying Common Starling numbers have been closely related to the location of the large roosts in the Maidstone area. Towards dusk and after dawn in the early 1990s, it was not unusual to see several thousands of birds, as they flew to and from these roosts. However, winter counts of a few hundred birds are now more usual and this may in part be due to this species' general decline (Marchant 1990).

The Hawfinch is an attractive, large finch and although it was only ever an infrequent visitor, its decline is a sad loss.

Annual bird/day totals for Hawfinch (a bird/day total is calculated by adding together each day's count):

| 85 | 86 | 87 | 88 | 89 | 90 | 91 | 92 | 93 | 94 |
|----|----|----|----|----|----|----|----|----|----|
| 4  | 11 | 18 | 11 | –  | 2  | 1  | 1  | 1  | –  |

Winter counts of Tree Sparrows vary from single figures in some years to 75 in others, with mean peak counts of around 30. Although the breeding population has declined markedly since 1990, this cannot be said for the wintering numbers.

Another fascinating aspect of this study has been the discovery of at least three different hybrid House x Tree Sparrows (Taylor 1994). Two were similar in size to a House Sparrow, with cheek patches of varying contrast, while one showed a small dark chin patch. The other was more like a Tree Sparrow in size, with a grey forehead, dark cheek patch and large darkish chin and throat patch. Although hybrids are rare, a similarly plumaged Somerset example is described in Harris *et al.* (1989).

The numbers and variety of finches present during January and February are again determined by the availability of the seeds on which they feed. A peak count of 100 Chaffinches was noted in January 1985, but the mean peak counts vary between 40 and 50, while Bramblings are relatively scarce during the winter months. Flocks of up to 50 or more Greenfinches have only been noted in two winters and the mean monthly peaks are nearer 20. Similar numbers of Goldfinches usually overwinter, but exceptionally there were up to 300 present throughout the mild winter of 1993/94. Siskins are regular winter visitors, attracted by the alders around the lake and along the marsh. The January mean peak count is 40, with up to 100 present early in 1986 and an isolated maximum of 150 on 9th January 1994. Linnets can be completely absent during the winter months, but small flocks occur occasionally, and exceptionally there were up to 100 present in January

1986 and 80 from mid-February 1993.

The Common Redpoll, like the Siskin, is often to be found feeding in alders, as well as silver birches, but this species has shown a dramatic decline in the latter years of this study, with a bird/day total of only 10 in 1994, when there were no winter records. Until that year the mean winter peak was 25-30, with an exceptional count of 120 feeding in a strawberry field in February 1989. The BTO Common Birds Census results also show a marked decline in Common Redpoll numbers.

As with the finches, Yellowhammer wintering numbers have varied considerably, with an exceptional maximum of 150–200 in January–February 1993, compared with mean monthly peaks of 35–50.

During the first seven years of the study, the Reed Bunting was rarely seen in the winter months, but once the reedbed became established a few started to roost there, with peaks of 11 in both 1993 and 1994. During the day, they can sometimes be seen feeding with the finch and sparrow flocks.

It is always interesting to compare different local study areas, and one species that is missing here but which was seen quite regularly at Langley, is the Corn Bunting. Its distribution within Kent has changed in recent years and it is no longer seen between the greensand ridge and the North Downs, but is has probably always been absent in this area of the Weald.

## March – May

Spring weather has a marked influence on the pattern of bird life. Warm spells in March and April may encourage early nesting and the early arrival of summer visitors. In contrast, cold spells in April and May can delay migration and suspend breeding, while torrential rainstorms and strong winds may have a devastating effect on breeding success. Examples of all these weather patterns were evident during the spring months of the study.

Different aspects of bird behaviour also become part of the annual cycle. Some I particularly look forward to. I have observed the display flight of the Lesser Spotted Woodpecker from January through to May, but most frequently in March. Sometimes three birds become involved and it is the short butterfly-like flights, ending with a raised-wing glide, that I find most attractive.

The threat behaviour of two opposing male Green Woodpeckers is also fascinating to watch, as they move up and down opposite sides of a tree trunk, peering at each other, or inching along a large branch, swaying their heads in an almost figure-of-eight pattern, occasionally touching bills.

Noting the dates on which you first hear song from different species can provide interesting comparisons from year to year. The Blackbird is much more selective than Song and Mistle Thrushes, often not singing until a warmer spell in late February or early March. However, not all song is related to the establishment of territory and one of the pleasures I enjoy each spring is hearing the beautiful fluty, descending phrases of four to five semitones uttered by migrant Redwings. Snatches of Siskin song are another welcome sound.

Early March is unlikely to produce many summer migrants. Exceptionally, two Chiffchaffs arrived on 28 February 1994 and were busy establishing their territories during the next week. However, while anticipating early migrants there is much to observe. Willows are in bud, the Blackthorn is in blossom and flowers such as Primroses, Lesser Celandines, Wood Anemones and even Bluebells may begin to bloom, while a warmer spell may encourage some butterflies to come out of hibernation. In 1990 Small Tortoiseshell, Comma, Peacock and Brimstone were all seen by 14 March.

In March 1989 the first Bluebells were blooming by the 9th, the first Chiffchaff sang on the 10th and by the 11th numerous toads were croaking and a Comma fluttered by.

Mid-March can produce early migrants, and four in particular may be anticipated. The earliest dates on which they have been seen are as follows:

| | |
|---|---|
| Northern Wheatear | 12 March |
| Blackcap | 15 March |
| Black Redstart | 17 March |
| Sand Martin | 18 March |

Spring ploughing invariably attracts small flocks of Pied Wagtails, but I also scan the newly turned sods in the hope of finding other species, such as Northern Wheatear, or maybe a Black Redstart. The Sand Martin will appear at the reservoir, while the strains of the first Blackcap song may come from the nearby woodland. A wintering Water Rail may become more evident at this time, calling occasionally from the dense undergrowth along the stream. The only other annual spring migrant that has been seen in March is the Common Cuckoo. Surprisingly, one was present from 30 March 1992.

March has produced one extremely rare species, a Rustic Bunting. It was present for ten days from 19 March 1993 and was the first away from the coast and only the sixth record for the county. Less common observations include a lone Curlew flying south-west in 1987; seven Dunlin at the reservoir and six Shelduck flying north on the same date, also in 1987; a group of five White-fronted Geese flying north-west in 1991; an immature drake Goldeneye performing its neck-stretching display in 1992; a Brent Goose that joined the resident Canada Geese for nearly three weeks and a Whooper Swan on the reservoir in 1993. Stonechats have appeared on just eight dates, four of which have been in March, and the figures for Black Redstart are precisely the same.

Unusual aspects of behaviour add further interest. On 19 March 1989 a Little Owl was seen undulating low over the ground, pursued by an aggressive Blackbird that virtually knocked it to the ground where it sat for a short while, looking somewhat abashed (Taylor 1989). On 23 April 1992 an equally aggressive Mistle Thrush kept flying at a perched Common Kestrel, in the end knocking it out of the tree. On both occasions I presumed that the aggressors were nesting close by, and that they were behaving defensively.

It was interesting, on another occasion, to observe Jackdaws perched on the backs of deer. They were pulling out strands of hair with which to line their nests. Once I was intrigued for several minutes by the sparring of a Magpie and a Stoat. The Magpie was sitting on the top wire of a fence; when the Stoat lunged, the Magpie sprang up and in turn dived at the Stoat, but neither touched the other.

In the springs of both 1993 and 1994 a male Blackcap confused me many times. Its ability to mimic different phrases of song was quite remarkable, imitating snatches of Common Nightingale song and then Sedge Warbler. Short phrases of Blackbird and Song Thrush song also flowed from this one individual, who would occasionally lapse into his own song.

More confusion was experienced during the same two springs when the drumming of a Lesser Spotted Woodpecker was heard, or what sounded like drumming. Tracking the sound back to its source, it was found to be coming from the throat of a Carrion Crow. The sound was virtually identical in both rhythm and intonation. For two consecutive years I was often fooled into thinking I was hearing a Mistle Thrush in song, only to discover that it was a Common Starling giving an excellent imitation.

One is sometimes aware of a perceptible increase in Redwing and Fieldfare numbers during March, and in the case of the latter species sometimes in early April, as returning migrants join the wintering flocks.

As March turns into April I eagerly await new spring migrants, but in recent years my hopes have often been dashed by a period of cold northerly winds, effectively stopping migration. In 1988 there were five Chiffchaffs by late March, but no other migrants were seen until the first Swallow on 9 April. During the next week there were daily additions to the year list. In 1994, although March had produced Chiffchaff, Blackcap, Northern

Wheatear and Black Redstart, and an early Willow Warbler on 2 April, there were no more migrants until a fall of Chiffchaffs and Blackcaps on the 12th. The earliest Hobby then followed on the 16th, but it was not before the 19th that new spring arrivals started to appear more frequently.

A later stage in the farming cycle is the planting of seeds and this has a great attraction for a number of species. It tends to concentrate the attention of all the finches and sparrows in the area. This focal point produces the peak monthly counts. Seed planting was responsible for attracting the largest spring flocks of about 500 House Sparrows and 400 Linnets as well as 87 Stock Doves, during 16–18 April 1985, and about 400 Greenfinches in early April 1992. It is worth searching for a few Bramblings amongst the Chaffinches, as the former often occur during late March and early April on their return migration to northern Scandinavia.

By mid-April, depending on the prevailing weather conditions, one anticipates new summer migrants arriving almost daily. A summary of the mean arrival dates recorded for this study area, with the earliest dates in brackets, follows:

**March**

| | |
|---|---|
| 16th | Chiffchaff (28/2) |
| 29th | Black Redstart (17/3) |

**April**

| | |
|---|---|
| 4th | Blackcap (15/3) |
| 6th | Willow Warbler (1/4) |
| 9th | Northern Wheatear (12/3) |
| 12th | Barn Swallow (8/4) |
| 13th | Common Cuckoo (30/3) |
| | Sand Martin (18/3) |
| 19th | House Martin (11/4) |
| | Yellow Wagtail (11/4) |

**April** (continued)

| | |
|---|---|
| 25th | Turtle Dove (17/4) |
| 26th | Lesser Whitethroat (16/4) |
| | Common Whitethroat (15/4) |
| 29th | Common Sandpiper (15/4) |

**May**

| | |
|---|---|
| 3rd | Hobby (16/4) |
| | Common Swift (25/4) |
| | Garden Warbler (25/4) |
| 5th | Spotted Flycatcher (1/5) |
| 15th | Whinchat (1/5) |
| 18th | Reed Warbler (11/5) |

An analysis of the arrival dates suggests that the spring migration of 1993 was earlier than most, with seven of the earliest dates being recorded in that year, three of them in mid-March.

The diurnal passage of three more species can provide further evidence of the changing seasons. An easterly movement of Chaffinches has only been noted in two springs, with a peak of just 50 on 13 March 1993. However, between mid-March and mid-April there is usually a northerly passage of Meadow Pipits, although it has been less marked in recent years. The mean spring passage totals are 33 and 9 respectively for 1985-89 and 1990-94, while the highest day total was 27 north on 29 March 1986. By far the most obvious is the northerly passage of Lesser Black-backed Gulls from mid-March to late May, with peak bird/day totals of 78 in both 1986 and 1994, and a maximum day total of 48 north on 15 April 1986.

Other gull species become increasingly less frequent during March, with relatively few at all from April until July. However, since Herring and more recently a few Lesser Black-backed Gulls have started breeding at the nearby Parkwood Trading Estate, these two species now occur quite frequently throughout the spring and summer.

The wintering Golden Plover flocks have already been mentioned, but in spring 1986 there was an exceptional spring passage. A field adjacent to the study area attracted up to 460 between 22 and 25 March and up to 590 between 11 and 13 April. It was interesting to observe small flocks leaving this large gathering, flying off north-eastwards, presumably on migration to their breeding grounds.

Although comparatively few are seen or heard, Whimbrel and Greenshank are almost annual on spring passage. Only one to three Whimbrel are normally seen, but flocks of seven and 11 flew north and east on 23 April 1993 and 24 April 1991 respectively. An afternoon visit to the reservoir on 20 April 1989 was rewarded with another surprise, five Ringed Plovers and a Greenshank had arrived during the day.

Observing spring migration like this, at an inland site, is much appreciated, but witnessing an arrival of migrants is rare. I got close on 25 April 1989 when I made two visits to the area. A cold northeasterly wind was blowing and there were heavy showers. In the morning, some 30 Sand Martins and the first five House Martins of the year flew northwest and the earliest Garden Warbler was singing. But when I returned in the afternoon the reservoir had attracted an unprecedented 100 Sand Martins, a White Wagtail and a flock of 20 Yellow Wagtails. The flock comprised 17 Yellow *M. f. flavissima*, two Blue-headed *M. f. flava* and one Yellow-headed *M. f. lutea*. It was an exciting period and migration was in full swing. The next morning two scarcer spring migrants, a male Common Redstart and a male Pied Flycatcher were present. The latter remained until the 27th when the Sand Martins panicked as a Hobby suddenly appeared, and the presence of a summer plumaged Bar-tailed Godwit on the reservoir island all day was an unexpected bonus. A southeasterly wind now blew and the showers continued, as did the migration, unabated. The first Turtle Dove and the earliest Common Swift were seen, while a total of 44 Lesser Black-backed Gulls and an unprecedented flock of 17 Common Terns all flew north-west.

During the study period a total of 21 wader species has been recorded, a high percentage of them attracted to the reservoir. A monthly analysis shows, in particular, how many different species pass through during the spring.

Monthly occurrence of wader species:

| J | F | M | A | M | J | J | A | S | O | N | D |
|---|---|---|---|---|---|---|---|---|---|---|---|
| 7 | 8 | 9 | 14 | 14 | 8 | 9 | 11 | 8 | 5 | 6 | 7 |

Other April highlights included an Oystercatcher and a fall of three male Pied Flycatchers in 1985, one of which sang; an adult male Hen Harrier, a female Peregrine, a Dunlin, and a 'reeling' Grasshopper Warbler in 1988; a male Marsh Harrier and a male Ring Ouzel in 1990; a pair of Hobbies displaying over the park in 1992; another male Ring Ouzel and a Firecrest in 1993; a Short-eared Owl and four Little Ringed Plovers in 1994, when a pair of Bar-headed Geese paid a brief visit, looking just like genuine vagrants as they grazed.

During the study a dozen or so 'escapes' have been seen, such as Snow and Barnacle Geese, Black Swan, Chiloe Wigeon, White-cheeked and Yellow-billed Pintails, Yellow-bellied Parrot, Cockatiel and Canary, as well as several hybrid ducks.

Not only are summer visitors arriving at this time, but winter visitors are departing and it is interesting to compare dates from year to year. The mean departure dates for five species that winter regularly, with the latest dates in brackets, are:

| | | |
|---|---|---|
| **March** | 17th | Water Rail (26/4) |
| | 25th | Siskin (14/4) |
| **April** | 6th | Brambling (16/4) |
| | 9th | Redwing (29/4) |
| | 24th | Fieldfare (15/5) |

Of these, only the Fieldfare has occurred in May, with two on the 7th in 1985, two on the 1st in 1989 and one on five dates up to the 15th in 1990.

A new feature for this area, as a result of human intervention, is the now annual arrival of Reed Warblers to breed, rather than just on migration. A few rhizomes of *Phragmites* were planted in 1987 and Reed Warblers have bred annually since 1992. Not surprisingly, their arrival dates have become progressively earlier, from 11 June in 1985 to 11 May in

1992.

Spending 16 hours on the patch as part of the *Birdwatch* magazine initiative on 1 May 1994 was a rewarding experience. Some aspects of that day's structure and a few of the high points are described.

'A Common Cuckoo called at 0400, but it was 0455 before the Barn Owl flew back to its nest box. A Nuthatch was the 20th species at 0510. A Green Sandpiper was still present at the reservoir, where a pair of Little Ringed Plovers had established a breeding territory for the first time. A Mistle Thrush was the 50th species at 0637, but the 60th species at 0827 was a most unexpected surprise, a Firecrest in song. Searching some Holm Oaks, we eventually discovered a pair of roosting Tawny Owls, having failed to hear them hooting before dawn. A Common Swift, my first for the year, then flew north. Another surprise was the discovery of the earliest Spotted Flycatcher for the area. Around 1100, I sat on the reservoir bank, dividing my attention between watching for overhead migrants and studying the Little Ringed Plovers.

'The male of the pair is busy, attending the nest scrape. He then stands up on the edge of the hollow, spreading his wings, while the female creeps in and sits underneath him. She then walks away, he follows, fluffing out his white flank feathers, tapping the ground with his feet, as he stretches his head proudly high (looking very bustard-like) before mounting her.

'A Sparrowhawk appeared and circled, gaining considerable height before dropping like a stone, but it was 1127 before the first Common Kestrel was seen – number 65. At 1135 two Hobbies circled and dived at each other. Another walk around the area produced a Coal Tit – number 69 at 1423 – but Grey Heron, Turtle Dove and Common Sandpiper had failed to appear. At 1755 I eventually found a hen Northern Wheatear – number 70 – but the next 90 minutes failed to produce anything new and I called it a day, well pleased with the total achieved.'

The month of May can be one of the most exciting in the calendar. There will still be a few of the later summer migrants to add to the year list, such as Spotted Flycatcher and possibly Whinchat, while the breeding populations of species such as Turtle Dove and Common Swift will also be arriving. One of these may well feature as the 100th species for the year. Although the earliest 100 was achieved on 20 April 1993 with a Hawfinch, the average for the ten years is 20 May.

Most resident species, together with the early migrants, will be busy with various aspects of nesting activity. By early May this may include the feeding of newly fledged young. As part of my study, I monitor the breeding populations of selected residents and summer migrants. This involves plotting nesting activity on a map, such as song, nest building and carrying of food, in order to establish how many different territories or breeding pairs there are. This will certainly continue into June and, for some species, even into July. However, although I find this a fascinating part of working my own local patch, May also has a reputation for producing rarities.

An analysis of the 27 species that have only been recorded once shows that seven were in May, six in September and four in June. Mention has been made of waders migrating overland and in May 1994 three new species, out of a total of nine different waders that month, were all seen at the reservoir. There were three Avocets on the 7th, a Spotted Redshank on the 13th and a Turnstone on the 16th. As the water level was exceptionally low there was quite an extensive mud bank that spring. This not only proved attractive for the migrants, but also for a pair of Little Ringed Plovers to make their only attempt at breeding. Sadly, their clutch of four eggs disappeared shortly before hatching.

The only record of drake Garganey occurred on 22 May 1989 and a Montagu's Harrier flew low to the north-east on 18 May 1992, but 26 May 1991 is probably the most memorable date in my birdwatching calendar:

'At around 1030, I made a second visit to the reservoir, on the offchance that a pair of duck that I had seen drop in might have been Garganey. As I started to walk round the reservoir, I was surprised to see a large swift flying low over the water, with a few Common Swifts. My first thought was that it might be an Alpine Swift, then I saw a whitish looking back and wondered about a partial albino, but as it reappeared from behind the island, an excellent view revealed deep metallic blue wings and a large white vent. I knew then that I was looking at a needle-tailed swift – a bird that I had never seen before, nor even dreamt of seeing in England, let alone on my own local patch!!

'With the adrenalin flowing and the excitement reaching heights that I cannot remember experiencing in my 40 years of birdwatching – it was such a fantastic looking bird – thoughts were racing through my mind: I haven't got my camera with me; I must phone Birdline; Martin Woodcock is the nearest birdwatching friend and he probably has experience of this species; are there other, similar species? I must note enough details to confirm the identification, in case it disappears. This last I did first, but I only allowed myself a few minutes, before heading off to collect Martin and Barbara. We were back within ten minutes and the bird was performing superbly, flying low over the water, with the trees and reservoir bank providing an excellent backcloth. Martin confirmed that it was a White-throated Needletail. We watched it for a further ten minutes, then I left them and headed home, stopping briefly to give Mark and Janice Hollingworth the amazing news. Of the five people I attempted to phone, I only got through to Richard Millington of Birdline and Tim Loseby.

'I returned to the reservoir before 1130 and was able to take several photographs, as did Tim Loseby who arrived a few minutes later. The seven of us were enthralled by the superb views of this quite magnificent bird, but it flew off at noon, some minutes before the first of several hundreds of hopeful twitchers arrived.'

With so many eyes on the sky for much of the afternoon, it was not so surprising that another rarity was seen; a lone Honey Buzzard drifted slowly north-west.

Other less common May occurrences include a male Common Crossbill feeding in a Scots pine in 1989; two Whimbrel resting on the reservoir bank in 1990; Common Nightingales singing in 1990 and 1993; an Arctic Tern feeding over the reservoir and an Oystercatcher flying north-east in 1993; and a Golden Oriole singing from poplars in both 1993 and 1994. Other less than annual occurrences include single Whinchats in four years, and a Blue-headed Wagtail at the reservoir in 1991. A good example of returning migrants occurred on 18 May 1994. A period of continuous rain eased early in the morning and two Common Terns were seen flying north. A short while later small flocks of House Martins started to appear out of the low clouds, until eventually about 230 were feeding low over the reservoir, with about 50 Barn Swallows and a Sand Martin. On another occasion, in strong winds, a group of obviously tired migrant Barn Swallows rested on a strand of barbed wire by the reservoir.

Many delightfully enjoyable moments are experienced when newly fledged young are seen. In late May 1987 I stumbled across a group of five juvenile Common Treecreepers clinging like a feathered fist to the bark of an oak, revealing their orange gapes as a parent came to feed them.

## June – July

My descriptions of the weather for these months reveals an amazing range, from 'one of the wettest Junes on record', through 'unsettled, with thunderstorms', 'periods of heavy rain and strong winds', to 'predominantly dry' and 'very hot and dry, producing drought conditions'. Such are the vagaries of our climate.

Much of June is spent watching and recording the success, or otherwise, of the breeding species, particularly the later migrants. But there are other interesting events to note. Lapwings often commence their post-breeding dispersal fairly early in June and flocks can sometimes be seen flying over, while the bank of the reservoir occasionally attracts loafing flocks during the summer. There were peaks of about 220 in mid-July 1985 and 1994, years when the water level was low. As at Langley, there are a few mid-summer records of Common Teal, a pair being present for a week in June 1992. Common Kingfishers only occur as the young birds disperse from their breeding areas, such as the nearby Loose stream, and the first sightings each year are in June or July. In contrast, the last adult Common Cuckoos are seen in June, while juveniles (all those bred in the area are hosted by Dunnocks) or migrants occur between July and September. Another feature of the summer season is the gathering of newly fledged Common Starlings into post-breeding flocks which feed in the park. Usually 200-300 are involved, but in 1989, when a mild winter followed by a mainly dry and hot summer produced good breeding conditions, about 1,000 were present.

June has also produced unexpected excitements, including the only record of a Fulmar that flew south-west in 1988; the only records of Long-eared Owl and Marsh Warbler in 1988 and 1989 respectively; and the only record of Red-footed Falcon, which was seen twice in June 1989. A Quail has only been heard twice, in June and July 1988, while there are six records of single Golden Orioles, including four between 5 and 10 June. Five Common Crossbills flew WNW in July 1985; a Buzzard flew south-west and a juvenile Water Rail was present at the lake in July 1987; a Siskin was seen in June 1988; single Hawfinches were found in June 1988 and 1990; two Common Terns were present in both June and July 1989; a Great Crested Grebe visited, on single June or July dates between 1990 to 1992; a drake Common Pochard was present in June 1990 and July 1991; and a flock of nine Greylag Geese was seen in June 1992, followed by a flock of eight Mute Swans the following month.

The list of species that bred successfully, or attempted to breed, is long, but a few of them only bred occasionally, while six species bred just once. A summary of some of the more interesting breeding records follows.

A pair of Great Crested Grebes bred in 1993, hatching three young in mid-July, but the young were presumed to have been taken by an introduced terrapin! Sadly, none returned in 1994. One to three pairs of Little Grebes breed annually and they are a real delight to watch as they scramble on and off their parents' backs. Although pairs of Mute Swans summer occasionally, they have not yet attempted to breed. Canada Geese numbers have fluctuated considerably, with just one pair breeding in 1986, increasing to five and six pairs respectively in 1990 and 1991, but decreasing to one successful pair in 1993 and none again in 1994. During the summers of 1989 to 93, flocks of up to 30 birds remained to moult. Tufted Duck breeding numbers have also varied considerably, with a peak of six pairs in 1993 and none at all in three years.

A pair of Sparrowhawks attempted to breed in 1993, but the nest was deserted following a torrential thunderstorm on 14 June. One or two pairs of Common Kestrels breed successfully each year. A pair of Hobbies is seen each summer, but they breed elsewhere, sometimes bringing their young into the area in the autumn. It is a species that could breed within the study area one day.

Partridge species were rarely seen. A pair of Red-legged Partridges hatched seven young in 1993, fledging three of them successfully, but there was no other evidence of breeding. The Grey Partridge also bred just once, in 1985, although pairs were present again in 1992–94.

In May 1990 a group of four newly hatched Coot were seen on the lake. On closer inspection, amongst the four was a lone Moorhen chick. Could a Moorhen have laid an egg in the Coot's nest, or was the youngster just an opportunist feeder? According to BWP (Cramp 1980), Coot parents will occasionally adopt chicks similar in appearance to their own, but after a while they recognize their own young individually and the stranger is no longer tolerated.

Early in this study, I observed Coots apparently making second nests before their broods had hatched. When I referred to BWP, I discovered that this species sometimes makes a brood-platform, on which their newly hatched young can roost safely (Cramp 1980). On another occasion, in 1988, one pair successfully hatched three broods which, according to BWP, is unknown (Cramp 1980). There were two resident pairs of Coots at the lake; by 17 April they had broods of three and four young, eventually fledging two each. On 8 June, second broods of four and seven were hatched, while one of the pairs hatched five more young on 4 August.

Single pairs of Lapwings bred successfully in both 1985 and 1989, the former in a field of barley and the latter among strawberry plants.

Tawny and Little Owls breed annually. A breeding pair of Barn Owls, using a nest box in a Dutch barn, was known to breed successfully in 1993 and 1994, and may well have done so for several years judging by the accumulation of pellets in the nest box. In 1986, a nest among hay bales was inadvertently destroyed and following this two nest boxes were erected. However, for several years there was no evidence that they were being used.

All three woodpecker species breed annually, but the secretive nature of the Lesser Spotted during the breeding season can be frustrating. On leaving the nest they either leave the area, which seems unlikely, or become impossible to locate.

Although the Yellow Wagtail has not bred, there were some mid-summer records during 1985–1989, when fields of lettuces attracted a few birds. In July 1988 three were present. They were respectively showing characteristics of a male Yellow Wagtail *M. f. flavissima*, a female Blue-headed *M. f. flava* and a singing male, with a pale yellow head, possibly of the eastern race *M. f. lutea*. This, or another yellow-headed male, was present again the following summer.

The breeding of Reed Warblers, following the planting of some *Phragmites* is a success story that has already been mentioned. The fluctuation in the numbers of other breeding warbler species has, however, been beyond our influence.

Annual numbers of breeding territories:

|                  | 85 | 86 | 87 | 88 | 89 | 90 | 91 | 92 | 93 | 94 |
|------------------|----|----|----|----|----|----|----|----|----|----|
| Garden Warbler   | 1  | –  | 1  | 2  | 4  | 5  | 4  | 4  | 5  | 6  |
| Blackcap         | 9  | 8  | 9  | 7  | 15 | 17 | 11 | 13 | 17 | 14 |
| Chiffchaff       | 2  | 1  | 5  | 9  | 9  | 10 | 6  | 11 | 11 | 9  |
| Willow Warbler   | 5  | 6  | 2  | 4  | 8  | 6  | 7  | 2  | 1  | 1  |

The numbers of both Garden Warblers and Blackcaps increased to early peaks of five and 17 pairs respectively in 1990, in line with national trends. The number of Chiffchaff territories also increased significantly to 10 by 1990, again in line with the national trend, particularly on farmland. In contrast, Willow Warbler numbers have declined dramatically from the peak of eight in 1989 to just one singing male in 1994. Curiously, this decline seems to be mainly in southern Britain, the regional differences being a 47%

decline in the south and only 7% in the north (Peach *et al.* 1995).

Goldcrests bred successfully in 1989 and, following a dramatic decline in 1990, the numbers slowly increased and they bred again in 1994. Spotted Flycatchers, however, breed annually, although their numbers show an interesting rise and fall. The recent decline is in line with the national trend.

Annual numbers of Spotted Flycatcher breeding territories:

| 85 | 86 | 87 | 88 | 89 | 90 | 91 | 92 | 93 | 94 |
|----|----|----|----|----|----|----|----|----|----|
| 7  | 9  | 13 | 15 | 21 | 17 | 10 | 10 | 5  | 6  |

Long-tailed Tits nest annually and commence their breeding cycle early, often starting to build their nests in early March but still carrying feathers to line them more than three weeks later.

My experiences with Marsh and Willow Tits on this site show clearly how both species have declined.

Annual bird/day totals:

|            | 85  | 86  | 87  | 88  | 89 | 90 | 91 | 92 | 93 | 94 |
|------------|-----|-----|-----|-----|----|----|----|----|----|----|
| Marsh Tit  | 26  | 37  | 30  | 28  | 10 | 3  | 1  | 1  | –  | 1  |
| Willow Tit | 115 | 111 | 173 | 111 | 99 | 84 | 72 | 12 | 38 | –  |

Willow Tits bred annually until 1991 and again in 1993, but the only breeding record for Marsh Tit concerns a unique example of hybridisation. In June 1988 a male Marsh Tit and female Willow Tit fledged at least two young and all four birds were colour ringed. The female Willow Tit continued to breed annually, with her own kind, until 1991 and was last seen on 31 July of that year, by which time she was at least five years old.

The success of the Magpie is confirmed by a steady increase in numbers, and their breeding success has also improved, which is bad news for a number of passerines. In 1985, there was only one record between late April and early September, but breeding has been attempted in at least five years since the first nest was built in 1987. On several occasions the nests have been robbed by Carrion Crows, but at least one pair bred successfully in 1994.

Tree Sparrows appear to be decreasing as a breeding species. They reached a peak of 20 pairs in the good breeding season of 1991, but declined to a low of just five pairs in 1993, with six pairs the following year.

The Common Redpoll is another species which has declined quite dramatically. It has never been a regular breeding species, but there was evidence of breeding in four of the years between 1985 and 1989, following which there has been a complete absence of summer sightings.

The Reed Bunting bred successfully between 1992 and 1994, possibly influenced by the attraction of the reedbed as a winter roost site, which has certainly produced an increase in the number of annual bird/days recorded.

Annual bird/day totals for Reed Bunting:

| 85 | 86 | 87  | 88 | 89 | 90 | 91  | 92  | 93  | 94  |
|----|----|-----|----|----|----|-----|-----|-----|-----|
| 29 | 29 | 118 | 50 | 16 | 83 | 177 | 420 | 452 | 331 |

During July one becomes aware that the long period of autumn passage is commencing. At Langley, the Whinchat passage was a feature, but at Boughton Park and Wierton Hill Farm the passage by comparison is almost neglible, with just over 100 bird/days in the ten years. The extreme dates are 20 July – 21 September. Another regular autumn migrant that is also scarce in spring is the Sedge Warbler. Its extreme dates are 26 July – 29 September. Flocks of Common Swifts also start moving and a peak of 270 flying south-west was noted in mid-July 1991.

Compared with Langley a greater range of migrant waders can be expected as the reservoir is a more attractive staging post than Langley's reed-fringed lake. Green and Common Sandpipers are annual visitors, Ringed and Little Ringed Plovers are seen occasionally, Common Redshank and Greenshank have both occurred once in July, while Curlew and Whimbrel fly over almost annually.

Less common autumn migrants that may occur towards the end of July include passerines such as Tree Pipit, Common Nightingale, Wood Warbler and Pied Flycatcher.

## August – October

During the autumn different weather conditions produce certain species, or particular patterns of behaviour. Black, thundery clouds may be preceded by large flocks of House Martins, or Common Swifts. A flock of about 360 House Martins drifted south-west on 26 October 1989 and another of about 170 flew west on 19 September 1990, both under heavy rain clouds. The martins are attracted by the insects concentrated in the upcurrents of air.

In the autumn, House Martins often gather on south-facing roofs or walls, and on 16 August 1994 about 90 were 'sunbathing' on the walls of Boughton Monchelsea Place. In contrast, on 11 October 1987 in cold, wet conditions, I saw about 25 huddled two or three deep on a narrow window ledge, presumably to keep warm.

Falls of passerine migrants are relatively scarce, but rain during the night, following clear skies, may well produce an increase in numbers, as on 19 August 1986, when about 25 Willow Warblers were present, together with the two Garden Warblers, a Wood Warbler and a Reed Warbler – the first for several weeks. On another occasion, early on 16th August 1994, several newly arrived migrants were concentrated in one small clump of brambles. These included three Blackcaps, three Chiffchaffs, two Willow Warblers, a Common Whitethroat and a Garden Warbler, as well as four tit species.

The autumn wader passage is already well underway by August, and although April and May attract a greater range of species, August's total of 11 is impressive. Coastal as well as freshwater species migrate overland, as in spring. Eight Whimbrel flew south-west in 1985 during the early to mid-August peak period; two Ringed Plovers visited briefly in 1988; single Curlew flew over in three years; three Greenshank visited in 1994, with singles in other years; Green Sandpipers accumulated a total of 78 bird/days, only October having more; and the Common Sandpiper total of 104 bird/days makes August the peak month for this species.

Three terns have occurred in August: two Black Terns visited the reservoir in 1986, an Arctic Tern flew around the reservoir, before flying off west in 1989, while one and two Common Terns flew north-east and south-west respectively in 1992.

Other unusual August records include a Black Redstart and a Stonechat in 1987; a female Marsh Harrier flying north in 1990; and the exceptional sighting of an Ortolan Bunting on 26 August 1991, the first to be seen away from the coast in Kent.

Single Grasshopper Warblers have been seen in three autumns, all in August which is also the peak month for several almost annual migrant passerines, including Tree Pipit, Yellow Wagtail, Whinchat, Sedge Warbler and Wood Warbler.

Summary of monthly bird/day totals:

|               | A  | M  | J  | J  | A   | S  | O  |
|---------------|----|----|----|----|-----|----|----|
| Tree Pipit    | 2  | 3  | 1  | 7  | 33  | 19 | –  |
| Yellow Wagtail| 76 | 49 | 23 | 32 | 130 | 33 | 1  |
| Whinchat      | –  | 4  | –  | 12 | 54  | 42 | –  |
| Sedge Warbler | 2  | 1  | –  | 4  | 28  | 18 | –  |
| Wood Warbler  | 1  | 1  | –  | 2  | 18  | 1  | –  |

Another annual event in late summer is the flocking of Mistle Thrushes. Twenty or so are seen fairly regularly, with an exceptional flock of 50 on 24 August 1985.

On 4 August 1994 I saw two juvenile Grey Herons flying towards the reservoir, one of which alighted on the water and swam for a short while, before flapping its wings and taking off without any undue difficulty. BWP states, 'exceptionally recorded swimming and diving for food' (Cramp 1977).

Another unusual feature of the 1994 autumn was the incidence of Clouded Yellow butterflies, particularly around the reservoir during August. There were up to four on any one day for the best part of three weeks.

The highest counts of Canada Geese have occurred in August and September, with a peak of 240 in August 1987 and September 1994. In some years flocks spend time there, in others the highest counts are isolated peaks.

That most attractive of falcons, the Hobby, has already been mentioned. Its range is expanding in the British Isles and it is becoming more numerous. This is reflected in the increasing annual bird/day totals here.

Annual bird/day totals for Hobby:

| 85 | 86 | 87 | 88 | 89 | 90 | 91 | 92 | 93 | 94 |
|----|----|----|----|----|----|----|----|----|----|
| 8 | 11 | 11 | 15 | 17 | 29 | 14 | 32 | 20 | 58 |

Monthly bird/day totals for Hobby:

| J | F | M | A | M | J | J | A | S | O | N | D |
|---|---|---|---|---|---|---|---|---|---|---|---|
| – | – | – | 12 | 27 | 24 | 25 | 53 | 74 | – | – | – |

The September total doubled in 1994 when a pair with their two young was seen quite frequently between the 4th and 29th.

The southwesterly passage of Barn Swallows and House Martins is witnessed most autumns during late September and early October. The peak count of Barn Swallows involved 300 on 27 September 1994, but House Martin numbers are usually greater, with peaks of 700 on 27 September 1994, and 720 in less than an hour on 6 October 1988, including one loose flock of about 500.

There is also a small southerly passage of Meadow Pipits each September and occasionally, when there is suitable feeding habitat, flocks form and remain for several weeks. The peak count involves 120 in late September 1989.

September has also produced its share of rarities, with a group of four Little Stints flying over the reservoir in 1985; a Ring Ouzel in 1987; two Sandwich Terns flying northwest in 1988; a Corncrake and a flock of 13 Eurasian Wigeon in 1989; a Red-crested Pochard on the reservoir and two Arctic Skuas flying high south-west in 1991; an Osprey for three weeks in 1993; and four Mandarin Ducks in 1994.

In September 1991 in the marsh, an adult Water Rail suddenly flew up into the low, overhanging branches of an alder. It walked confidently among the thin branches, appearing to peck for insects, although I could not be sure what it was eating. BWP (Cramp 1980) describes a Water Rail flying into an apple tree to remove fruit, but I had not seen this species feeding in trees before (Taylor 1994a).

Recording the departure dates of summer migrants is another aspect of a local study and by the end of September a number of species will have flown south. The mean departure dates and the latest recorded dates (in brackets) are as follows:

**August**
  10th  Common Cuckoo (18/9)
  19th  Wood Warbler (3/9)
  29th  Reed Warbler (11/9)

**September**
  7th  Sedge Warbler (29/9)
  9th  Common Sandpiper (26/9)
  10th  Common Swift (9/10)
     Garden Warbler (11/10)
     Tree Pipit (24/9)
  11th  Pied Flycatcher (29/9)
  14th  Willow Warbler (5/10)
     Lesser Whitethroat (30/9)
     Whinchat (21/9)

**September** (continued)
  15th  Common Whitethroat (22/9)
  16th  Hobby (29/9)
     Yellow Wagtail (4/10)
  24th  Spotted Flycatcher (25/10)
  25th  Turtle Dove (30/9)
  26th  Sand Martin (14/10)
  27th  Northern Wheatear (10/10)

**October**
  17th  House Martin  (29/10)
  19th  Barn Swallow  (2/11)
     Blackcap  (20/11)
  24th  Chiffchaff  (18/11)

Each autumn small flocks of finches are another regular feature, as adults and young gather to feed on seeding plants. The peak counts occur in October, with 250 Linnets in 1989, 350 Greenfinches in 1985 and 500 Goldfinches in 1994.

In October much change takes place. Overnight frosts and cold northerly winds remind one that winter is not far off, although in some years the warmth of an Indian summer helps to postpone those thoughts.

In October 1993 a popular breeding site was lost when an ancient White Poplar finally keeled over. It was once the home of a pair of Barn Owls and during the study period a regular nesting site for Common Kestrels, Jackdaws and Stock Doves, as well as Common Treecreepers.

The annual overland Brent Goose movements are eagerly anticipated. They coincide with the species' arrival in the Swale from across the North Sea, often in light northeasterly winds. The biggest movement involving a total of 470 birds, in three flocks, flew south or south-west on 28 October 1988, in a light southerly wind. On occasions, other species can be seen moving with them, as on 25 October 1988 and 9 October 1992, when flocks of 11 and 17 Pintail flew south and south-west respectively.

Westerly movements of Common Starlings, finches and winter thrushes, which often follow the greensand ridge, are witnessed almost annually. Among these are regular autumn visitors such as Fieldfare, Redwing and Brambling, while Siskins are also annual in varying numbers, and Water Rails occur in most years. The mean arrival dates for these species, with the earliest recorded dates (in brackets) are as follows:

**September**
  27th  Siskin (13/9)

**October**
  3rd  Redwing (25/9)
  9th  Fieldfare (13/9)
  11th  Brambling (6/10)
  19th  Water Rail (8/9)

The peak movements have been spectacular: 3,340 Fieldfares flew west on 2 November 1986; 820 Fieldfares and 535 Redwings flew west in just an hour on 8 October 1990; 2,740 Fieldfares and 1,350 Redwings passed west during four hours on 20 October 1991; and 1,345 Redwings flew west on 15 October 1993.

Chaffinch movements have not been witnessed so regularly, but there was a peak of 200 west on 27 October 1986. A few Brambling sometimes get caught up in these westerly movements, but the highest counts have involved feeding flocks. There were exceptional numbers present in late October 1986, with up to 20 for nearly three weeks and an isolated peak of 50 on 14 November. The analysis of the monthly bird/day totals, show that this species is more a passage migrant than a winter visitor here.

Monthly bird/day totals for Brambling:

| J | F | M | A | M | J | J | A | S | O | N | D |
|---|---|---|---|---|---|---|---|---|---|---|---|
| 13 | 27 | 32 | 37 | – | – | – | – | – | 198 | 151 | 19 |

In October 1991 a hot-air balloon flew rather low over the reservoir, causing all the duck to fly up, together with a Green Sandpiper and, quite unexpectedly, two Common Snipe. I had not been aware that the two Common Snipe were roosting on the island. About ten days later, now aware of the possibility, I discovered one or two resting on the island each day for a few days.

Lapland Buntings are fairly regular around the coast of Kent, but inland records are exceptional and to find one feeding with Skylarks on 27 October 1985 was quite unexpected; to see another – or the same? – on 10 October 1986 was amazing, but frequent visits bring such rewards.

Unusual October sightings include a Ring Ouzel in 1987; a Black Redstart in 1988; single Woodlarks in both 1989 and 1992 (the former flew west with thrushes and finches, while the latter was flushed from a pathway); single Stonechats in 1990 and 1994; and a lone Bewick's Swan, which called evocatively as it flew over in 1992.

## November – December

The weather during these last two months is varied. In my report for that year I described November 1993 as a month of extremes, the coldest for many years, with snow but also with a very mild spell. This was followed by the wettest December in Kent for 60 years. A succession of depressions is not unusual, sometimes with heavy rain and strong winds. In contrast, a high pressure zone over the Continent may well produce cold, wintry conditions, as in November 1993 and earlier in December 1991.

Few additional species for the year list can really be expected, the average being just two for November–December, but in December 1991, when the high pressure produced a period of extremely cold weather, four new species were added.

It is the weather, more than anything, that determines the numbers and variety of species recorded. In some years, it seems that October extends into early November, when movements of Brent Geese, winter thrushes and finches continue early in the month, while a few summer migrants may linger on. Three summer migrants have occurred in November and their latest dates (with the year in brackets) are as follows:

| Barn Swallow | 2 November (1986) |
|---|---|
| Chiffchaff | 18 November (1990) |
| Blackcap | 20 November (1991) |

On 13 November 1988 in a light northwesterly wind, there was a marked westerly movement along the greensand ridge which involved some 2,000 Starlings, 360 Fieldfares and 53 Skylarks. The highest count of about 100 Skylarks was noted on 12 November 1985 during a spell of low temperatures, when flocks of Lapwings were seen flying south-west. The same severe weather produced the only record of Scaup, when a duck arrived at the reservoir and remained for three weeks. Other unusual records for November include the first Mandarin Duck, and an Oystercatcher in 1987; a Hen Harrier in 1989; a Common Crossbill in 1991; a Dunlin in 1992; the highest count of 20 Common Snipe and a Firecrest in 1993; and a Merlin in 1994. Flocks of Lapwing and Golden Plover often fly over in late autumn, but the only two occasions when single Golden Plover have been seen on the ground, within the study area, were both in November. Single Woodcock have also been seen, but on just three occasions. A pair of Tawny Owls often choose a mature oak and will remain as long as the leaves provide some cover.

In 1985 and 1986, flocks of up to 100 Siskins were seen in November and December, while in the latter month there was a peak count of 100 Tree Sparrows in 1992. Other unusual records for December include the only occurrence of Great Grey Shrike, in 1986, although this bird was seen intermittently until March 1987. The first Merlin flew north in 1986; a duck Goosander flew over in 1988; another Firecrest was seen in 1989; the first Goldeneye visited the reservoir and another Oystercatcher flew south in 1991; seven Eurasian Wigeon dropped down to the reservoir in 1992; and an immature male Peregrine was present in the park on 13 and 15 December 1993.

In concluding this chapter, it is interesting to compare study areas. Not surprisingly, with its greater range of habitat, including the reservoir, and with the more frequent visits, Boughton Park and Wierton Hill Farm has produced 31 species that were not seen at my former study site, Langley Park Farm (Taylor 1985). However, it is particularly fascinating to realise that an additional 11 species were seen there: Common Bittern, Knot, Ruff, Cetti's Warbler, Bearded Tit, Red-backed Shrike, Woodchat Shrike, Raven, Twite, Snow Bunting and Corn Bunting. I wonder how many of these may yet be seen at my new study area?

I enjoy speculating about new species that might occur and in my 1994 report I included 'a storm-driven Kittiwake' as a possibility; this species is now on the list – an adult flew over in May 1995. I believe that the following are the most likely potential additions: Common Scoter, Ruff, Little Gull, Water Pipit, or perhaps Hoopoe, Waxwing or Yellow-browed Warbler, but high on the list is Red Kite. I am sure that one will eventually pay a brief visit, hopefully while I am there and looking in the right direction.

# May Bird Races

How many different species is it possible to record in one day? In August 1955 I was well pleased with a modest total of 83 species at Cley, Norfolk. During 1962-64, I spent two years in Canada, where Christmas Counts and Bird Races were already popular. It was there that I really got the bug for seeing as many species as possible in a day, and took up the challenge more seriously. At Point Pelee on 11 May 1963, with two Canadian friends, we managed to total 135 different species, and 55 of them were new species for me. The following May we again recorded over 130.

Since returning to England in the summer of 1964 and settling in Kent, a bird race in May has become an annual event, shared with first one, then two and, since the national inter-county competition was introduced, three friends. Billy Buck was my first companion, but our early attempts were somewhat casual. Billy was then a dairy farmer, so time in the field was restricted by his milking regime.

Our first trip took place on 13 May 1965. It was pure coincidence that on the same day David Pearson, in Suffolk, achieved his best total at that time of 126 species, using only a bicycle (Gooders 1974). We scored only a modest 102, visiting Aylesford, Detling, Stockbury, Sheppey and Stodmarsh. Since then, more and more thought has gone into the planning of the most productive route, and our totals have slowly increased, as has our time in the field.

Some years ago the BBC broadcast a series of dawn chorus programmes from different parts of the British Isles. I remember Minsmere, Suffolk, recording the highest number of songs. This encouraged me to think in terms of an inter-county bird race competition. I had been trying for some time to get this off the ground when in 1980, David Tomlinson, through *Country Life* magazine, organised a four man team to set a British record of 132 species, raising over £1,000 for the RSPB in the process. During the next three years there was an annual competition between the *Country Life* team and a team from the Flora and Fauna Preservation Society. The record was raised to 153 species and the sponsorship money also increased. As a Kent resident, David Tomlinson joined my team in 1985. In 1986, following further discussion, he organised the first County Birdwatch Championship. My Kent team, with Bob Bland, Andrew Henderson and David Tomlinson, won that year with 143 species.

In 1993, as part of the national inter-county competition the Great Kent Bird Race was inaugurated. Over 25 Kent teams take part, raising money for local and international causes. Chris Barker and the Kent Trust for Nature Conservation are behind this admirable move. My 'Kent Veterans' team lost our title in 1994, even though we managed to record 143 species again. The winning team, Motney Hill Posse, comprising younger birders, amassed a new county record of 145 species. However, experience is invaluable and we regained the title in 1995, with 141 species to their 139.

On 11 May 1996 three teams broke the Kent record. My team reached 146 and Chris Bradshaw's recorded 147, but it was Dave Wilson's team, with Trevor Manship, Dave Morris and Roger Thompson, which became the first to exceed 150 species in a single day in Kent, with a brilliant total of 151. Extremely detailed planning, good team work and some good fortune made it possible.

Our cumulative total of 200 different species during 31 bird races gives some indication of the variety of species that occur in Kent during early May. This is the best period for recording the most species. At this time the birds are at their most vocal and this is how many of the resident and migrant breeding species are located.

Planning such a day is vital. Check for yourselves beforehand, and do not rely on information from others. You need to pinpoint sites for difficult-to-find breeding species, such as Hawfinch, Willow and Marsh Tit, Common Redstart, Stonechat, Lesser Spotted Woodpecker, Long-eared Owl and Woodcock. This last species, rather surprisingly, did not appear on our May bird race list until 1983. In the early years, as I have explained, there were restrictions on our time and we were not sufficiently motivated to start at midnight and to continue until after dark. It was the competitive element of the inter-county bird race that encouraged us to take our May bird races seriously.

When working out the route, the elements of time, tide and weather, the location of those species that are best seen at dawn or dusk, and the preference for an early morning seawatch, all combine to produce a high total mileage. Until 1991 we used to drive up to 250 miles, but since then the distance has increased to nearly 350 miles during the day, in order to include those extra few species.

Ideally, the weather early in the day needs to be fine and dry, with little or no wind to restrict bird song. A light southeasterly wind at Dungeness improves the chances of a good seabird passage, while the timing of the tide is crucial for finding species such as Rock Pipit and Purple Sandpiper quickly.

The weather on our first May bird race was gloriously hot. A Wryneck called near Aylesford, a Wood Warbler sang from the beeches at Detling, Capel Fleet produced a splendid variety of passage waders including Whimbrel, Spotted Redshank, Ruff and Wood Sandpiper, as well as Black Tern, and at Stodmarsh we heard a Savi's Warbler. Returning to Aylesford at dusk, we heard a Quail calling. We did not visit Dungeness in that first year.

On 4 May 1971, we saw a number of late wintering birds, including a Pink-footed Goose at Lade Pits, a pair of Long-tailed Ducks and a Brent Goose on the ARC pit at Dungeness, a Eurasian Wigeon on Capel Fleet and our only Fieldfare near Bridge. Nowadays, Eurasian Wigeon summer regularly on Sheppey, while small flocks of Brent Geese are invariably still present in the Medway.

It was not until 14 May 1978 that we achieved what seemed then to be a magical total of 120. It was overcast when we set out, but still, with light rain which ceased shortly after dawn. We left East Sutton at 0230. Neither Tawny nor Little Owls were calling in the miserably damp conditions. During a brief stop at 0330 by the golf course east of Canterbury, we heard the first of a number of Cetti's Warblers singing. In Trenley Park Woods we added 40 species in the next two hours, including Little Owl and Jay, both of which have eluded us more than once. We arrived at Stodmarsh at 0530, where we always anticipate adding a number of species that we do not expect to see elsewhere. The first of these, the Bearded Tit, was quickly added, as several birds called and flitted from reed to reed alongside the Lampen Wall. The drumming of a Common Snipe was another welcome sound. A Common Redpoll called as it flew over, while a distinctive reeling song attracted us to another Stodmarsh speciality, Savi's Warbler, which continued to sing from a reed stem as we watched it. A Water Rail squealed from the reeds behind us, and was a welcome bonus. After a while we saw a drake Garganey and heard the more metallic reeling of a Grasshopper Warbler. Although not entirely unexpected, as it had been first seen the previous day, the presence of a Pallid Swift was an exceptional bonus and we spent about 20 minutes studying it. (This is definitely not on during a bird race, particularly when you fail to see a Glossy Ibis flying over your head!). No Common Bitterns had boomed, but we left Stodmarsh at 0825 feeling well satisfied with our 75 species and especially elated over the Pallid Swift.

We visited Church Wood near Canterbury next to search for the woodland species which are so important to add early in the day. We failed to find Common Redstart or Wood Warbler, but did add Willow Tit, Nuthatch and Tree Pipit. Minnis Bay was our next stop, where we saw a Stonechat and a migrant Whinchat, while at Foreness we added Fulmar, a lone Common Scoter and the summering flock of Common Eider. With the tide low in Pegwell Bay, the waders were too distant to identify with any certainty, so we headed south for Lade Sands. Arriving there around 1330, we saw Bar-tailed Godwits and Sanderling, our 100th species. We allowed ourselves 90 minutes for a seawatch, adding

Red-throated Diver, Gannet, Common Guillemot and Razorbill. This is the only occasion on which we have identified both these auks during a bird race. The Dungeness RSPB reserve produced Ruff and Whimbrel. We left there at 1715 and drove back to East Sutton, where I knew of a damson orchard favoured by Hawfinches. We found one – number 115. Several woodland species were missing and we had still not seen or heard a Little Grebe, so we put our faith in a small stretch of the Len Valley at Broomfield. Long-tailed Tit, Common Kingfisher and then Marsh Tit, followed by a Spotted Flycatcher, increased the total to 119 and at 2020 I eventually glimpsed a Little Grebe, as it dived below the lake's surface. It gave me an immensely satisfying feeling to achieve, at long last, my target of 120 species in a day in Kent. It had taken 15 attempts and, although on paper there always seem to be ample species in the county at that time, it had proved to be a considerable challenge. The evening was still and clear and I had every hope of adding Woodcock and possibly Nightjar in the nearby coppiced chestnut area of Kingswood, but it was not to be. Sadly, the latter species seems to have disappeared from this area. As the last of the evening light faded, it was a most pleasant end to a memorable day.

In the early eighties, because of the increased interest in May bird races and the fund-raising potential they have, I began to look at our efforts even more critically. In planning our route for 16 May 1982, I came to the conclusion that visiting woodland in south Kent, before doing an early morning seawatch at Dungeness, might well prove more successful.

It was still, with a cloudless sky, when we visited Challock Forest shortly before 0300. Both Nightjar and Common Nightingale were performing well, and we left for Hamstreet Woods. There, as dawn broke, we added a wide selection of woodland birds departing around 0600 with 50 species on our list. On the way to Dungeness we visited Dengemarsh and the ARC pit, where a Little Ringed Plover was a welcome bonus. The next hour or so was rather disappointing. After some good sea passage during the week, the flat calm and light wind were not conducive to seabird movement and we only added six more species. We failed to identify a total of four distant divers, although two were almost certainly Great Northern. There were few passerine migrants around the Observatory, but brief visits to Lade Sands, Lade Pit and then Dungeness RSPB reserve, enabled us to see our 100th species, a Sand Martin, at 1030. Lyminge Forest produced the expected Firecrest, followed by two Dotterel at Sandwich Bay, a Whimbrel at Pegwell Bay and Fulmars at Foreness. The highpoint of the day was the sighting of an Osprey drifting slowly up the Stour Valley, while Westbere produced four more species, including Savi's Warbler. Arriving at Elmley around 1900, with 117 already on our list, we added five more ducks and four waders, as well as the Glossy Ibis. With a total of 127 species, the new route had paid off handsomely.

The challenge now was to see 130 species. Another change was considered for 1984 – to start at midnight. For various reasons 6 May was selected, but the darkness of the heavily cloud-covered night sky and the cold, strong northeasterly wind prevented us hearing as much as we had hoped for in the Stour Valley. However, both Cetti's and Savi's Warblers sang well for us. Dawn was exceedingly slow in breaking over Fagg's Wood and although we heard a Woodcock roding shortly before 0430, the dawn chorus did not get underway until 15 minutes later. The Common Crossbills that were present had still not appeared when we left at 0600, but Hamstreet Woods again produced a good selection of woodland specialities, including Hawfinch and Lesser Spotted Woodpecker. We had to-talled 56 when we left there just after 0700, about an hour behind schedule. The seawatch commenced at 0800, by which time we had recorded 82 species, but it too was disappointing and we only added six more species, including Gannet and Arctic Tern – no sign of any divers, skuas or auks, not even a Kittiwake or Common Scoter. The trapping area was also quiet, although a Golden Oriole had been seen that morning. We added Stonechat, Northern Wheatear and Black Redstart, and a Common Sandpiper on the Long Pits, while a little more time at the ARC pit produced a lone Sand Martin – our only one of the day – and a Little Ringed Plover, but there was no sign of the Temminck's Stint that had been seen there earlier. We were now well behind schedule and cursing the strong wind.

Suddenly as we looked out to sea at the Brooks our luck seemed to change. We chose to go there primarily to see Common Eider and as we scanned the water at 1100 we saw a fine Slavonian Grebe in summer plumage, our 100th species. Five more species followed in quick succession, including Common Eider, Velvet Scoter and Red-breasted Merganser. Although we had left the Dungeness area by this time in 1982, it was noon before we reached 105 in that year. Our expectations took on a new look, particularly when we added five more species on the RSPB reserve, including a Black-necked Grebe, although we failed to see the Mediterranean Gulls that were there. Back to the ARC pit yet again and this time we found the Temminck's Stint. At last we were able to leave the Dungeness area, ticking off Knot on Lade Sands as number 112, at 1300.

From there on everything seemed to fall into place, as planned, apart from a little hiccup when we failed to stop at Sandling Park to try for that increasingly elusive Bullfinch – we never did find one. Several Firecrests were either calling or singing in Lyminge Forest at 1350 and we decided not to spend time searching for Common Crossbills there, but drove on to Pegwell Bay where we added Curlew and two more unexpected bonuses –Brent Goose and Avocet. The adrenalin was really beginning to flow. Thanet produced Ring-necked Parakeet and Purple Sandpiper, while a very brief visit to Stodmarsh enabled us to add Bearded Tit, but we did not stay long enough to hear Common Snipe or Water Rail. The Canterbury Grey Wagtails could not have been more obliging and 40 minutes later we were on Sheppey and looking at a Marsh Harrier. At 1800, as we drove towards the Elmley reserve with 122 already listed, we felt confident that we could exceed our 130 target for the first time. The Dotterel which had been there for some time were still present, a pair of Grey Partridge appeared and several Whimbrel called as they flew off. On the floods we added four duck species and three more waders, bringing the total to 132 by 1930. Two known localities in central Kent produced Long-eared and Barn Owl respectively, just before 2100 – marvellous climax to a superb day's birdwatching. A total of 134 had exceeded our highest expectations, and yet, as always, we had missed quite a number of common birds.

The next year we totalled 140 for the first time. Since then we have achieved 143 twice and our record of 144 once, in 1989. The bird race in 1994 was an exciting one, even though we came second. At the end of the day we had added five species that we had never before recorded during these May bird races, and we felt we might have reached that tantalising target of 150.

On 8 May 1994 it was drizzling at midnight and my local Barn Owls failed to appear, but a Grey Plover called as it flew over at 0045 and seven minutes later we heard the expected Little Ringed Plover as we walked round the small reservoir. The rain eased at New Hythe, where we were almost deafened by the volume of Common Nightingale song, but unfortunately the Cetti's Warblers failed to utter any sounds.

A Woodcock at Fagg's Wood was heard roding just after 0410, but after two attempts we failed to see a Barn Owl. In Fagg's and Hamstreet Woods we added several of the more difficult woodland species. We left there some 15 minutes behind schedule, with 55 species on the list, added a few more across the marsh and another 15 at the ARC pit, including four Avocets, which brought our total to 79 before starting the seawatch at Dungeness. The seabird passage was negligible, although we did add an encouraging 12 more species in just half-an-hour, including Gannet, Common Scoter, Red-throated Diver, Mediterranean and Little Gulls, plus four tern species. Somehow we managed to miss the Roseate Tern that was apparently roosting on the beach. Dengemarsh provided our first ever Hoopoe, plus Marsh Harrier, three late Golden Plovers and Red-legged Partridge – number 100 at 0922. Since 1986, the 100th species has invariably been seen at an earlier time, with the earliest being 0824 in 1988, when we totalled 137 species.

The Dungeness RSPB reserve produced both excitement and frustration. We saw Bar-tailed Godwits, but could not find Ruddy Duck and we learned later that we were within 20 metres of a Golden Oriole – strangely silent while we were there – but a summer plumaged Black-necked Grebe was a delightful addition. At about the same time, two more Golden Orioles and a Wood Warbler were present in the trapping area.

With the tide right in on Lade Sands, there were no shore waders to be seen, so we left the Dungeness area around 1040 and headed for Lyminge Forest, where we added both Firecrest and Tree Pipit. Elhampark Wood was scheduled to produce Marsh Tit, Common Redpoll and Common Crossbill, but only the last appeared, a flock of 11 flying over. The addition of a Sparrowhawk there, however, gave us more encouragement. With Marsh Tit, Common Redpoll, Hawfinch and Lesser Spotted Woodpecker still missing, we decided to make a brief visit to Larkey Valley Wood, but only managed to add Common Redpoll. We were now about an hour behind schedule, as we hastened to Funton Creek and Sheppey. The Brent Geese obliged rapidly and while parked on the river wall near Ridham Dock, we added our first Shag for a Bird Race day, plus Whimbrel and Little Tern. A Slavonian Grebe was still present on the Swale at Elmley, where we added three ducks, four waders and a Peregrine – 125 species by 1500. The Kingshill Farm Little Owl also obliged, before we headed into central Kent. Mote Park came up trumps. Although the resident Common Kingfisher failed to materialise, we added Grey Wagtail, Mandarin Duck, Nuthatch and Spotted Flycatcher. As we were still behind schedule, we should have headed straight for Dover, but we wasted a valuable 20 minutes searching for, but failing to find, a Common Kingfisher along the Len.

At Dover we could not locate the Black Redstarts that had been found there a day or two earlier. Near St. Margaret's we had some good fortune in finding a migrant Whinchat, but wasted more time searching for a Stonechat. We then decided not to go for the Rock Pipit and headed for Pegwell Bay, not having time, either, to visit Sandwich Bay for a possible Quail. We did, however, find both missing shorebirds, Sanderling and Knot, on the mud in Pegwell Bay. By this time we had made the decision not to visit Thanet, where there were three more species to be seen – Common Eider, Purple Sandpiper and Ring-necked Parakeet. We had set 1930 as the time to reach Stodmarsh, so we just had time to call in at Seaton where we knew we could expect a Ruddy Duck. It was still there, another first for our Bird Race days.

We reached Stodmarsh, back on schedule, with 136 listed and hopes of six more. As we walked along the Lampen Wall, we were greeted with "There's a Red-rumped Swallow up there". Within seconds we were all watching it. Then followed five of the anticipated species, including Common Snipe drumming, a Long-eared Owl perched and in flight, a prolonged call from a Water Rail, numerous Bearded Tits and fine views of a Hobby. As the sun set below a band of red sky, a noisy pair of Hobbies passed food. This seemed a fitting end to the day, but it was only 2100. Surprisingly, a Merlin then flew by, presumably going to roost. With all this good fortune, why wouldn't the Grasshopper Warbler reel? We had also missed a drake Garganey there. As we returned to the car, two of us heard what sounded like a Quail calling from an arable field, but the rhythm was not quite right. Maybe we should have stayed a little longer for the others to hear it too, but it didn't seem that it was going to call again. Our minds were thinking arable and Quail, but beyond the arable was the reedbed and two weeks later, in France, I heard the same call from a marsh – it was obviously a Spotted Crake.

We visited Westbere, where a Savi's Warbler had been heard singing, but it would not oblige for us and we could not hear any Nightjars in Challock Forest either. We returned home by 2340. Our total of 143 was pleasing, particularly with five new species for the 30 year cumulative total including such goodies as Hoopoe and Red-rumped Swallow. It had been a splendid day's birdwatching and the longest we had ever spent in the field. We had had some good fortune and had been so close to seeing a number of other species, that we really ought to have broken our record. However, we had also made some wrong decisions. It really has become an amazingly complex logistical exercise.

Extreme rarities have been seen on a number of occasions, but pride of place must go to the Laughing Gull, an American species that Billy Buck and I found at Lade Pit on 11 May 1966. At the time it was the first to be accepted for the British Isles, as was the Stodmarsh Pallid Swift. We also saw a Squacco Heron at Elmley on 13 May 1990 and a Black Stork there on 12 May 1991.

Over the years, the status of some species has changed. The Wryneck has disappeared as a breeding bird. The Common Redpoll appears to have turned full cycle; we failed to record it at all between 1965 and 1969, then it became increasingly more widespread as a breeding species and we had no difficulty seeing it annually, but during the nineties it has again become scarce; we missed it in 1991 and in 1995. The Hawfinch is also becoming less widespread. The Cetti's Warbler became regular from 1973, following its colonisation, but the hard winters of the mid-eighties have made it a more difficult species to record since then. After the mid-sixties, the Wood Warbler declined as a breeding bird and is consequently now hard to record. Most recently, the small breeding population of Grasshopper Warblers has become almost nonexistent.

On the plus side the number of raptors that can be expected has increased. The Marsh Harrier, which was first added in 1977, then seen again in 1984 and 1987, can now be seen annually since starting to breed in the county. Sparrowhawk did not appear on the list until 1983, but we now anticipate seeing it regularly, as its breeding population continues to expand. The Peregrine, too, now breeds and can be seen annually. In recent years, three more species have begun to breed regularly in Kent: the first Avocet was not included on the list until 1984, but since 1986 it has been impossible to miss. Mediterranean Gull was not seen until 1975, but since 1979, like the Firecrest, it has been seen almost annually.

I wonder what the future holds? Should we anticipate a few more breeding species? Scarlet Rosefinch, Bluethroat and Penduline Tit breed just across the Channel, and that stretch of water should not prevent the further expansion of their ranges. We may lose Savi's Warbler from the Stour Valley, but perhaps the Common Bittern will return.

# A Year in Kent: 1994

In *Birdwatching in Kent* (Taylor 1985), I described the excitements and frustrations of my experiences during 1977, when I managed to record 210 species in the county. In 1984 I raised my record to 230 and in 1988 to 241. I then promised myself that I would not try again, as it does make pressing demands on one's time, until I retired from teaching. This I did in the summer of 1993, and when I heard that in 1994 others were attempting to improve upon my best total, I took up the challenge once again, although it was mid-February before I heard this news! However, I had already made a reasonable start to the year.

Whenever possible, I like to spend the whole of New Year's Day in the field, trying to see as many species as possible. My best total so far is 110 species, within Kent, in 1986. During the years I have lived in this county I have been out birdwatching between dawn and dusk on 20 occasions on 1 January. My cumulative total for that date is a surprisingly high 153 species. (As a postscript, I added an amazing three more to that list on 1 January 1995 when, on the same route that I am about to describe, I saw Mandarin Duck, Common Buzzard and Dartford Warbler!)

The weather towards the end of December 1993 was atrocious, with heavy rain and strong winds from the south-west – not a good omen for a promising start to 1994. Nevertheless, I planned to follow a traditional route in the south-east of the county with three fellow enthusiasts.

## 1 January

With prior knowledge of a local Long-eared Owl roost and blessed with a full moon on a surprisingly still, almost cloudless night, we started at Langley at 0600. A Moorhen was the first bird we heard calling, followed by four thrush species that we disturbed from their roost in some blackthorn. Somewhat carelessly, I then disturbed two Long-eared Owls, without seeing them myself. However, the other three group members saw them clearly as they flew off. A Coot also called while we were still at Langley.

Shortly before 0700 we arrived at Sandling Park, where we planned to see as many of the woodland species as we could expect. We were surprised and dismayed at the volume of traffic noise from the nearby new motorway extension. However, several Tawny Owls were hooting, a Carrion Crow called and a Robin sang as we commenced our walk through this attractive wooded valley. We continued to hear new species calling and slowly added Mallard, Common Pheasant, Woodpigeon and Blue Tit, before seeing Common Kestrel, Black-headed Gull, Green Woodpecker and Common Treecreeper when the light improved. A Common Gull flew over, followed by a Common Starling and two Jackdaws, then a noisy Wren chattered and a Dunnock crept through some brambles. A Great Spotted Woodpecker flew overhead and we added Great Tit and Long-tailed Tit before flushing a Woodcock, a good species to get on the first day of the year. In past years we have often witnessed numbers of thrushes and finches flying from their roosting sites, but there was little sign of them on this occasion and the finches were slow to appear. A Chaffinch was next, then a Stock Dove and a Mistle Thrush to bring our total to 30 by 0820. It became more of a struggle after that and the next five species took another 25 minutes – Rook, Magpie, Goldcrest, Nuthatch and Lapwing. As we left Sandling Park we saw a Collared Dove. We spent half-an-hour in nearby Brockhill Country Park, where we added House Sparrow, Coal and Marsh Tits, Greenfinch, Bullfinch and Siskin, but failed to find Common Redpoll, Common Kingfisher or Grey Wagtail. Other species we might reasonably have expected by that time included Sparrowhawk, Little Owl, Lesser Spotted Woodpecker, Willow Tit and Jay. However, 43 species by 0920 was a reasonable start and we were feeling quietly confident, though aware that we were unlikely to have time to find any of the missing species elsewhere. In mid-winter there are less than ten hours of daylight.

Our next stop, Folkestone Warren, was an important one, as three species we hoped to find there were unlikely to be seen any farther south. Fulmar, Purple Sandpiper and Rock Pipit were all located within a few minutes, together with Herring Gull en route. Great Crested Grebe and Cormorant were seen on the sea. At Copt Point by 1000, we added Linnet, Ringed Plover – a species that is also scarce any farther south during the winter – Mediterranean Gull, Common Redshank, Great Black-backed Gull and Oyster-catcher. We had reached a total of 55 species by 1020 – about average for the ten years that I have followed this route.

Beside the chip-and-putt course at Hythe we found a pair of Stonechats, as well as Meadow Pipit and Pied Wagtail. In the Botolph's Dyke area we saw 23 Red-throated Divers on the sea, added Little Grebe and Mute Swan, had a brief glimpse of a Green Sandpiper flying over, good numbers of Golden Plover and several Common Snipe. Skylarks and two coveys of Red-legged Partridges were seen as we drove across Romney Marsh, but we failed to find any Grey Partridges. We were confronted with the problem of discovering where the waders were roosting, as the tide was virtually on the full. It was 1125 and we had 66 species on our list. The Greatstone Sewage Farm produced a flock of Curlew and a Grey Heron, while small flocks of waders were being disturbed from the shingle beach towards the southern end of Lade Sands. Here a dozen Brent Geese flew north, a welcome bonus at this time of year, while we were able to identify Knot, Dunlin, Grey Plover and Sanderling amongst the flocks of waders. Offshore, near the Lifeboat Station, there were two Black-throated Divers, several Kittiwakes and a Razorbill, bringing our total to 75 by 1245.

The only significant news at Dungeness Bird Observatory was of Firecrest and Blackcap at the Long Pits. We didn't feel that we had time to spend hunting for what can be extremely elusive 'little brown jobs', so we carried out another brief seawatch near the Patch. We only managed to add Gannet – 1315 and just 76 species. The earliest 100 that we have achieved was at 1343 in 1986. However, within 15 minutes, scanning over the ARC Pit and the New Diggings, we raised our total to 91, with Tufted Duck, Common Pochard, Goldeneye, about 80 Bewick's Swans, Gadwall, Common Teal, Canada Goose, Common Shelduck, Pintail, Shoveler, Ruff, two Ruddy Ducks, an unexpected Chiffchaff, Lesser Black-backed Gull and Smew. Driving onto the RSPB reserve we saw a flock of Corn Buntings. During our 80 minute visit there – a little longer than anticipated, but necessary to find a number of rarer species that were present – we saw Eurasian Wigeon, Slavonian Grebe, Goosander, another Black-throated Diver, Black-necked Grebe, Long-tailed Duck, a small flock of 11 Barnacle Geese on Dengemarsh and a Yellowhammer. We failed to find the wintering Black Redstart. The Yellowhammer was our 100th species, seen at 1450 – our second earliest 100. A dark-looking Common Kestrel almost got onto our list as a Merlin, until it flew. So this species eluded us.

We decided that a brief visit to Scotney Pit should be worthwhile and there we added Greylag Goose, a Hen Harrier and a lone drake Scaup. The light was now fading fast so we sped for the Woolpack reedbed, where at long last we added Reed Bunting, saw at least five Hen Harriers – including two superb adult males – unexpectedly heard a Bearded Tit calling and then heard and saw a flock of about 80 White-fronted Geese. They disappeared into the gloom as they flew towards their roost. This rounded the day off satisfactorily, with our total on 105. We might well have added Water Rail, Grey Partridge and Barn Owl, but whatever preparation you do, birds have a habit of not always being obliging, which adds to the fun of this competitive side of birdwatching.

# 3 January

I was back at Boughton Park and Wierton Hill Farm on the 2nd, but failed to add anything new for the year. It was the next day before I found Tree Sparrow and Little Owl; another visit to Langley Park Farm produced excellent views of two Long-eared Owls.

# 4 January

My first Sparrowhawk of the year on my local patch.

# 7 January

My 110th species for the year was a female Lesser Spotted Woodpecker.

# 17 January

News of two Red-necked Grebes wintering together encouraged me to visit Snodland. A drake Ruddy Duck was also present, but I failed to hear the Cetti's Warbler.

# 18 January

Having received news of a wintering Dipper in the county, I drove to Dover. The bird was attracted by the fast flowing stream running through the village of River, just below Kearsney Abbey. It is an attractive spot. I saw not only the Dipper, which sang a few phrases for me, but also Grey Wagtail and Common Kingfisher.

# 20 January

Not having made a visit into north Kent so far, there were up to ten additional species that a trip to Sheppey could produce. My timing was poor, as the tide was low when I arrived at Shellness. I saw a male Marsh Harrier and there were Bar-tailed Godwits and Turnstones feeding on the mud and mussel beds respectively. It was disappointing not to find any Twite or Snow Buntings near the hamlet, but the former was proving scarce this winter, which was continuing to be mild. With the tide so low I was unable to see any Red-breasted Mergansers either, but there were four Common Eider in the Swale. Along Capel Fleet there were flocks of some 44 Ruff and 30 Bewick's Swans. Only two young swans were present, indicative of a poor breeding season last year. A pair of Grey Partridges was the next addition to the list, bringing the annual total to 120, before I enjoyed the sight of a Merlin chasing a Common Starling.

# 27 January

I received the first 'rarity call' from Dungeness and I reached Greatstone within the hour. The weather had deteriorated and it was dull, with a light drizzle falling, but I was still able to find and study my first Kentish Ring-billed Gull. It was almost dark by the time I reached the seawatching hide and an Iceland Gull had just disappeared. At Dungeness I got news of another extreme rarity for Kent, a Lesser White-fronted Goose on Elmley, feeding with about 1,900 White-fronted Geese.

# 28 January

Although a strong westerly wind was blowing, the sky was almost cloudless, so the light was excellent as I scanned through the distant goose flock on Elmley. Nine Barnacle Geese were easy to pick out, but it took some time before Mike Buckland eventually spotted the Lesser White-fronted Goose. At that range I was only able to see the yellow eye-ring by looking through a Questar telescope. However, the diagnostic short bill, which gives the bird an almost flat-nosed profile, could be seen and its smaller size was obvious when it showed itself fully. I added several more species to my year list, including Peregrine, Avocet and Short-eared Owl.

As Mike had not yet seen the Ring-billed Gull, we headed for Dungeness again, and by 1530 we were studying it at close range in far better light. The dry conditions made some aspects of the bird's plumage look very different from its 'wet' appearance the previous day – an important consideration when writing a description.

The numbers of gulls wintering at Dungeness were impressive, and from the seawatching hide I was able to get good views of Iceland and Glaucous Gulls, both in first-winter plumage. I managed to identify an impressive total of ten gull species; several Common Guillemots were swimming on the sea.

## 30 January

Little Egret is becoming increasingly common in Britain, with small flocks wintering in several southern counties. Not to be outdone, Kent was hosting one, or possibly two birds, so I visited Cliffe Pools to add Little Egret to my year list – number 130. It was sharing a pool with a remarkably pink Chilean Flamingo. A Long-tailed Duck and a Red-throated Diver were also present and there were several Scaup in Cliffe Quarry.

In the afternoon I visited Cooling and Halstow marshes, as there were two Common Buzzards wintering in the area, together with several other birds of prey. I managed to see two Peregrines, a Sparrowhawk and two Hen Harriers, but failed to see the Common Buzzards.

## 7 February

Another species that is unusual during the winter months in Kent is Serin, but one was being seen quite regularly in King George VI Memorial Park in Ramsgate. It was mild and sunny and I spent four hours searching for the Serin, with no success. The only addition to my year list was the resident Ring-necked Parakeet, a number of which were screeching loudly as they flew around the park.

In the late afternoon I visited Stodmarsh, where I could not find the wintering Great Grey Shrike, but was able to add two more species: a Cetti's Warbler and several Water Rails. The latter's diagnostic calls made their presence obvious. It was also good to see another splendid adult male Hen Harrier.

## 9 February

A pair of Barn Owls was resident on my local patch, but they were particularly nocturnal! Late afternoon visits did not produce the anticipated sight of the pair hunting. One needed to wait patiently until after dark before one of the Barn Owls deigned to leave the nest box in which it roosted. It was not until my fourth attempt that I was at last rewarded, but it was only a shadowy glimpse as it left an ash branch on which I could barely make out its pale form.

## 11 February

Another visit was made to Capel Fleet with several friends who also wanted to see Lesser White-fronted Goose. The goose flock was feeding close to the Harty Road and eventually a Lesser White-front was located, a different bird from the one I had seen on Elmley. This one showed no belly markings and had only a small white blaze on its forehead. With a more powerful telescope than my own, I was again able to see the yellow eye-ring clearly. The flock was disturbed at one stage and I was able to pick out this individual on size as it flew back and landed again. I was also able to add Bean Goose to my year list, as we found three among the huge flock of Whitefronts, as well as Lapland Bunting – a single bird called as it flew overhead.

## 12 February

I visited the Halstow marshes again, but still failed to see the Common Buzzards.

## 13 February

It was bitterly cold, with a strong wind blowing from the east, but I felt I had to try to see the Common Bittern that was wintering by the Abbey Mead pit at New Hythe. I looked across the water towards the reedbeds, remaining until dark, but failed to see it.

## 14 February

During the morning I conducted the monthly census on my local patch and among the large numbers of finches I managed to find a lone Brambling. I visited New Hythe again in the afternoon, with the bitterly cold wind still blowing, although the sky was almost cloudless. As the light began to fade, I could just see a Common Bittern, as it climbed up some reeds.

By now I had decided that I was going to attempt to break my Kent record, so it was necessary to find those wintering species that were still missing from my list, particularly the rarer ones. It can get quite frantic in December if you are still missing some of the regular winter visitors!

## 18 February

I visited the lakes along the Stour at Bagham, having been told that one Shag was still present after a group of six had been seen there earlier. I could not locate it, so I headed for King George VI Memorial Park again and on this occasion I managed to locate the female Serin – only my second in Kent. On the way home I called in at Stodmarsh to discover that the Great Grey Shrike had been seen on the two previous days. It was absent today. However, I did find a drake Red-crested Pochard – number 140 for the year. I also counted 220 Corn Buntings going to roost.

## 20 February

This date was set aside for my annual Kent Ornithological Society field trip to Bewl Water and Bedgebury. As usual we spent the latter half of the day at Bedgebury and although we failed to find any Common Crossbills, I did manage to add two new species to my year list, Common Redpoll and Hawfinch. The former species has become more scarce in recent winters. I had still not seen one on my local patch and there had been up to 40 wintering there the previous year.

## 21 February

On my local patch I had a surprise addition to the list – that gem of a bird, a Firecrest. The weather was bright and sunny, so I headed for Knole Park hoping to hear Woodlarks singing, but no luck. I again visited Bedgebury and also a larch plantation at Round Green, but still failed to find any Common Crossbills.

## 22 February

The weather had deteriorated, but I had arranged to meet some friends at Stodmarsh. It proved to be worthwhile, as the Great Grey Shrike performed extremely well. I also visited Littlebourne and added a Water Pipit. On the way home I called in at Broomfield, where I saw at least seven Mandarin Ducks, another new species for the year list.

## 24 February

One of my favourite north Kent spots is Funton Creek when the tide is almost full. Here you can get close views of Pintail, Brent Geese and numerous waders, including Avocet in the winter months. Another species that is regular here is the Red-breasted Merganser, which I still needed for my year list: there were 10 present. I then drove along to Motney Hill and saw at least 15 Black-tailed Godwits, another first for the year. They were feeding on the mud in Rainham Creek as the tide dropped.

## 25 February

Although the weather was dull and damp, I visited Knole Park again and was rewarded with the delightfully melodic song of a Woodlark. Two others were calling as they chased each other over an open area, virtually cleared of trees following the great storm in October 1987. Another species that has been attracted to these heath-like areas is the Stonechat. It will be interesting to see how long they remain.

In the afternoon I made yet another unsuccessful attempt to see the Common Buzzards on Halstow marshes. However, I did enjoy studying a small flock of White-fronted Geese, and was impressed by the increased numbers of Pintail now being attracted to the newly flooded section of the RSPB reserve, below Eastborough Farm.

## 26 February

Having not yet seen any Snow Buntings, I visited Whitstable in the afternoon and had pleasingly close views of two birds perched on a breakwater, part of a flock of 17. This species featured as number 150 for the year, but a wintering Black Redstart failed to show itself. I next visited Oare Marshes where I had excellent views of a wintering Spotted Redshank, still showing the attractive pale greyness of full winter plumage.

## 27 February

At 0600, just before dawn, I was once more overlooking Halstow marshes and Northward Hill, anticipating that a Common Buzzard would fly from its roost just after dawn. It apparently chose to roost elsewhere, or slipped out without my seeing it. The clouds of corvids flying from the roost were most impressive, and there were strange 'grunts' from the Grey Herons, which were already tending their nests in the large heronry.

Still missing Common Crossbill, I thought an afternoon walk along the North Downs Way, near Chilham, might be worthwhile. Plantations of larch are favoured by this species, as well as by Siskins and Common Redpolls, and a flock of Siskins provided good viewing in one such plantation. Eventually one Common Crossbill called a few times as it flew over.

## 28 February

Had spring really arrived so early? Two Chiffchaffs were singing and chasing each other around an alder copse on my local patch, while a lone Shelduck flew north-east. The Chiffchaffs remained to establish territories, some nine days earlier than in any previous year.

There was news of a Common Buzzard wintering on Dengemarsh, so I headed south later in the morning and my luck changed. I found the Common Buzzard sitting in a field with grazing sheep – much more obliging than the birds on the Thames marshes. Earlier that morning there had been a small up-Channel passage of Common and Velvet Scoters, but the sea was quiet, apart from a few flocks of Brent Geese flying east and a few Gannets. However, a Great Northern Diver obligingly swam around the Patch, providing me with good views and another addition to my year list.

The end of February saw a total of 154 species – a promising start to the year. Among those species recorded in the county that I might have seen were Whooper Swan, Pink-footed Goose, Shag, Velvet Scoter, Jack Snipe, Greenshank, Little Gull, Black Redstart, Blackcap, Willow Tit and Twite. However, I anticipated being able to add most of these species during March, leaving only the first two. These would be difficult to find during the last quarter of the year, but I would just have to hope for a cold spell in December.

## 2 March

The Shag is becoming more common around the Kent coast and a few had been seen regularly on the Swale near Ridham Dock, so I set out to try and find one. I approached the Swale from Sheppey and on arriving at Elmley Hills I located an immature, seeing an adult a short while later. In the same area at least three Short-eared Owls were hunting over the wet grassland, while a ringtail Hen Harrier flew through.

## 5 March

A phone call the previous evening aroused considerable excitement. A Ross's Gull, a first for Kent if accepted, had been reported over the Patch at Dungeness. Quite a crowd had assembled there by dawn, but there was no sign of it during the first two hours of daylight (and no description was ever received of it). There were good numbers of Common Guillemots on the sea, along with a few Red-throated Divers and a lone Shag, while a few small flocks of Common Eider flew west. The only addition to my year list was Common Scoter, hardly a substitute for a Ross's Gull. I returned again for the two hours until dusk, hoping that it might repeat the previous day's performance, but it was not to be.

## 10 March

Twite had been particularly scarce, so I thought I would see if there were any remaining at one of their favoured localities. I visited the saltings at Sayes Court and did manage to find four. I then walked along the seawall to the Swale NNR, where about 1,000 White-fronted Geese were resting. It was a fine sight, even though I could not find either of the Lesser Whitefronts among them. The reserve was looking extremely attractive for spring waders and about 20 Avocets and 50 Black-tailed Godwits were already making use of it for roosting.

## 13 March

I attended the KOS/BTO Conference in Canterbury on 12th, when I missed hearing a Blackcap in song by about five minutes. I also learned that a Spoonbill was present at Elmley. This species was far more important to add to my year list than a Blackcap in early March, so I visited Elmley and eventually located it feeding by a fleet overflowing with flood water, and occasionally disappearing from view. Spoonbill is very much a bonus species for the year list – although it occurs annually in the county, it is difficult to see.

## 15 March

As a belt of rain cleared, the weather looked more promising for an afternoon visit into west Kent. I had been told of a pair of displaying Goshawks. This is one of just two annual species, the other being Red Kite, that I have yet to see in my home county, so the visit had a double purpose. During the 90 minutes that I scanned the area, I only saw a single Sparrowhawk, so another visit was going to be necessary, perhaps when the wind dropped and the weather was more settled.

## 17 March

An almost cloudless morning, and although the strong westerly wind was still blowing, I headed into west Kent again. I scanned over the same woodland area between 0800 and 0820, when a heavy-looking hawk came into view and started to perform a display flight. As it climbed, it made Jay-like wing flaps, before plunging in a rather Woodpigeon-like display loop. It performed like this for several minutes before dropping into the wood. It may well have been the much sought-after Goshawk, but it was too far away to be sure. I walked over the farmland footpaths and through some most attractive mixed woodland to find vantage points with the sun behind me, but I failed to see any sign of the hawk again. However, I did glimpse a small male Sparrowhawk, as it flew rapidly along a woodland edge.

## 18 March

It was time to put Jack Snipe on my year list, as the wintering numbers are augmented by passage migrants in March. My choice of site was Conningbrook gravel pit. I flushed four, at close range, from a small patch of lakeside *Juncus*. I then decided to visit Dungeness for some early spring migrants and found three female Black Redstarts by the lighthouse – number 160 – while nearby there were two male Northern Wheatears. A few Sandwich Terns had already been seen, but I saw none during a short seawatch. However, it was good to see that the Great Northern Diver was still feeding offshore by the Patch. There was news of a Common Crane flying south-west over Folkestone earlier in the morning, so I drove over parts of Romney and Walland Marshes, just in case it had dropped down to rest or feed. I failed to find it, but it was relocated the next day, just over the border in Sussex, while Goshawk and Red Kite – both needed for my Kent list – were also seen that day in the Bough Beech area.

## 24 March

A dry day with sunny periods was forecast, so I headed for west Kent, deserting my local patch even though a west wind was still blowing quite strongly. I selected a suitable vantage point, looking north, and watched the sky above the wooded landscape between 0815 and 1145. Common Kestrels and Sparrowhawks performed intermittently, but it was not until 1100 that a male Goshawk put in an appearance, gliding from high above the wood, flapping occasionally and eventually passing some 200 metres distant before it disappeared over another stretch of wood. Success at last. It was a large hawk and showed a distinctly rounded tail and markedly white undertail-coverts. A small male Sparrowhawk, seen just a few minutes later, lacked the whiteness on the undertail-coverts and showed a proportionately longer, square-ended tail. After a while a female Sparrowhawk displayed, spreading her white undertail-covert feathers, but only making a couple of slow flaps. I now believe that the displaying bird I saw on the 17th was indeed a female Goshawk.

I spent the next two weeks on holiday in Thailand.

## 11 April

Back on my local patch, where the only addition to the year list was a male Blackcap in song. The previous day, Bob Bland had glimpsed what he thought might have been a Little Bunting, so we headed for Riverfield Trout Farm, near Staplehurst. There was no sign of the bunting, but I did see three more species to add to my year list: Little Ringed Plover, Yellow Wagtail and Barn Swallow. A Scandinavian Rock Pipit provided a testing identification challenge.

## 12 April

There was a hard overnight frost, but the previous day's cold northerly wind had dropped and the morning became pleasantly warm. I found no new migrants on the local patch. Riverfield Trout Farm was extremely quiet, with no migrants apart from a White Wagtail, which had also been present the previous day. There was no sign of the Rock Pipit.

The unseasonal, bitterly cold spell of weather persisted, with more sleet and hail showers. It was as though a high wall had been dropped into the English Channel and virtually nothing was attempting to fly north over it.

## 16 April

Still cold and damp, but a hint of change, maybe, when I discovered a migrant Hobby on my own patch.

## 20 April

At long last the weather had changed, the persistent cold northerly wind being replaced by a light southerly as a front moved through. However, I noticed surprisingly little change during the morning, when I conducted the monthly census on my local patch. I had anticipated the first Common Cuckoo and a few other new migrants, but I had to be content with two Willow Warblers in song, my first in Kent this year, along with a migrant Yellow Wagtail. Most unexpected was a Short-eared Owl, the first to be recorded there in the ten years of the study.

In the late afternoon, I received a call about a Rose-coloured Starling in Aylesford. It had been visiting a garden regularly for about a month, but it failed to turn up while I was there.

## 22 April

I failed to see the starling between 0530-0615, but I heard later that it had appeared at 0630 and had performed well for the next 90 minutes. I was then visiting my local patch where there was still little evidence of new migrants. I next headed for Dungeness. The wind there was southwesterly rather than south and, apart from a Wryneck that had been trapped earlier, which I missed, there were very few migrants to be seen. However, there was a steady sea passage, and during a period of about three hours I managed to add seven species to my year list. There were 20 or so Common Terns feeding on the Patch, with a few Sandwich Terns coming and going, while a few of both species were observed moving up-Channel. The Sandwich Tern was number 170 for the year. I also saw five Arctic Skuas and one Great Skua, a party of Whimbrel flew by, four Little Terns flew west towards the Patch and a lone Little Gull flew east. Other passage birds included about 150 Common Scoters – there had been over 1,000 before I arrived – about 170 Brent Geese, 95 Bar-tailed Godwits, 27 Gannets, six Red-breasted Mergansers and a first-summer Mediterranean Gull.

## 22 April

A beautiful warm, sunny day, with a southeasterly blowing during the afternoon, but there were no new migrants to be seen on my local patch. Nor could I find the Rose-coloured Starling among the flocks of Starlings near where it roosted. A brief visit to a gravel pit at Aylesford, however, did produce my first Sand Martin of the year, probably my latest 'first-date' ever.

## 23 April

A very light southeasterly blew and some light rain fell as I visited my local patch, but there still appeared to be little increase in the numbers of migrants. It was some while before at long last I heard my first Common Cuckoo of the year. The weather conditions suggested that a trip to Dungeness ought to provide a chance to increase my year list. As I drove down, the front moved through, bringing rain, but it ceased soon after I arrived. There were good numbers of terns moving, along with a sprinkling of other species, while nearly 400 Common Terns were feeding over the patch. I failed to find any Arctic Terns among them, but I was able to see my first Black Terns of the year. A few Arctic Skuas were moving up-Channel throughout the day, but I decided to visit the trapping area around 1530 to see if I could add any passerines to my list. It was a wrong move; within five minutes of my leaving, the first Pomarine Skua of the year flew by. In the trapping area I failed to see a Pied Flycatcher and also missed Common Whitethroat.

During this period, several scarce migrants had been seen in the county, including Kentish Plover, Hoopoe and Alpine Swift, but none had stayed long. If my luck changed, I could reach 200 by the end of the month, but it was more important to catch up with a few of these scarcer migrants – bonus birds, as I call them.

## 24 April

The wind remained in the southerly quarter and more rain had fallen in the night, but there still appeared to be no sign of the missing summer visitors on my own patch. The exception was a single House Martin at the reservoir, where a lone Sand Martin and four Barn Swallows were also feeding. A migrant Yellow Wagtail flew east, but it remained a disappointing visit, and I felt that so much more should have been happening.

A visit to Great Heron Wood did not produce the expected Common Nightingale and there were no signs of any Willow Tits either. This last was the only resident species still missing from my year list, but it is becoming increasingly scarce within the county.

I felt sure that Dungeness would provide several more additions: it would have, had I been there for an early morning seawatch. All four skua species had been seen and another flock of Velvet Scoters flew up-Channel. The wind had veered south-west, which is not as productive as a southeasterly. I managed to identify a single Arctic Tern amongst all the Common Terns feeding over the patch, while a walk around the RSPB reserve enabled me to add both Reed Warbler and Common Whitethroat. Later in the day I heard that both Black Kite and Osprey had been seen during the afternoon at Bough Beech. An Osprey also flew in off the sea at Dungeness in the early evening.

## 25 April

As I arrived on my local patch a Hobby flew over. A short while later I discovered my first Lesser Whitethroat of the year, and towards the end of my visit I located a male Common Whitethroat. It was singing quietly in the area where one pair had bred the previous year. Apparently, Common Nightingales flooded in overnight, a signal to commence the countywide Nightingale Survey.

## 28 April

The morning visit to my local patch was particularly enjoyable. Two pairs of Little Ringed Plovers were displaying at the reservoir and I also added three more species to the year list for Boughton Park and Wierton Hill Farm. The next, surprisingly, was a lone Common Redpoll – particularly scarce this year, followed by a pair of Grey Partridges and then the gloriously rich notes of a Common Nightingale singing. The latter was also an addition for my Kent year list.

## 29 April

Another beautifully warm, sunny day, as a zone of high pressure slipped through. Garden Warblers had come in overnight, as there were three singing on my local patch. One pair of Little Ringed Plovers was still present, but I was a little surprised not to add species such as Turtle Dove and Common Swift.

## 30 April

The high pressure continued to dominate and the day was again hot. I eventually heard a Turtle Dove purring, making the total 186 by the end of the month. This was somewhat below what I had anticipated, as the final week of April had been quiet. I saw a pair of Bar-headed Geese on my local patch; they are a splendid species when seen 'in the wild', rather than in a collection. In the recent countrywide survey only one had been reported from Kent. These individuals were unringed, so where they had come from remains a mystery. The species is not accepted on the British list and any individuals seen are presumed to be escapes, although the species may be breeding ferally.

## 1 May

I spent nearly 16 hours birdwatching on my own patch, part of an initiative supported by *Birdwatch* magazine. A high had settled over Britain and the night was clear and starry, with light from a half moon. Cloud increased during the morning, with a cold wind from the east-north-east, but during the afternoon it became almost cloudless again. I managed to see 70 species, a good score for a small, inland site. The highlights included a Firecrest in song, a pair of Little Ringed Plovers displaying and mating, three Hobbies and two Kent list firsts for the year – Common Swift and Spotted Flycatcher.

## 2 May

With a southeasterly wind forecast, it was obvious that I needed to visit Dungeness again, but after such a tiring day the day before I did not arrive until 0830. A Long-tailed Skua went through before 0700, along with a total of 17 Pomarine Skuas. Fortunately, I saw a group of four Pomarine Skuas flying up-Channel around 0930 and I also heard my first Greenshank of the year – number 190. On the RSPB reserve I saw my first Sedge Warblers, but failed to find the Ring Ouzel that was present. Roseate Terns had been reported either on the Patch or the reserve, but I failed to find them at either site. I then heard news of four Dotterel at St. Margaret's, so I decided that it had to be worth a visit, despite the bank holiday traffic. It was to no avail as they had been seen flying out to sea some two hours before I arrived.

## 6 May

On my daily visit to Wierton Hill reservoir, I was pleased to find the first Common Sandpiper of the year, as well as a new Willow Warbler, but the only Common Whitethroat so far had disappeared. I received a phone call mid-morning to say that a Whiskered Tern was present on the reserve at Dungeness. I was there within the hour and enjoyed the bonus of seeing such a splendid bird in full breeding plumage. On the same sandy spit was an Arctic Tern, also in full breeding plumage. There were others on the Patch, where I failed to find the Roseate Tern that had been seen earlier in the day. Even so, it was a good day for terns, with several Black and Little Terns also present, as well as Sandwich and Common Terns.

## 7 May

Much of the previous week had been spent preparing for the Great Kent Bird Race and a number of summer visitors had not yet been seen. The morning's excitement did not add any species to the year list, but I saw three Avocets on my own patch for the first time.

## 8 May

The Great Kent Bird Race turned out to be one of the best race days we have experienced and is fully described in the May Bird Races chapter. I added five new species to my year list: Hoopoe, Tree Pipit, Willow Tit (at long last), Whinchat and the Red-rumped Swallow; we might also have added Golden Oriole and both Savi's and Grasshopper Warblers, which would have been a fitting end to the day and a good time to reach 200 for the year, rather than 198.

## 12 May

News eventually reached me that I had missed another Golden Oriole, this time on my own patch, on the 9th.

I had still to see a number of regular spring migrants and summer visitors, including Garganey, Nightjar, Common Redstart, Ring Ouzel, Grasshopper, Savi's and Wood Warblers, Pied Flycatcher and waders such as Curlew Sandpiper, Little Stint and Wood Sandpiper.

## 13 May

The visit to my local patch was delayed until mid-morning. I was just leaving the reservoir when a Greenshank called and two waders dropped out of the sky, alighting on the wet mud at the water's edge. The second was a Spotted Redshank in its attractive, black summer plumage. Both were new for the local patch year and the latter a first for the study area. Three Little Ringed Plovers were also present. The *Tringa* waders only stayed for about five minutes, before flying off WNW. Fortuitous moments like these provide the necessary excitement that is just one of the attractions of studying a local patch. Had I been there at my usual earlier time, I wouldn't have seen them.

## 14 May

I made another visit to Dungeness as two Roseate Terns had been present on the Patch the previous morning, but there was no sign of them. It started raining around 1030 and continued until after dark. I was feeling quite sorry for those teams that were taking part in the Great Kent Bird Race on this date, but I should not have been – one group of youthful enthusiasts broke my team's Kent record with a total of 145 species.

The only addition I managed was Temminck's Stint – at the time thought to be number 199, but in fact the 200th for the year (14 May is the earliest date I haved reached 200). There were two on the ARC pits, where I should have stayed as a Kentish Plover arrived later. Instead, I went to Pegwell Bay, where a Kentish Plover had been seen the previous day, but it was not to be found. It was raining too hard to attempt to hear the Quail at Sandwich Bay, so I visited Stodmarsh where I was unable to find any Garganey either – a fruitless trip.

## 18 May

I received a telephone call from Dungeness late morning and I sped down there, eating a picnic lunch on the way. A Thrush Nightingale and an Icterine Warbler had been trapped and released in the Moat. There was no sign of the latter at all and the former failed to sing while I was there. I did get a fleeting flight view of the Thrush Nightingale, but it was insufficient for me to identify it safely. However, I managed to find a female Ring Ouzel.

## 20–22 May

I was in Pas de Calais, preparing for and taking part in our annual bird race there and I missed the visit of a Long-tailed Skua to Bough Beech, but there was a significant bonus – in France I managed to clinch the identification of the bird that I had heard calling at Stodmarsh on the 7th, enabling me to add Spotted Crake to the year list.

## 24 May

With a number of breeding summer visitors still missing from my year list, I visited east Kent, starting in Church Wood, Blean. Here I had good views of a singing male Redstart, but failed to hear any Wood Warblers. In the Stour Valley, the weather deteriorated and I was unable to hear or see either Grasshopper or Savi's Warblers, but I did enjoy a good view of yet another Hobby.

## 26 May

It was about the time to add Montagu's Harrier to the list, so I headed for Sheppey in the morning. With good fortune on my side I was rewarded with splendid views of both a male and a female, as well as seeing up to 15 Marsh Harriers and, somewhat surprisingly, a pair of Peregrines as well.

I also learned that a Great Reed Warbler was singing at the Hookers Pits, Dungeness. It took me about an hour-and-a-quarter to drive to Dungeness: fortunately the Great Reed Warbler was still singing and showing itself well. It was only my second in Kent. Earlier in the day both Melodious and Icterine Warblers had been trapped and the former was seen and heard singing in the trapping area until around 1330, when I was still on Sheppey. I spent about an hour trying to relocate these secretive birds, but without any luck. In the evening I visited New Hythe and heard snatches of song from two Cetti's Warblers and saw a Common Kingfisher – two species that had eluded us during the Great Kent Bird Race.

## 27 May

I made another trip into the Stour Valley to try to find Savi's and Grasshopper Warblers. Both were proving to be elusive and time was running out, unless I could discover where pairs were breeding. Seeing the former on autumn migration is virtually impossible, while even the latter cannot be guaranteed. Despite several hours of listening in areas where they had both been heard, I still had no joy. However, from the Lampen Wall at Stodmarsh, I was rewarded with distant views of an Osprey – number 205.

## 28 May

One of my favourite warblers, the Wood Warbler, was still missing from the year list. I returned to Oldbury Hill having learned that, since the great storm of 1987, Wood Warblers had not returned to Hungersall Park in Tunbridge Wells. Here they could once be virtually guaranteed. Soon after I arrived on the hill, which is a most attractive wood, I heard the trill of a Wood Warbler, located a pair and observed them for a while. I then visited New Hythe anticipating that I would be able to find one of the Marsh Warblers that had recently returned, but no, not a breath of song. I drove to Elmley next, hoping that I might be able to see the drake Garganey that had been reported the previous day, but it, too, remained elusive.

## 29 May

Soon after 2100, I arrived at Oaken Wood for my annual appointment with Nightjars. It was a still night with an attractive glow in the sky. Shortly after 2115 a Nightjar called and then performed its 'wing-clapping' display, before settling on a branch and churring. A roding Woodcock flew over, and in the distance a Tawny Owl hooted. Birdwatching at dusk has a special charm all of its own, especially on a peaceful night like this.

## 30 May

News via Birdline suggested that both Melodious and Icterine Warblers were present in St. John's Cemetery, Margate. However, by the time I got there both had apparently disappeared. There was no sign of them during the four hours I spent there. On the plus side, two Common Crossbills were feeding in a pine, and they provided some consolation, giving excellent close views. Another visit to Westbere was again unsuccessful: no Savi's or Grashopper Warblers.

## 2 June

The previous day had been hot and sunny with a southerly wind – the first real taste of summer. But the wind blew from the south-west in the morning, increasing during the afternoon, when there were heavy showers along the coast. I headed for St. Margaret's, knowing that I would be able to see and listen to my first Marsh Warblers of the year. I was also hoping to find a Greenish Warbler and hear a Quail, both of which were present there on the 1st. I did enjoy seeing the Marsh Warblers, but I had no luck with the other two species.

Back on my patch in the late afternoon, I bumped into my co-patch watcher and he gave me news of a second Thrush Nightingale at Dungeness. He had heard it singing around midday and had also managed to see it. I decided to give it a try, as I had been so close to adding it to my year list the previous month. Although it was not in full song in the early evening, it did utter one short phrase which came from an extremely dense bushy area comprising aspens and osiers. Peering through the leafy foliage, along with a good many other birdwatchers, I had great fortune. The bird suddenly appeared within three or four metres of me and I had brief but good views.

## 6 June

I visited Dungeness again, hoping to see the Roseate Tern that had been present on the reserve during the previous two days. I was able to study four tern species closely, but there was no sign of the Roseate. The most interesting of the terns present was a first-summer Arctic Tern in what is known as 'portlandica' plumage, in which some juvenile feather tracts are still retained.

In the evening I received a phone call which caused me to speed to Sandwich Bay, but I failed to hear either the Quail or the Corncrake that had been calling from the 100 acre field near the point. Had they stopped calling and flown, or were they simply resting during the hour or so that I was there? I heard later that I was just unfortunate not to hear them, for they remained in the area.

## 15 June

I made another attempt to hear a Quail calling in the early morning, arriving at Sandwich Bay shortly after 0600. I walked the paths among crops of barley, rape and potatoes for nearly two hours, in the area where it has been calling for several weeks and as recently as the previous day, but it didn't call for me.

I wondered whether number 210 for the year would be one of the missing summer visitors, such as Quail, Golden Oriole, Garganey, Savi's or Grasshopper Warblers, or maybe a more exotic rarity that the month of June has a habit of producing. Some of the rare species that I have seen during June in Kent include Red-footed Falcon, Black-winged Stilt, Collared Pratincole, Terek Sandpiper, Caspian Tern, Whiskered Tern, Great Reed Warbler, Greenish Warbler, Lesser Grey Shrike and Woodchat Shrike.

## 26 June

Another visit to Sandwich Bay, hoping to hear a Quail, but with more interest focused on looking at and photographing orchids. With a modicum of good fortune, which is much needed when aiming for an annual species list of 250 in Kent, I was enjoying a picnic lunch with my wife when a Quail uttered a few distinctive 'wet my lips' call notes; number 210 for the year. Strangely enough, Quail was also number 210 in 1988, my previous best year.

Six months gone and six to go. With 210 already recorded, a total of 250 looked possible, although this did mean seeing nearly 90% of all the species recorded in the county during the year. At this time my total represented approximately 85% of those that I knew had been recorded to date. However, quite a few of the 30 or more species that I had missed should be added with little difficulty during the autumn. In the immediate future I was now looking forward to the return wader passage and some movements of shearwaters off Dungeness.

## 6 July

A phone call on the 4th brought unexpected news of a pair of Savi's Warbler at a new breeding site in Kent. A visit in the evening two days later was successful, although it was 2130 and the light was fading before I heard any reeling.

## 11 July

Reports of a Marsh Sandpiper at Cliffe attracted me there in the morning, in very hot conditions under a clear blue sky. The pools were particularly wet, with very little in the way of muddy fringes to attract the waders. Consequently, they were tending to hide in the wet vegetation. If the Marsh Sandpiper was still present, it did not show itself. However, there was a good selection of 14 different waders, including my first Curlew Sandpiper for the year, an adult bird still in its attractive orange summer plumage, as were about 250 Black-tailed Godwits. A few Ruff and an almost black Spotted Redshank were also sporting colourful summer plumages.

## 13 July

Another visit to Cliffe proved more successful, although the weather following an overnight thunderstorm was decidedly gloomy and overcast. After nearly three hours I found the Marsh Sandpiper, having already added Little Stint. The latter was an adult in worn summer plumage, and showed a distinctly orange/buff face and nape, which had me wondering about Red-necked Stint for a while. I had identified 17 species of wader and I was sure that I would be back quite frequently during the autumn, as the habitat looked so promising.

July can be a surprisingly productive month for rarer species; I have seen species such as Great Spotted Cuckoo, Stilt and Pectoral Sandpipers and Spoonbill. On 15 July 1995 Dungeness really excelled for me, with the third Kentish Laughing Gull on the beach, a summer plumaged White-winged Black Tern on the reserve, a Mediterranean Shearwater on the Patch and a Woodchat Shrike in the trapping area – all species I failed to see in 1994.

## 20 July

A phone call to Birdline the previous evening got the adrenalin flowing again with news of a Broad-billed Sandpiper on the Brickfields scrape at Elmley. The adult bird was still there in the morning and provided me with good views as it fed with a few Dunlin and a Little Stint. This was just the 13th Kent record, ten of which have been in May, so this was quite a bonus for the year list, which was now on 215. I then visited Cliffe again in the hope that it, too, might have attracted something new. With the tide high, some 500 Dunlin were roosting and among them were at least 15 Curlew Sandpipers. Several other birders were there looking for the Marsh Sandpiper, but no-one could find it. However, Chris Wheeler relocated a Pectoral Sandpiper which provided us with excellent close views. This was another good bonus species for me, as very few had been seen in Kent in recent years.

News reached me that a summer-plumaged Spotted Sandpiper had been seen about a month ago. It had turned up on a privately owned inland site and the local observer had not been able to arrange for a mass influx of birdwatchers. I wondered whether I could look forward to a spate of American waders in the autumn, as there had been in 1984.

## 25 July

I made another visit to Cliffe in the afternoon, during the high tide period, in the hope that maybe a Wood Sandpiper would be there to add to the year list. I did not add anything new, but enjoyed seeing 21 different wader species on just one of the pools, while a single call was almost certainly made by a Temminck's Stint. I had excellent views of the Marsh Sandpiper, together with 38 Avocets, about 15 Curlew Sandpipers and a Little Stint.

## 27 July

A brief visit to the Brickfields at Elmley produced the sixth additional wader species this month, a better total than I had anticipated. There were three or four Wood Sandpipers amongst a dozen wader species present, bringing my annual total to 217.

## 3 August

On returning from a short trip to Holland late on the 2nd, I phoned Birdline to discover that a Lesser Grey Shrike had been found at Sandwich Bay during the afternoon. I collected my friend Peter Stoodley, and together we drove down to the observatory, arriving at around 1100. Though the heat haze made viewing difficult when the bird was perched close to the ground, it showed well when it flew onto nearby electricity cables. It was an adult in full breeding plumage. It was only the fifth record for Kent this century and the first since 1980. We searched for a Garganey near New Downs Farm, but could only find a few Common Teal. An attractive flock of at least 25 Whimbrel was feeding on the golf course nearby. News reached me that a Dartford Warbler had been seen at St. Margaret's, but we had to return home, so that species, as well as the Garganey, would have to wait for another day.

## 4 August

I visited St. Margaret's but failed to relocate the Dartford Warbler, finding only a few Common Whitethroats, together with the resident Stonechats and a migrant Whinchat.

## 12 August

With news of a Barred Warbler and several Pied Flycatchers at Dungeness the previous day, I made a brief visit there in the morning. There were few passerine migrants to be seen and just a single Arctic Skua on the sea. However, a phone call at around 1800 raised the adrenalin once again and within the hour I was enjoying excellent views of an adult White-rumped Sandpiper at Cliffe.

## 14 August

I made another visit to Cliffe during the afternoon high tide. Some 800 waders of 20 species were roosting or feeding on the flooded pools and both the Marsh and White-rumped Sandpipers were still present. When a Hobby suddenly appeared and selected a Dunlin for its quarry, virtually all the waders got up as the falcon harried the frightened wader. The Dunlin kept dropping onto the water as the Hobby dived at it, but it could not escape the falcon and eventually they both disappeared over the treeline, the unfortunate Dunlin in the Hobby's talons. It was a most impressive spectacle and as the waders started to drop down, additional species such as Knot and Bar-tailed Godwit were more easily identified. A good number of the 170 or more Grey Plovers were still in their resplendent summer plumage, but few of the 180 Black-tailed Godwits now retained their colourful orange feathers. Probably well in excess of 200 Dunlins, and some 100 Ringed Plovers were the other waders present in three-figure numbers. At the nearby quarry I added Wood Sandpiper to the day's wader list and saw two Little Egrets, but failed to see the albino Sand Martin that had been reported there. However, I did see an albino Coot, looking most strange with its all-white plumage and pale pink bill.

## 16 August

A phone call just before lunch encouraged me to visit the Swale NNR on Sheppey, where I had only poor flight views of a Red-necked Phalarope. Sadly, I was unable to relocate this attractive wader, but constant searching of the wet areas of the scrape eventually revealed three Garganey – number 221 for the year. The highlight of this session was the opportunity to study and photograph an adult Wood Sandpiper from the hide.

## 22 August

With the wind ENE in the Thames Estuary a visit to Allhallows for a seawatch seemed worthwhile. Virtually no seabird movement was evident, although a Long-tailed Skua had been seen farther up the Thames the previous day in a very light easterly wind. A visit to Cliffe during the afternoon found the Marsh Sandpiper in almost full winter plumage, with very pale grey upperparts.

## 26 August

News came of a White Stork at Conningbrook, near Ashford. I spent the best part of an hour watching the adult stork feeding in a field which a farmer was ploughing; it was eating large earthworms. After a while it flew towards Conningbrook water, making a number of swimming Canada Geese panic as it flew low over them. By the time it landed on the grass the geese had their necks stretched and, as one, they 'marched' towards the stork which took little notice of them.

One of the visiting birders had been speaking to local inhabitants, who said they were a little surprised that the White Stork was attracting so much attention. They went on to say that a Roller, which they had seen in the same area quite recently, would surely have attracted many more birders. Another one that got away?

## 27 August

News of another Red-necked Phalarope at Elmley provided reason enough for a visit, but it proved unsuccessful and only a limited range of waders was present, including some 35 Spotted Redshanks and a single Curlew Sandpiper.

As I was about to leave, a friend with a pager announced the arrival of a Buff-breasted Sandpiper at Cliffe. I spent an hour or so studying this splendid American wader, the first in Kent since August 1986.

## 31 August

With early morning rain and the wind now in the northeast, it looked promising for a passage of seabirds in the Thames estuary. However, all I saw during about 90 minutes was a lone Fulmar. There were no signs of any passerine migrants at Warden Point either, apart from one Lesser Whitethroat, so I headed for Elmley, where the juvenile Red-necked Phalarope performed extremely well, much to my delight.

I was about to leave Elmley when I heard there was a juvenile Red-backed Shrike at nearby Eastchurch. I arrived some 15 minutes later and was able to enjoy the subtleties of its plumage.

## 1 September

After an overnight deluge accompanied by earth-shaking claps of thunder, few passerine migrants seemed to have arrived, but the wind had backed from northeast to north. The weather conditions suggested that a seawatch at Shellness should be interesting and I spent four hours there. During that time I counted 319 Black Terns, saw a flock of 14 Gannets, but only one Great and two Arctic Skuas flew into the Swale. At Warden Point I managed to see two Pied Flycatchers – number 225 for the year – and the Red-backed Shrike was still at Eastchurch.

## 2 September

The wind remained in the north-west during the morning, but I did not commence seawatching at Shellness until 1000, by which time two Sooty Shearwaters had flown into the Thames. I had to content myself with 66 Gannets, 16 Arctic, four Great and two adult

Pomarine Skuas, and just four Black Terns before the wind backed west.

## 4 September

A call to Birdline Southeast revealed that a juvenile Common Rosefinch was present at Swalecliffe. It showed well when I arrived at 1630; another bonus species for the year list.

## 15 September

The promise of a northwesterly wind and rain in the Thames estuary tempted me to seawatch there. When I arrived, the wind was WNW and there was no evidence of any sea passage. However, as the wind veered north-west a few Great and Arctic Skuas started to appear. During a period of nearly six hours, some 53 Great Skuas were seen, but only nine Arctic, plus a small, elegant, light brown skua that showed the wing/tail proportions that I associate with Long-tailed Skua. Its central tail feathers were almost as long as the tail again, indicating that it was an adult. When it alighted on the sea it was too distant to ascertain any plumage detail, but it showed extensive white upperwing flashes. It was not until I returned home that I found a note and photographs of a Long-tailed Skua with a similar amount of white on the bases of the outer primaries. I feel convinced that it was a Long-tailed Skua, but the accurate identification of small skuas is still a developing skill. The highlight of the seawatch, however, was the sighting of a Sooty Shearwater, another addition for the year list. A flock of 19 Gannets flying out of the Swale was an impressive sight too.

## 16 September

The discovery of a Tawny Pipit at North Foreland the previous day attracted me to that locality in the morning. The wind was north-west, force 6-7, and I was unable to locate the pipit. With such a strong northerly wind, I felt that a spell of seawatching must offer an opportunity to increase my tally, so I visited the seawatching hide at Foreness Point. Very little had been seen, although distant skuas and Gannets were obviously flying into the Thames estuary. However, while I was there, a Manx Shearwater flew east – another addition to the year list.

I went back to the seaweed-strewn field at North Foreland and my luck was in. A small group of birders was obviously watching the Tawny Pipit. I located it and had excellent views of the bird – another first for the year – which was in immaculate juvenile plumage, with fine, sparse streaking on the breast.

A Wryneck had been seen at Reculver the previous day, so I headed in that direction in the early afternoon, hoping too that a seabird passage would be visible from the Towers. This is now a much favoured seawatching point when northerly autumn winds blow. Just before I arrived a Richard's Pipit had been located. However, I and a few others failed to find it at our first attempt. I then looked for the Wryneck and obtained brief flight views – number 230 for the year.

Seawatching had been producing good numbers of skuas, including three Long-tailed. My luck was obviously in, as good numbers of seabirds continued to fly west towards the Swale, many only 400-800 metres offshore. Within about half-an-hour of arriving, another juvenile Long-tailed Skua – my fourth new species for the year – flew past with three Arctic Skuas. It was shortly followed by another. During the two hours that I was there, the totals were 53 Gannets, 25 Great Skuas, 13 Arctic, the two Long-tailed and a lone adult Pomarine Skua – all four skua species within an hour. Those who watched all day totalled 140 Great, 130 Arctic, 5 Long-tailed and 1 Pomarine Skua. It was a memorable sea passage, in dry conditions with excellent visibility.

Just before I left, two of us made a second attempt to relocate the Richard's Pipit. With good fortune it was found and I had excellent close views of another scarce pipit in pristine juvenile plumage. I had not seen one of this age before. It had been a classic day, as I had never seen four skua species nor two scarce pipits in a single day in Kent.

The autumn months of September and October can really make or break a challenge for a lengthy year list. I had a purple period in September 1984, when I added White-rumped and Buff-breasted Sandpipers, Purple Heron and Long-billed Dowitcher, while in September/October 1988 I added Oriental Pratincole, Baird's Sandpiper, Dotterel, White Stork, Sabine's Gull and Wilson's Phalarope.

## 17 September

The wind was forecast to be north, force 4-5, so I arrived at Reculver at around 1030, anticipating more seabirds, with the possibility of a Sabine's Gull or a Leach's Petrel. However, on arrival the wind was blowing from the west. There was very little activity over the sea, but I enjoyed good views of a Manx Shearwater which alighted not far offshore, and the Wryneck showed well for a while.

## 21 September

Rain and a north-east wind, with high pressure extending across Scandinavia should mean an interesting fall of migrants, so I headed for St. Margaret's. There was a good sprinkling of Common Redstarts and Pied Flycatchers around the coast and I saw several at St. Margaret's and on the Wantsum Marshes later in the day. Wrynecks and Ring Ouzels were reported too, but I was content to see the Reculver Wryneck well, once again. I was about to head home when I heard that a Dotterel had been seen the previous day, so I spent another 90 minutes or so scanning the numerous fields across the Wantsum Marsh, but without success. The best bird occurring in this fall was an adult male Red-breasted Flycatcher at Warden Point. Would it remain overnight?

## 22 September

It did. I managed to get to Warden Point in the afternoon and had splendid views of this superb, delicate flycatcher. It was immaculate in its full adult male summer plumage, with a subtle blue-grey hue around the lores contrasting with the soft orange of the chin, throat and breast. The white tail-sides were particularly striking when the bird flew.

## 25 September

A damp, misty afternoon, but I could not take a chance on Yellow-browed Warblers occurring in reasonable numbers this autumn, so I headed for Bishopstone where one had been found the previous day. It was still present, but during a 90 minute stay I only heard and glimpsed it briefly. I had to content myself with better views of both Pied Flycatcher and Firecrest.

## 8 October

I sped to St. Margaret's again, this time in search of a Dotterel that had been seen there early in the morning. It had disappeared by the time I arrived and much searching of the cliff-top fields proved fruitless. I had now missed this attractive wader on three occasions. The one compensation, apart from the fine weather, was the sighting of another Yellow-browed Warbler which provided excellent views on this occasion. Several had been found in Kent during the morning, following an easterly airflow that looked promising for many more passerine vagrants during the next few days.

## 9 October

The first October Turtle Dove for my local patch seemed a good omen for the day and I headed for St. Margaret's again. The Dotterel had apparently been seen late yesterday afternoon, in the fields that I had been diligently scanning. Efforts on this occasion were equally unrewarding and, apart from another Yellow-browed Warbler, there were relatively few passerine migrants of interest.

I drove from St. Margaret's to Dungeness, hoping that there might have been a fall there, but there were very few migrants at all in the trapping area. However, another Yellow-browed Warbler at the Hooker's Pits provided some pleasing views. Sadly, two Penduline Tits seen flying over on the 7th do not appear to have settled in the area.

Almost three weeks had passed without any additions to the year list, and at a prime time for autumn vagrants and seabird passage. One brief period of northerly winds had failed to produce the anticipated Sabine's Gull or Leach's Petrel, but a Puffin was seen in the Thames. Unfortunately, I was unable to get out on that date.

# 14 October

I was attracted to Sandwich Bay in the morning, as a Short-toed Lark had been seen there the previous evening. It was seen again early on, but it disappeared into thick fog and was never relocated. I also failed to see a Barred Warbler at Bishopstone in the afternoon.

# 15 October

Late on the 14th, a Radde's Warbler was discovered near St. Margaret's, so I drove into east Kent again in the morning. Thick fog enshrouded the coast, not clearing, as before, until nearly noon. The warbler was not found. I did see an adult male Siberian Stonechat that had been present for a few days, but there was little else of interest there. News reached me of the Barred Warbler showing well at Bishopstone, so I drove there again during the afternoon. It continued to show briefly while I was there, so I was able at long last to add number 235 to the annual list. This attractive area of coastal scrub and woodland also produced a juvenile Red-backed Shrike, as well as one, possibly two, more Yellow-browed Warblers; I have never before seen this species so frequently in one autumn.

# 16 October

News of a Sabine's Gull and a petrel being taken by a Great Black-backed Gull at Shellness made me realise that the north-east wind had strengthened considerably and I should have been there. An afternoon visit was not very productive, although three adult Little Gulls flew out of the Swale, a late Sandwich Tern flew by, about 150 Common Scoter could be seen distantly and some 140 Brent Geese arrived from the north-east.

# 17 October

I learned that I should have stopped and had a word with Dennis Tayler, whom I had seen at Leysdown the day before. He had been trying to film a Pallas's Warbler. It was seen again in the morning but I failed to find it, even though I spent two-and-a-half hours searching the area in the afternoon. An hour or so of seawatching failed to produce anything new either. The wind was not strong enough to encourage the appearance of a Sabine's Gull or Leach's Petrel. A number of Little Gulls were moving and I saw a lone Great Skua and my first Red-breasted Mergansers and Red-throated Diver of the autumn.

# 18 October

After a clear sky overnight there was little hope of the Pallas's Warbler remaining, but I still worked the site again for another hour in the morning. I discovered about ten unringed Goldcrests, obviously new arrivals as virtually all yesterday's birds had been caught and ringed, and had dispersed along with the Pallas's. Two Shore Larks had been seen briefly at Swalecliffe on the 17th, so I searched the beach at Shellness, but without any joy, just finding a late Yellow Wagtail and a few Rock Pipits. Another Pallas's Warbler was found at Warden Point in the evening.

A strong southerly wind was forecast, so I thought that a visit to Dungeness would be a good choice for the morning, with the chance of a Sabine's Gull and maybe a few other seabirds. However, I might need to visit Warden Point first.

## 19 October

As I walked round my patch, the southeasterly wind did not appear to be as strong as forecast and there was little of interest locally. A phone call produced negative news from Warden Point, so I headed for Dungeness as planned. However, the wind was SSE, force 4, and although a two-and-a-half hour seawatch produced nothing new, I did see three Black-throated Divers, five Gannets, 19 Brent Geese, nine Common Teal, a Pintail, seven Common Scoter, a Pomarine Skua, a Little Gull, 11 Kittiwakes and two Common Guillemots.

News from elsewhere included the relocation of the Warden Point Pallas's Warbler and another one at St. Margaret's. I headed for Warden Point, arriving there at 1500. At 1645 the Pallas's was found in a sycamore and although it was incredibly active, I was eventually able to build a complete picture of this superb, brightly plumaged Siberian rarity. The final glimpse, as it hovered, revealing its tiny, square, pale yellow rump was classic, and worth every minute of the five-and-a-half hours of searching.

## 21 October

I visited Dungeness again, hoping that a seawatch might be more productive, but the south-east wind was not really strong enough and I saw little of interest. With the north and east of the county attracting eastern rarities, the south-east should surely produce something of interest. I searched the attractive habitat around the ARC Pit and at the Airport Pits, but my reward was just four Goldcrests, and not even an autumn Jack Snipe.

## 23 October

Strong SSW winds were again forecast, so I headed for Dungeness in the morning, in heavy rain. The wind was no more than force 3 and there was virtually no seabird movement. When I returned to the Observatory I found a note saying 'Pied Wheatear at Tesco's, Sheerness'. I was there in just over an hour, to find that the wheatear had last been seen some 40 minutes earlier. I and many others searched the area to no avail until 1430, when news of a Rough-legged Buzzard near Capel Fleet came through on a pager. This bird, too, had disappeared by the time I reached Capel Fleet, where I saw a single Hen Harrier and several Marsh Harriers, including one handsome adult male. I returned to Tesco's around 1600 and some 40 minutes later the Pied Wheatear was refound and I enjoyed some excellent close views of a splendid first-winter male. This was not only a new Kent species for me, but also a lifer.

Off Thanet, a Cory's Shearwater had been seen in the late afternoon, as well as another Rough-legged Buzzard which apparently went to roost in Northdown Park.

## 27 October

More Rough-legged Buzzards had arrived on the 24th and 25th, so I visited Sheppey, a favoured locality for this species in past years. Although I spent some time in the Capel Fleet area, my rewards were restricted to good views of commoner species such as Merlin, Hen and Marsh Harriers and towards dusk six Short-eared Owls, two of which were heard calling on several occasions. One was uttering a squeaky grunt while being mobbed by a Carrion Crow, while the other uttered a screech-like call. At Shellness I had an interesting encounter with a Knot showing a strange horn-like growth on its upper mandible. It was also in an intermediate plumage with which I was not familiar. The wings and upperparts were a mixture of pale grey and very dark brown, while the sides of the breast and the flanks were marked with bold black spots. The Knot-like jizz and the retained pale buffy-orange underparts ruled out any other species.

There was news of a Shore Lark at Kingsdown and a Rough-legged Buzzard at Cliffe. Later I heard that a Penduline Tit had showed well at the Hooker's Pits, Dungeness.

## 30 October

Heavy rains and strong southwesterly winds were a feature of the weekend. I visited Sheppey in the morning and was rewarded with some fine views of two Rough-legged Buzzards below Harty Hill. I then headed for Reculver, where I was able to study a fine adult male Shore Lark, my first in Kent for some years.

I have already mentioned that September and October are key months, virtually dictating whether you reach 240 or 250. In October 1988 I added 11 species, including such rarities as Common Crane, Little Auk, Olive-backed Pipit and Isabelline Shrike, while in 1994 only five species were added.

## 3 November

A fine day with a southeasterly blowing, which looked good for a visit to Dungeness. I arrived there at about 1100 and heard news of two more Pallas's Warblers at Brett's the day before and one in the trapping area in the morning. These brought the Dungeness autumn total to a record five. Also the previous day a Penduline Tit had flown over, a Sabine's Gull had flown west and a Dartford Warbler had been seen. I went in search of the Dartford Warbler. Luck was with me, and within the hour I had encouraged it, by 'pishing', to show itself in a large gorse bush. This was in a different area from where it had previously been seen. The glimpses were only fleeting, but the richness of the vinous-red underparts suggested that it was an adult male. I felt quite elated as this species is such a skulker. The seabird passage had dropped off by noon, so I searched the Hooker's Pit area in the hope of finding a Penduline Tit, but my luck had run out. My total was now 240, but with a month in South America from mid-November, the possibility of reaching 250 was diminishing rapidly.

## 4 November

With the wind still in the south-east, I headed for Dungeness again in the morning. I joined Ray Turley for a two-hour seawatch, but the seabird passage was slow. He had already seen a flock of nine Velvet Scoters, so I was particularly pleased to see two more amongst a distant flock of Common Scoters – number 241, equalling my best year yet. Other interesting species included over 200 Brent Geese, a total of 12 adult Little Gulls, five Red-throated Divers and two Red-necked Grebes, all flying west, while an adult Mediterranean Gull and several Gannets were feeding off the point.

As we walked back to the Observatory a Merlin disturbed several hundred Greenfinches. Although there had been a small fall of Blackbirds, Robins and Goldcrests, nothing of particular interest had been trapped. Nevertheless, we explored the trapping area bushes for the next two hours, seeing a Sparrowhawk and the fresh remains of a Water Rail, a Firecrest and a late Northern Wheatear, but we failed to find any scarce migrants.

When we returned, there was news of a Penduline Tit seen at the Hooker's Pits earlier in the day. I spent another 30 minutes there towards dusk, hearing Water Rails squealing, seeing a distant Short-eared Owl hunting and thousands of starlings gathering to roost in the reedbeds, but still no Penduline Tit. I had had a series of similar close encounters back in 1985.

## 5 November

Heavy rain fell as I drove to Dungeness again, and I arrived at the Hooker's Pits around 1030. The rain eased about an hour later by which time I had found no sign of the Penduline Tit, but I did see four Bearded Tits well, glimpsed a Water Rail and had good views of a female Hen Harrier.

At Dungeness Observatory two Pallas's Warblers had been trapped and ringed, so I spent some time in the trapping area, eventually having excellent views of a third, unringed Pallas's Warbler. It was proving to be an outstanding autumn for this species, with a record 18 in Kent, since 16 October. A short seawatch produced a lone Long-tailed Duck flying east, with at least 60 Kittiwakes, 22 Gannets and a Red-throated Diver flying west.

## 9 November

I received a phone call during the evening of the 8th informing me that a Short-toed Lark had been found at Cliffe around noon, but it had not been seen later in the day. I arrived there at 0810, just as light rain started to fall. I did not see another birder during the next two hours, but within the hour I relocated the Short-toed Lark. I was able to enjoy studying it at close range for the best part of an hour, although it seemed to enjoy running through the *Salicornia* and completely disappearing every now and then. The greyness of the plumage suggested to me that it might be of the eastern race *C. b. longipennis*. This was another new species for my Kent list and, as number 242 for the year, it set a new record annual total for me.

## 14 November

Time to close the diary for a month. It might seem strange to be going away at this stage of an exciting year in Kent, but I had been planning a trip to South America with Tony Prater for some time. I hoped to add another 17 species to my world wader list, visiting both Argentina and Chile.

## 16 December

Back in Kent to news of no unusual winter visitors, as the weather had been so mild, and just one rarity missed – a first for the county. Before I left, a Tawny Pipit had been claimed at Seasalter and, when the finder returned to look at it more closely, he decided that it was a Blyth's Pipit. However, it had not been seen since 11 December.

A Blackpoll Warbler was present at Bewl Water just over the county border in Sussex. It stayed there for 12 days, until 21 December.

## 28 December

Vague rumours of two Red-breasted Geese in the Medway on Boxing Day encouraged me to leave my patch and venture farther afield, although the exceptionally mild weather was disappointing for late December. A strong southwesterly blew and there were occasional heavy showers, none of which was conducive to attracting rarer winter visitors from the east.

The tide was dropping when I reached Funton Creek and very few Brent Geese were visible. However, that most elegant of ducks, the Pintail was there in good numbers and I could see a flock of at least 65 Avocets. What did surprise me was seeing a large flock of 1,000 or more Golden Plovers flying from pasture on Chetney to rest on the mud.

I headed for Sheppey in the hope that I could find a large wintering flock of Brent Geese there, amongst which I could search for the rare Red-breasted Goose but I was unable to locate a flock. Apparently, a human goose-scarer had been hired by the local farmers.

Flocks of White-fronted Geese and Bewick's Swans were generally quite distant, as was a possible immature Whooper Swan. I failed to relocate it when I tried to get closer views. The strong wind did not encourage the wintering raptors to fly, so the visit was not as rewarding as I had hoped.

## 31 December

The weather was dry, cold and sunny early on, splendid conditions for a final day's birding in North Kent. Funton Creek looked most attractive, with a very high tide and numbers of Brent Geese and Pintail at very close range.

I also visited the Capel Fleet area of Sheppey and had good views of one of the three wintering Rough-legged Buzzards, together with several Marsh and Hen Harriers. Small flocks of grey geese were arriving from the north-east, and late in the afternoon one flock of at least 500 could be seen feeding in the fields. With them were three Barnacle Geese. At least 30 Bewick's Swans were feeding with a larger flock of Mute Swans, but I could not see any sign of a Whooper Swan, although there were reports of one or more being present.

Offshore, at Leysdown, there were three Velvet Scoters, which provided much more pleasing views than those I had experienced at Dungeness in early November.

With cold weather forecast, it was likely that several hard weather visitors might arrive early in the New Year, but too late to be added to 1994's impressive tally. I had set out to improve on my previous best total and that I had achieved. I would like to give credit to Roger Thompson, who achieved an outstanding total of 246 in the same year (86% of the 285 species recorded in Kent in 1994), while others reached 235 and 236. It seems that 250 species in Kent in a year should be possible.

I estimate that I doubled my normal annual mileage during 1994, from around 10,000 to over 20,000 miles – possibly 50 miles for each bird seen? Each year that I have attempted a year list I have improved on my annual tally. The totals reached by the end of selected months are as follows:

|      | Jan | Mar | May | Aug | Oct | Dec |
|------|-----|-----|-----|-----|-----|-----|
| 1977 | 123 | 140 | 175 | 194 | 204 | 210 |
| 1982 | 138 | 143 | 195 | 207 | 216 | 220 |
| 1984 | 140 | 149 | 203 | 211 | 226 | 230 |
| 1988 | 119 | 154 | 204 | 213 | 237 | 241 |
| 1994 | 130 | 162 | 207 | 224 | 239 | 242 |

# Birdwatching Calendar

The annual cycle of bird seasons is a pattern we can enjoy, knowing that essentially it is constant. We have our resident species, some that winter with us, others that come to breed, while some simply pass through on migration. Each spring we can look forward to hearing the Willow Warbler sing and the Common Cuckoo call, or watching the Great Crested Grebe displaying. Field trips can be arranged, as necessary, to enjoy these and many other events year after year, although it is often the unexpected that adds a little spice to this absorbing hobby.

In this chapter, I include a summary of expected events for each month. I then describe a selection of possible trips within Kent, which, over the year, should produce an interesting variety of birds in different habitats. Most of the localities mentioned warrant frequent visits throughout the year, but that would defeat this chapter's objective. You may feel that some sites feature too frequently, while others do not feature enough. These are simply my suggestions based on my own experiences. Ultimately the choice is yours.

Planning trips in advance can be fun and quite challenging. I suggest that you consult the Systematic List, which gives information on where and when each species is most likely to be seen. You can then select the time of year and site accordingly. You should also bear in mind that the state of the tide must be considered for coastal outings, while falls of migrants and seabird passage will be influenced by the weather. This means that flexibility in your planning will improve your chances of seeing particular species. Six-figure map references (prefixed with the letters OS and based on the Ordnance Survey Landranger series) usually indicate car parking areas. All sites are listed in the Gazetteer in Appendix III.

## January

This is usually a month of stability. Certainly, in mild conditions, little change can be expected. Visits to the coastal marshes will produce wintering waders and wildfowl, plus a few passerines, while inland, in addition to our resident species, there may well be Long-eared Owl roosts. Winter thrushes, such as Fieldfare and Redwing, and finches such as Brambling and Siskin can be seen. But, when hard frosts persist, survival becomes crucial and birds will seek food wherever it is available. Snow and severe frosts locally may well restrict or prevent feeding. These conditions may initiate cold-weather movements of Lapwing and Skylark. Severe weather on the Continent may cause an influx of Red-necked and Slavonian Grebes, rarer geese such as Barnacle or Bean, and diving duck, such as Smew and Goosander, while northerly gales will bring seabirds wintering in the North Sea, such as divers and auks, closer to our shores.

### Elmley RSPB Reserve
Merlin, Peregrine, Hen and Marsh Harriers, wildfowl and waders. White-fronted Goose flocks sometimes feed and roost. Short-eared Owls – more often seen in late afternoon.

### Sandwich Bay, Stonar Lake and Pegwell Bay Country Park
Snow Buntings, roosting waders at high tide. Wintering geese in more severe weather. Enquire at the Observatory. Check Stonar Lake for diving duck and possibly rare grebes. Pegwell Bay Country Park for waders, best on a rising tide.

### Dungeness and Walland Marsh
Grebes and ducks on the pits, including Smew and Goosander. Check the gull flocks for Glaucous Gull, at the high tide roosts or on Lade Sands as the tide drops. The Woolpack Inn area attracts Bewick's Swans, with Hen Harriers gathering at dusk to roost in the reedbed there (OS 978244), where Water Rails and

possibly Bearded Tits may call. Short-eared Owl and Barn Owl both occur. Golden Plover often favour the pasture in the Fairfield area.

### Stodmarsh

In icy conditions, Common Bitterns and Water Rails are more easily seen. Bearded Tits feed and call amongst the reeds. Siskins frequent the alders. If you are fortunate a Great Grey Shrike might perch on the tops of hawthorns. Roosting Hen Harriers can be observed towards dusk. Park at OS 222609. Check the logbook entries and chalk board information at the toilet block.

# February

A cold spell early in the month frequently produces numbers of wintering wildfowl, but as the month draws on, it becomes less and less likely to produce much change. Warmer, sunny days will stimulate some species to sing. Grey Herons return to their heronries to repair nests, and possibly commence breeding.

### Shelness, Swale NNR and Capel Fleet

Park near the hamlet and check the beach area for finches and buntings. Twite are sometimes by the car park (OS 052683). Either side of high tide is best for watching the flocks of waders flying to and from their roosts – view from the point, or the block house. Brent Geese feed in the fields as well as on the mud. White-fronted Geese sometimes feed on the reserve, which attracts wintering duck. Great Crested Grebe flocks swim offshore, as do Red-throated Divers. Common Eiders may be seen on the mussel beds. Look for a Merlin, perched in a field, or harrying a flock of Dunlin. Capel Hill and the Harty Road provide numerous viewing points for scanning the fields for Bewick's Swans, White-fronted Geese and Golden Plovers, as well as raptors – Marsh and Hen Harriers, Merlin and Peregrine. Walk to the Swale from Sayes Court for Twite on the saltmarsh and waders roosting at Harty – often close to the Ferry House Inn. Short-eared Owls and possibly Barn Owls hunt towards dusk.

### Bedgebury Pinetum

Find a high point to scan over the forest for Sparrowhawk. Visit the pinetum in the late afternoon to see the finches coming in to roost, particularly Hawfinch, along with Brambling, Siskin and occasionally Common Crossbill, which often favour larches. The Hawfinches roost in cypress trees (OS 718334) on an east facing slope, but often alight in the leafless oaks, or perch on top of the conifers on arrival.

### Northward Hill, Cooling Marshes and Cliffe Pools

The heronry is impressive late in the month. White-fronted Geese, Pintail, Hen Harriers, Common Buzzard, Merlin, Peregrine and Golden Plover occur on Cooling Marshes – view from the river wall, from various footpaths, or Eastborough Farm (OS 770765), which overlooks the extension of the RSPB reserve bordered by Decoy Fleet. Grebes and ducks at Cliffe Pools, where the Ringed Plover high tide roost is worth checking. Cliffe quarry also attracts a good selection of ducks, a rare grebe occasionally and possibly Little Egret.

### New Hythe and River Medway

Park at Snodland (OS 707614), near Brookland Lake. Walk around the various pits on both sides of the railway and along the river. Wintering grebes and ducks. Common Bitterns and Bearded Tits winter occasionally and a Cetti's Warbler may call. Dunlin and sometimes Ruff feed on the river mud at low tide.

# March

Early spring is a good time to visit broadleaved woodland to become familiar with our resident species, before the summer migrants return. A period of change usually commences about mid-month, when the earliest summer migrants, such as Chiffchaff, Northern Wheatear, Sand Martin and Little Ringed Plover begin to arrive, while resident birds show signs of breeding behaviour – Long-tailed Tits often start nest-building at this time. Wintering wildfowl and waders steadily disappear from the North Kent Marshes, with the last White-fronted Geese, for instance, usually leaving during the third week. The up-Channel passage of seabirds off Dungeness commences.

### South Medway – Chetney Marshes to Riverside Country Park
Brent Geese, Red-breasted Mergansers, Avocets and other wintering grebes, ducks and waders. Either side of high tide is best as it brings birds closer to the shoreline. Some good spots, such as Funton Creek for Avocets, are close to the road, while short walks will take you to others, such as Chetney Marshes, Ham Green, from which to view Half Acre, favoured by Goldeneye, or Motney Hill for viewing Bartlett and Rainham Creeks, usually good for Black-tailed Godwits. The Riverside Country Park and Horrid Hill, at Gillingham, provide distant views of Nor Marsh, now managed by the RSPB and good for roosting waders.

### Bough Beech Reservoir
Late wintering duck. Possibly an early Little Ringed Plover. View the Nature Reserve and the reservoir from the road across the north end.

### Dungeness
Early migrants, including Black Redstart, Northern Wheatear and Firecrest. Sea passage of Red-throated Divers, Brent Geese and Common Scoters, with other species such as Red-breasted Merganser and Sandwich Tern towards the end of the month.

### Sevenoaks Wildfowl Reserve
(OS 519567) Ducks, possibly Common Kingfisher and migrant waders, along with early passerine migrants. A carefully managed gravel pit reserve, with hides and a mile-long Nature Trail. Check visiting arrangements with the warden (see Appendix IV).

# April

Traditionally a time of great change, when spring takes over from winter. In recent years, however, cold spells have frequently delayed not only the breeding behaviour of resident species, but the departure of winter visitors and the arrival of summer migrants. By mid-month though, you can expect a considerable increase in the volume and variety of song, as the Common Nightingales and warblers arrive. Each visit to any coastal site, gravel pit, lake, park, or woodland will produce something different at this exciting time of year.

### Pegwell Bay Country Park and Thanet
Essentially for waders. Include some time watching from the hide in Pegwell Bay, as the tide rises bringing the waders closer. Then visit North Foreland, Foreness Point or Botany Bay, towards high tide, when Purple Sandpipers and other waders roost. Fulmars nest here, providing wonderful close views, while Common Eiders can sometimes be seen offshore. Visit Northdown Park (OS 380702) or Port Regis (OS 393701) for Ring-necked Parakeet.

### Elmley RSPB Reserve
Migrant waders, raptors and possibly Garganey.

### Dungeness
For passerine migrants and sea passage. Mediterranean Gulls, Sandwich Terns

and possibly Garganey on the RSPB reserve.

### Sandwich Bay and Stodmarsh

Visit Sandwich Bay in the morning for migrants generally – enquire at the Observatory. At Stodmarsh check the log entries. If you remain until dusk, you may hear a Common Bittern booming, and they sometimes fly at this time. The Common Snipe's display flight is also worth seeing and hearing.

# May

A most exciting month. Large numbers of breeding summer visitors arrive, while some resident birds will have fledged young. Some species that breed within the Arctic circle stop off briefly to feed, or fly up-Channel. A warm southerly airflow brings with it the promise of rarities. With such a variety of species in the county and many of them in song, this is a good opportunity to test your ability to identify birds by sound. Trying to unravel the complex sounds of the dawn chorus, though, can be bewildering until you have sorted out the songs of all the resident species.

### Fagg's Wood and Parkwood Picnic Site

Fagg's Wood is predominantly coniferous, with associated species such as Goldcrest, Coal Tit and possibly Common Crossbill, but with clearings that may attract Tree Pipit and various warblers. A few pairs of Willow Tits are resident. The car park (OS 986347) is clearly signposted. Parkwood Picnic Site (Great Heron Wood) is managed by the KCC, and also has a car park (OS 954318). It is an attractive, mainly broad-leaved woodland, with a heronry on the southern edge. Usual woodland species, including Willow Tit and Marsh Tit, Common Nightingale, warblers, Sparrowhawk and Hobby.

### Dungeness

A must in early May for the Pomarine Skua passage, plus numerous passerine migrants. The right weather patterns are essential for seabird passage (ideally a southerly wind after a period of northerlies) and falls of migrants (cloud developing during the night and rain around dawn). Study the terns on the Patch, or while they roost on the shore. Passerine migrants may be found anywhere – check the gully along the Dengemarsh road, while any of the pits may attract a rarer wader or tern.

### Stodmarsh and Westbere

Bearded Tits feeding young. Hobby and possibly Marsh Harrier, with rarer species such as Osprey occasionally. Freshwater waders may be observed from the Marsh Hide at Stodmarsh. The dawn chorus is a splendid mix of woodland and marshland species, and may include Common Bittern booming, Water Rail squealing and Common Snipe displaying. At Westbere, check the wood by the railway for Lesser Spotted Woodpecker. Follow the river, on the north bank, between Fordwich and Hersden lake, listening for Grasshopper and possibly Savi's Warblers.

### Elmley Reserve and Swale NNR

Waders galore, including breeding Avocets, but one of the great attractions in May is seeing the birds in full breeding plumage, particularly Ruff.

# June

A little less hectic than May, but there is still a great deal to be seen and always the possibility of a southern rarity or two. This is the best time to study some of the breeding species that arrive late, such as Nightjar.

### Knole Park and Oldbury Hill

Common Redstart, Tree Pipit and all three woodpeckers in Knole Park (OS 541524), where the great storm of October 1987 created an almost heath-like habitat for a few years, attracting Stonechat and Woodlark. The mixture of oak and birch on Oldbury Hill (OS 577559) suits the Wood Warbler well.

### Church Wood RSPB Reserve
An alternative to the above for Common Redstart and Tree Pipit, plus Common Nightingale. May attract Wood Warbler and Common Crossbill, while Nightjar and Woodcock also breed. Various walks, all well marked. The car park (OS 124594) is clearly signposted from Rough Common.

### Dungeness RSPB Reserve
Breeding Mediterranean Gulls, Common and Sandwich Terns and more recently Cormorants.

### Challock Forest, Bedgebury Forest or Hurst Wood, Mereworth
Nightjar and Woodcock – evening visits required. Both species are most easily located by listening for their unique calls towards dusk. Areas of youngish sweet chestnut or conifer, particularly with bracken, are favoured. Bedgebury (OS 741335); Hurst Wood (OS 625560).

# July

The long period of autumn migration commences for Arctic breeding waders, and some of the adults can be seen in good plumage as they pause on their southern journey. It is a busy time for local breeding birds, some attending their second broods. A chance, too, to become familiar with the differences between adult and juvenile plumages of various species that sometimes cause identification problems.

### Oare Marshes Nature Reserve
Reed and Sedge Warblers, returning freshwater and shore waders, raptors. An attractive reserve beside the Swale and the Saxon Shore Way, managed by the KTNC. Information Centre open at weekends.

### Bough Beech Reservoir
Young Great Crested Grebes, returning waders, particularly Common and Green Sandpipers by last week, and terns. Call in at the Visitor Centre, managed by the KTNC, for information.

### Stodmarsh
Fledgling Reed and Sedge Warblers in the reedbeds, with Bearded Tits, broods of various waterfowl, including Great Crested Grebes, returning freshwater waders and terns; maybe Hobbies hunting for food.

### Dungeness Reserve and the Patch
A good chance to study tern plumages.

# August

As the month progresses, increasing numbers of migrant visitors can be seen. Wader flocks are forming around the coastal marshes. Winds from the east will encourage the arrival of Scandinavian night migrants, such as Pied Flycatcher and the rarer Wryneck, mainly around the coast, but occasionally inland. Frequent visits to localities all around the coast are tempting, but check the weather pattern.

### Yantlet Creek and Stoke Lagoon
Little Terns flock at the mouth of the creek, roosting on the shingle at high tide. Follow the creek south from its mouth for about three kilometres to find Stoke Lagoon on your right. Migrant freshwater waders and possibly Garganey.

### Elmley RSPB Reserve, Swale NNR or Cliffe Pools
Excellent for waders at this time of year, including Little Stints and Curlew Sand-

pipers, as well as rarities from either west or east – White-rumped, Buff-breasted, Pectoral, Broad-billed and Marsh Sandpipers were all seen in 1994. Marsh Harrier and probably Hobby.

### Shellness
Winds from the northerly quarter, later in the month, will bring Arctic Skuas into the Thames and Swale. They can be seen well from the point, and there is the possibility of other seabirds, along with increasing numbers of shorebirds which can be seen well on the mud, either side of high tide.

### Isle of Grain
With the wind in the north-east, the scrub between the village and the shore can be good for migrant passerines. It is also a good seawatching point, in a north-east wind, but the tide needs to be high, otherwise the birds will be very distant.

## September
During the month there is a subtle change in the mixture of migrants. The majority of Swifts will already have gone, and this is the peak time for departing Barn Swallows, followed by House Martins, while migrant Willow Warblers are slowly replaced by Chiffchaffs. By the end of the month summer migrants are becoming scarce and are being replaced by a more autumnal mixture of Robins, Goldcrests and Firecrests. Seabird movements tend to include a greater variety of species, while wader flocks should constantly be checked. Scarce eastern and northern warblers, as well as other passerine migrants, may drift west and land around the coast, if the weather conditions are right.

### Dungeness
Mainly for passerine migrants in the trapping area, but an opportunity to study the terns and gulls on the Patch again, with immature and adult plumages – moulting from summer into winter – to sort out. A strong southeasterly wind and showers may produce a movement of Sooty Shearwaters.

### Allhallows, Shellness, Reculver or Foreness Point
As in late August, when the wind veers into the northerly quarter, seabirds fly into the Thames, sometimes hugging the north coast and flying up the Swale. Gannets, skuas and shearwaters can be expected and later in the month, often in stronger winds, rarer species such as Leach's Petrels and Sabine's Gulls may appear.

### Elmley RSPB Reserve or the Swale NNR
More migrant waders to sort out, many in fresh juvenile plumage. The estuary feeders also come in at high tide to swell the numbers, which can be impressive.

### St. Margaret's Bay
Passerine migrants, with rarer Scandinavian vagrants in the right weather conditions. Park at the end of St. Margaret's/Seaview Road (OS 358436), before the road turns to the lighthouse. Follow the various footpaths down and around the head of the valley. On good days stop on the edge of the valley and watch the migrants, either flying along the valley or working their way up the valley through the trees.

## October
This can be another exciting month in the birdwatching calendar, marked by constant change. The last summer visitors leave and winter visitors start to arrive in large numbers. The passage of diurnal migrants, such as Chaffinches and Common Starlings, can be most impressive, not only around the coast. On the sea, northerly gales may produce rarer seabirds, such as Leach's and Storm Petrels, or Sabine's Gull, as well as Gannets, Manx and Sooty Shearwaters, Pomarine Skuas, Common and Velvet Scoters, and Brent

Geese. Regular seawatchers may also identify Short-eared Owls and migrant raptors such as Hen Harrier, Merlin and Sparrowhawk, or even a Rough-legged Buzzard, coming in off the sea. Look at the weather map for a large high pressure zone over Asia and eastern Europe; then eastern rarities, such as Pallas's and Yellow-browed Warblers, can be anticipated.

### Allhallows, Shellness, Reculver or Foreness Point
Seawatching, when the wind moves into the northerly quarter. Visible passerine migration.

### Dungeness
Visible migration of thrushes and finches. Falls of migrants may include Ring Ouzels, Black Redstarts and Firecrests. Seabird passage – best seen here in south-easterly winds.

### Sandwich Bay or Thanet
A spell of easterly winds late in the month may produce rare warblers amongst the Goldcrests, Firecrests and Chiffchaffs – search any coastal scrub or copse.

### St. Margaret's Bay
Visible migration, with passerine vagrants in easterly weather conditions. Clear skies over the North Sea in the evening, followed by increasing cloud cover and rain during the night, will produce optimum conditions for a fall of passerine migrants.

## November

Winter thrushes are now widespread and virtually no summer visitors remain. Seabird movements have a more wintry mixture and may include flocks of Bewick's Swans and more Brent Geese, with divers, Common Eider and the rarer Long-tailed Duck, plus various auks. November is usually the best month for Little Auks and Puffins. The numbers of wintering wildfowl and waders on the North Kent Marshes and elsewhere increase during the month. A cold spell may bring an early influx of the rarer grebes, wintering geese and diving ducks, such as Scaup, Goosander and Smew.

### Sandwich Bay
First week is the peak time for Pallas's Warblers. Check the weather pattern. Snow Buntings should have returned.

### Allhallows, Shellness, Reculver or Foreness Point
Seawatching in strong northerly winds with rain.

### Hollingbourne to Harrietsham and Leeds Castle
This is one of many downland walks along the North Downs Way, where you might see a Sparrowhawk, or possibly a Common Buzzard. Conifers will have Coal Tits and Goldcrests, while the beech-mast may attract Bramblings. The lake by the aviary at Leeds Castle can be approached along the footpath from the Broomfield road and usually has a variety of wildfowl, plus Common Kingfisher and possibly Common Snipe.

### South Medway – Funton Creek to Riverside Country Park
Brent Geese, Red-breasted Mergansers, Avocets and wintering grebes, ducks and waders (see March).

## December

As in January, a severe spell of weather on the Continent can produce an influx of rarer grebes, geese and ducks. In milder conditions such species as White-fronted Goose, Smew and Goosander may not arrive in any numbers until the New Year. Large flocks of Lapwings and Golden Plover will be present on the coastal lowlands, and at various inland localities, while rarer visitors such as Great Grey Shrike, Shore Lark and Lapland Bunting may be much sought after, particularly if they were not found earlier in the year. Your choice of localities this month may well be influenced by what you missed the previous winter.

### Reculver to Minnis Bay and Chislet Marshes
Shore waders and ducks. Hen Harriers over the marshes. Possibly Shore Lark or Lapland Bunting. Chislet Marsh can be viewed from Marshside, or a higher vantage point, to locate any wintering geese or swans. Various footpaths cross the marshes.

### New Hythe and River Medway
Abbey Mead, the large flooded pit between the railway and the river, often attracts wintering grebes and large numbers of ducks. Cetti's Warblers are resident here, while at Burham Marsh, on the opposite bank of the river, Bearded Tits often winter and Common Bitterns occur almost annually.

### South Swale Local Nature Reserve
Brent Geese and waders; best either side of high tide when they feed on the mud close to the shore. At high tide scan the mouth of the Swale for wintering Great Crested Grebes and possibly Red-throated Divers or Velvet Scoter. Park near the Sportsman Inn and walk west along the seawall – a KTNC reserve. Hen Harrier and Short-eared Owl may be hunting over Graveney Marshes, while you might with luck find a few Snow Buntings or even a Shore Lark.

### Folkestone Harbour, Copt Point and the Warren
Gulls roost in the harbour at high tide, with the Mediterranean Gulls at Copt Point – on the cliff-top grass, on the rocks below or feeding offshore over the sewage outflow. Purple Sandpipers frequent the concrete apron below the Warren and sometimes roost on the harbour walls at high tide. Fulmars can be seen prospecting along the chalk cliffs. Rock Pipits also favour the apron. Passerines such as Chiffchaff and Firecrest may overwinter in the Warren, while Black Redstarts may be found around old buildings along the coastal strip.

# A Summary of Interesting Events
# 1985 – 1994

In the previous chapter I gave examples of the normal pattern of events month by month, but in most years extreme conditions of one sort or another occur and it is these conditions that create much of the excitement.

The Systematic List, which forms the next chapter, includes bar charts to show when each species occurred during this ten year period. What they cannot show, particularly for some of the less common species, is what lay behind the occurrences. The British Isles enjoy a varied climate. This, along with Kent's close proximity to the Continent, is largely responsible for the wide variety of species that we can anticipate in the county – and sometimes one or two that we don't.

For each year, I have selected examples of usual and extreme weather patterns.

## 1985

Early in the year there were Arctic conditions. Snow fell towards the end of the first week of January and again at the beginning of the third. Some unprecedented bird movements were associated with both these periods. As often happens, certain species move ahead of approaching severe weather. On this occasion there were exceptional counts of 20,000 Redwings, 8,000 Fieldfares, over 2,000 Skylarks, over 1,000 White-fronted Geese, 150 Common Snipe and 15 Little Auks arriving or moving west around the coast before the first fall of snow. The second fall was influenced by a Siberian airflow with freezing temperatures, and produced 190 Scaup, the highest number since 1962/63, and record numbers of 1,000 Common Eiders and 230 Goosanders, along with nearly 1,000 Red-throated Divers off Foreness and an influx of Red-necked and Slavonian Grebes. Single Red-breasted Geese arrived with each cold spell, while virtually all the Golden Plover and Lapwing flocks dispersed. The severity of the weather caused the loss of the east Kent's Cetti's Warbler population.

The temperatures rose during the last week of January and the mild weather continued into early February, but a deep anticyclone to the north-east of Britain again produced strong easterly winds, more snow and two more weeks of freezing conditions. During this time there were record numbers of Bewick's Swans and several small flocks of the rarer Whooper Swan in the county. The Margate wader roost attracted record numbers of 760 Sanderlings and 875 Turnstones and up to 20 Hen Harriers were roosting on Sheppey. In early March a Sociable Plover was found, 4,000 kilometres west of its normal wintering range.

As the summer's series of depressions started tracking on a more northerly course, a southerly airstream developed in early September. This produced an unprecedented flock of 19 Dotterel and an Ortolan Bunting. Later in the month a large anticyclone settled over the Continent and the easterly influence was soon felt with the arrival of a Purple Heron and over 100 Curlew Sandpipers. It also produced outstanding numbers of migrant Siskins and Common Redpolls, followed from late September and throughout October by an unprecedented influx of over 60 Yellow-browed Warblers. There were also six Pallas's Warblers and four Red-breasted Flycatchers. These species continued to arrive because the anticyclonic conditions persisted during October. There were staggering numbers of Pied Wagtails around the coast, with 1,800 at Foreness on one day. High numbers of Lapland Buntings were also arriving on the coast, and one was discovered inland at Boughton Park.

There was also a record influx of Pomarine Skuas, a number of which remained to winter in Kent for the first time. During the ten years, the best three Pomarine Skua autumns, 1985, 1988 and 1991, have coincided with three good lemming years in the arctic, and in those years there were a good proportion of juveniles amongst the skuas and the movements were later.

Exceptional numbers of Little Auks were seen between late October and late November, driven south in northerly gales. During this same period, numbers of Lapland Buntings continued to arrive, increasing the wintering flock at Allhallows to 123, the highest ever recorded in the county.

## 1986

January was generally mild, but cold northeasterly winds brought snow late in the month, when 10,500 Kittiwakes flew west into the Thames estuary and the numbers of White-fronted Geese on Sheppey increased to 1,550. In contrast, February was dominated by an anticyclone to the north-east of the British Isles, which brought the coldest conditions in Kent since 1947. Not unexpectedly, numbers of wildfowl increased with the White-fronted Goose flock on Sheppey reaching a record total of 2,700, while there were above average numbers of Scaup, Smew and Goosander, as well as up to 2,000 Red-throated Divers around the coast.

The latter half of May and much of June was cool and unsettled, but it was the influence of the previous cold winters that caused the absence of breeding Stonechats and Goldcrests. Wrens were down to less than 50% of their 1984 numbers and few Common Kingfishers survived to breed.

## 1987

There was a long period of typically autumnal weather with numerous depressions, but at times their centres moved north along the continental littoral and over the North Sea. This produced a succession of northerly winds and, in consequence, seabird movements from mid-September (Davenport 1989).

Strong northerly winds in the northern North Sea will precipitate seabird passage, but where and when they will be seen from the Kent coast will be determined by the local wind directions. Off Dungeness, on 13 September, there was an unprecedented westerly movement of 263 Arctic Skuas, flying into a force 4, south-west wind, most passing after frontal rain had cleared.

A force 3, north-west wind veered north-east on 18 September and watchers at Shellness identified a Leach's Petrel, 15 Manx Shearwaters, and 74 Arctic, 22 Pomarine and 18 Great Skuas. The wind veered ESE on the 19th and the focus switched to Foreness, where 52 Great, 31 Arctic, four Pomarine and an adult Long-tailed Skua flew east, while another 51 Arctic Skuas flew west at Dungeness.

However, it was early October that produced something really special. On the 9th a force 5, south-west wind blew at Dungeness and flocks of Manx and Sooty Shearwaters started passing west during the late morning, continuing through the afternoon as the wind backed and increased to SSE, force 6. By the end of the day unprecedented counts of 408 Sooty and 241 Manx Shearwaters had been totalled, along with the first county record of Little Shearwater. Other species included one Storm and two Leach's Petrels, 28 Great and two Pomarine Skuas and two Sabine's Gulls. The wind continued the next day and another good movement of seabirds flew west.

The great storm in the early hours of 16 October was the meteorological event of the decade, with a SSW wind force 10 gusting to force 15. As a result large numbers of seabirds were blown inland in the south-east of Britain, although relatively few were seen in Kent. However, a Sabine's Gull flew over Rainham on the 16th, when Leach's Petrels appeared inland at Sevenoaks Reserve and Mote Park, while on the 17th there was a Leach's Petrel on Dungeness Pits and a Grey Phalarope at Elmley, with two more on Scotney Pits.

Towards the end of November and the beginning of December, a change to colder north-east winds produced further seabird movements in the Thames estuary. There were a number of later than usual records of petrels, shearwaters, Little Auks and Puffins, as well as the usual late autumn arrivals of Common Guillemots and Razorbills. An influx of 21 Little Auks was not unexpected, but a total of 17 Leach's Petrels over a period of four days, when the wind was at its strongest, was surprising so late in the autumn.

## 1988

The weather this year was about as 'normal' as one can expect. There were the usual cold northeasterly winds in early April, which held up the arrival of spring migrants, while north-east winds in October resulted in a large influx of *Phylloscopus* warblers. At Reculver on 2 October there were 410 Chiffchaffs, 14 Yellow-browed Warblers and a Bonelli's Warbler, with ten more Yellow-browed at Foreness the next day. These birds were part of a record Kent autumn when 97 Yellow-browed Warblers were seen.

## 1989

This year six new species were added to the Kent list. In the majority of cases it is not easy to attribute their arrival to particular weather conditions. In January two North American warblers were discovered – a Golden-winged Warbler at Larkfield attracted one of the largest 'twitches' so far seen in Britain, while the presence of a Common Yellowthroat was not broadcast. A Desert Wheatear in early April did not stay for others to see. A Bonaparte's Gull in mid-April was found by a visiting Sussex birder, before being seen by regulars at Dungeness. A Lesser Crested Tern in May was also seen from three Sussex sites as it flew east presumably on its way to the Farne Islands for the seventh year in succession. A Blue-cheeked Bee-eater in July was another colourful surprise, enjoyed by just two fortunate observers.

March was considerably warmer than normal, with temperatures at Folkestone of 16°C on the 6th and 19°C on the 28th. These mild conditions produced a number of early migrants. The first Northern Wheatear and Ring Ouzel on the 6th, followed by Willow Warbler, Sand Martin and House Martin by the 14th, Barn Swallow, Yellow Wagtail, Tree Pipit and Sedge Warbler by the 28th, and the county's earliest ever Grasshopper Warbler on the 29th.

During a period of light north-east winds, there was a record easterly movement of 241 Black Terns off Dungeness on 10 May. Between the 8th and 10th a total of 950 either visited the pits there or flew east. In similar weather conditions in early May 1990 and in 1993, high numbers were again present, with a new record 283 east on 10 May 1993.

## 1990

Apart from occasional, brief, cooler spells, the first quarter was mild, with heavy rain and strong winds at times. The mildness may well have been responsible for attracting the county's earliest ever Sand Martin to Seasalter on 22 February, and even more remarkable the earliest ever Spotted Flycatcher to Darenth on 17 March. A number of other early migrants were seen, including a very early Garden Warbler at Sutton-at-Hone on 31 March.

In October a period of east or south-east winds brought warm weather. There were 700 Goldcrests at Dungeness and nearly 400 Little Gulls flying east at Reculver. There were also two additions to the county list, with the first Two-barred Crossbills at Bedgebury and a Parrot Crossbill at Sandwich Bay. There were comparatively large influxes of both these species into Britain at this time.

# 1991

During the first two weeks of February, a deep anticyclone over the Continent produced cold north-east winds and hard frosts, with two heavy falls of snow. The wind-blown snow was quite sufficient to block minor roads. Virtually all the Lapwing and Golden Plover flocks deserted the county to find less harsh conditions farther west, as did many Skylarks and winter thrushes. Being late in the season, many divers, grebes, ducks, geese and swans were relatively unaffected, although large numbers of Scaup and a good number of Smew arrived, while an increase in the numbers of Barnacle Geese supported claims of genuine vagrancy. There was also an influx of Jack Snipe and Woodcock from across the Channel. An unprecedented gathering of 100 Woodcock on recently cleared ground in Quex Park must have been an amazing sight. A flock of Common Redpolls in Church Wood increased to 300, amongst which two diligent observers identified up to four Arctic Redpolls, a rare vagrant to Kent.

This severe spell, together with unfavourable weather conditions during spring migration, meant that the breeding season was poor for a number of resident and migrant passerines. The Wren and Goldcrest breeding populations were again vastly reduced, there was no evidence of Firecrest nesting and both Willow Warbler and Spotted Flycatcher numbers were low.

At the end of October an area of high pressure over Spain produced warm southerly winds across the Continent, which brought Kent's first Desert Warbler to Seasalter – there were three in Britain at this time. Three weeks later the second Kentish Desert Wheatear was discovered at Langdon.

# 1992

Much of May was dominated by settled anticyclonic conditions, with easterly and warm southeasterly airflows which brought an unprecedented influx of Red-footed Falcons into the county from the 14th: seven at Stodmarsh and a probable total of 22. There were already up to 14 Hobbies present at Stodmarsh towards the end of May when a Black Kite appeared. Other rarities probably influenced by this weather included Kent's first Cattle Egret at Stodmarsh, a Purple Heron at Dungeness, two White-winged Black Terns on the Swale NNR, European Bee-eaters at Sandwich Bay and Foreness, a Red-rumped Swallow at Abbot's Cliff, a Red-throated Pipit at Foreness and a Great Reed Warbler on the Hoo peninsula.

On 6 September, in fresh SSE winds, there was a remarkable westerly passage of terns off Dungeness, with 2,000 Common or Arctic Terns, including at least 120 Arctic, and an unprecedented 10,215 Black Terns.

A break in a period of almost continuous southwesterly gales in November, when the wind backed to south-east, produced exceptional numbers of ducks flying west off Dungeness, particularly on the 9th. These included peak counts of 700 Common and 43 Velvet Scoters, 331 Red-breasted Mergansers, 285 Pintail and 51 Scaup. In addition, 238 Avocets flew past.

# 1993

In June a stationary anticyclone over the Continent, with the consequent easterly airflow, produced a number of southern rarities. This year was a good example of this weather pattern, with a White Stork over Cheriton and Dungeness, a European Bee-eater and Red-rumped Swallow at St. Margaret's, a Woodchat Shrike and Black-winged Stilt at Dungeness again, and a Common Rosefinch at Stodmarsh, all in the space of nine days. Within a week two Greenish Warblers were discovered at Capel-le-Ferne.

In mid-September, an anticyclone over Scandinavia and the Baltic produced north-east winds, pushing Continental migrants westwards as frontal systems moved east across southern Britain. These conditions saw an unprecedented raptor passage, with at least 24 Common Buzzards, 17 Honey Buzzards and a Rough-legged Buzzard between the 11th and 19th. At St. Margaret's there were also peak numbers of 600 Blackcaps and 134 Tree Pipits.

On 14 October, with a force 6 NNE wind, there was another excellent seabird movement along the north coast. At Foreness 2,550 Kittiwakes flew east and at Shellness there were high skua totals of 260 Great, 55 Arctic and 25 Pomarine, along with 130 Little and two Sabine's Gulls.

## 1994

The seabird passage on 16 September in a force 6, north-west wind along the north Kent coast has already featured in 'A Year in Kent' (pp.65-66). During October, a continental high produced a period of easterly winds and a record number of Pallas's Warblers; a Radde's Warbler at St. Margaret's and Kent's second Pied Wheatear at Tesco's, Sheerness were also observed.

In contrast to coolish weather in September and October, early November was one of the warmest on record. The combination of an anticyclone to the north-east of Britain and low pressure to the south and west, produced a warm southeasterly airflow. There were seven more Pallas's Warblers at Dungeness during the first two weeks, and two sightings of Penduline Tit there. A Red-breasted Flycatcher was present at St. Margaret's, a Short-toed Lark was discovered at Cliffe, and a Blyth's Pipit, found at Seasalter, was a first for Kent.

# Systematic List

The list includes all species satisfactorily identified in Kent during 1985-94 and the comments relate to this period. The names of the additional 38 species on the county list, recorded before 1985, are included in Appendix I.

The weekly bar charts are based on an analysis of the records received by the Kent Ornithological Society for 1985-94, a selection of which is published annually in the Kent Bird Report. With this in mind some skulking species, such as Water Rail and Common Nightingale in late summer may well be present but not seen or heard, and will therefore be under-recorded. The charts are designed to show at a glance when a species is most likely to be seen.

Where appropriate, I have indicated where you may see particular species, and some hints on how to see them.

In the descriptions of the species' principal status, the following terms have quite specific meanings for the period 1985-94:

|  |  |
|---|---|
| Very rare | 1 – 10 records |
| Rare | 11 – 25 records |
| Scarce | 26 – 50 records |

## Key to Bar Charts

Each month is divided into four 7 or 8 day periods. To avoid creating a false impression regarding frequency, individuals making long stays, such as early or late migrants, or those overwintering, may only be shown in the arrival or departure week:

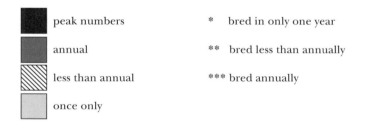

peak numbers     *   bred in only one year

annual     **   bred less than annually

less than annual     *** bred annually

once only

# Red-throated Diver
*Gavia stellata*

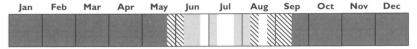

| Jan | Feb | Mar | Apr | May | Jun | Jul | Aug | Sep | Oct | Nov | Dec |

**Common winter visitor and regular passage migrant**

May be seen all round the coast and occasionally on inland waters. In rough weather, favours sheltered localities, such as estuaries, or freshwater pools near the coast, like the pits at Dungeness or Cliffe Pools. Wintering flocks off Leysdown to Thanet sometimes exceed 100, and more rarely 300, while higher three-figure movements occur in extreme winter conditions; day totals in excess of 1,000 were noted in February 1986. During spring passage off Dungeness three-figure day totals most often occur in March and early April, but passage continues into May.

# Black-throated Diver
*Gavia arctica*

| Jan | Feb | Mar | Apr | May | Jun | Jul | Aug | Sep | Oct | Nov | Dec |

**Winter visitor and regular passage migrant**

Winters on coastal and occasionally inland waters. Most regular on spring passage off Dungeness, where day totals rarely exceed 30.

# Great Northern Diver
*Gavia immer*

| Jan | Feb | Mar | Apr | May | Jun | Jul | Aug | Sep | Oct | Nov | Dec |

**Passage migrant and occasional winter visitor**

The rarest of the three wintering divers, regular on spring passage off Dungeness in late April and May. Sometimes winters in the Medway estuary, but rare on inland waters.

# White-billed Diver
*Gavia adamsii*

**Very rare vagrant**

The second and third county records were of singles seen flying S off Ramsgate in December 1991 and flying E at Dungeness in April 1993. The first was one found dead in November 1969.

# Little Grebe
*Tachybaptus ruficollis*

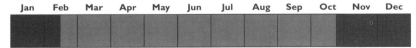

| Jan | Feb | Mar | Apr | May | Jun | Jul | Aug | Sep | Oct | Nov | Dec |

**Resident**                                                                                                    ***

Commonly seen on most inland waters, breeds on small lakes and in ditches. Flocks form during the winter months, with peaks of over 100 on Cliffe Pools, and occasionally at Murston.

Great Crested Grebes

# Great Crested Grebe
### *Podiceps cristatus*

| Jan | Feb | Mar | Apr | May | Jun | Jul | Aug | Sep | Oct | Nov | Dec |
|-----|-----|-----|-----|-----|-----|-----|-----|-----|-----|-----|-----|

**Resident and winter visitor**     ***

Breeds on larger inland waters and gravel pits. Coastal flocks of 100-500 form during the winter, the favoured localities being between Dungeness and Hythe, from Sandwich Bay round Thanet to the mouth of the Swale, and the south Medway.

# Red-necked Grebe
### *Podiceps grisegena*

| Jan | Feb | Mar | Apr | May | Jun | Jul | Aug | Sep | Oct | Nov | Dec |
|-----|-----|-----|-----|-----|-----|-----|-----|-----|-----|-----|-----|

**Winter visitor and uncommon passage migrant**

Severe weather brings influxes. May be seen around the coast and on inland waters. Most regular on the pits at Dungeness.

# Slavonian Grebe
### *Podiceps auritus*

| Jan | Feb | Mar | Apr | May | Jun | Jul | Aug | Sep | Oct | Nov | Dec |
|-----|-----|-----|-----|-----|-----|-----|-----|-----|-----|-----|-----|

**Winter visitor and uncommon passage migrant**

Usually singly, but between two and four sometimes occur together around the coast and on inland waters. As with the previous species, influxes follow severe weather on the Continent.

# Black-necked Grebe
### *Podiceps nigricollis*

| Jan | Feb | Mar | Apr | May | Jun | Jul | Aug | Sep | Oct | Nov | Dec |
|-----|-----|-----|-----|-----|-----|-----|-----|-----|-----|-----|-----|

**Winter visitor and early autumn passage migrant**

Usually seen in ones and twos, but occasionally four or five occur together in early autumn. Favours reservoirs and gravel pits.

# Fulmar

*Fulmarus glacialis*

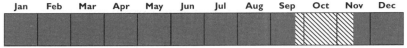

| Jan | Feb | Mar | Apr | May | Jun | Jul | Aug | Sep | Oct | Nov | Dec |

**Annual visitor, some birds virtually resident** \*\*\*

Up to 40 pairs nest on the cliffs between Thanet and Folkestone. Prospecting birds and those breeding return from late November and depart during August. Can also be seen on passage in the Channel and in the Thames estuary, with day totals of 200+ off Dungeness in spring and an exceptional 1,049 E there on 13 May 1985.

# Cory's Shearwater

*Calonectris diomedea*

| Jan | Feb | Mar | Apr | May | Jun | Jul | Aug | Sep | Oct | Nov | Dec |

**Very rare passage migrant**

A rare reward for regular seawatchers. All ten records involved singles off the coast between Dungeness and Reculver.

# Great Shearwater

*Puffinus gravis*

**Very rare vagrant**

One off Dungeness in January 1990 is the seventh Kent record, and the first since 1968.

# Sooty Shearwater

*Puffinus griseus*

| Jan | Feb | Mar | Apr | May | Jun | Jul | Aug | Sep | Oct | Nov | Dec |

**Annual passage migrant**

An average of 35 per year, excluding 1987 when there was an unprecedented movement off Dungeness in October, involving peaks of 409 W on 9th and 143 on 10th.

The best chances to see this species are in inclement weather, particularly in northerly gales, from seawatching points such as Foreness, Reculver and Shellness; also may be seen in southerly winds with frontal rain off Dungeness.

# Manx Shearwater

*Puffinus puffinus*

| Jan | Feb | Mar | Apr | May | Jun | Jul | Aug | Sep | Oct | Nov | Dec |

**Annual passage migrant**

Annual totals range from 43–1023, with an average of 336. Day totals very rarely exceed 100, but there was a composite total of 488 along the north coast on 27 August 1989, 338 flew S off North Foreland on 15 July 1988 and 241 flew W off Dungeness on 9 October 1987.

Best seen from suitable seawatching vantage points in the Thames estuary, around Thanet and at Dungeness, where small flocks can occasionally be seen during summer.

# Mediterranean Shearwater
## *Puffinus yelkouan*

| Jan | Feb | Mar | Apr | May | Jun | Jul | Aug | Sep | Oct | Nov | Dec |
|-----|-----|-----|-----|-----|-----|-----|-----|-----|-----|-----|-----|

**Scarce annual passage migrant**

Ones and twos most often seen off Dungeness, but occasionally in the Thames estuary and off the Thanet coast. The form concerned is *P. y. mauretanicus.*

# Little Shearwater
## *Puffinus assimilis*

**Very rare vagrant**

The first county record concerns one flying W off Dungeness in October 1987.

# Storm Petrel
## *Hydrobates pelagicus*

| Jan | Feb | Mar | Apr | May | Jun | Jul | Aug | Sep | Oct | Nov | Dec |
|-----|-----|-----|-----|-----|-----|-----|-----|-----|-----|-----|-----|

**Rare visitor**

1–4 in six years, but 10 in 1987. Usually associated with northerly gales.

# Leach's Petrel
## *Oceanodroma leucorhoa*

| Jan | Feb | Mar | Apr | May | Jun | Jul | Aug | Sep | Oct | Nov | Dec |
|-----|-----|-----|-----|-----|-----|-----|-----|-----|-----|-----|-----|

**Annual in autumn and occasional in winter**

In 1987-89 severe conditions produced exceptional annual totals of 42, 39 and 88 respectively. The average is around 15 per year, though only one was seen in 1994. As with Storm Petrel, usually associated with northerly gales.

# Gannet
## *Sula bassana*

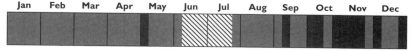

| Jan | Feb | Mar | Apr | May | Jun | Jul | Aug | Sep | Oct | Nov | Dec |
|-----|-----|-----|-----|-----|-----|-----|-----|-----|-----|-----|-----|

**Passage migrant**

May be seen all round the coast, but peak day totals exceeding 200 are usually recorded in late autumn in the Thames estuary, off Thanet and off Dungeness.

# Cormorant
## *Phalacrocorax carbo*

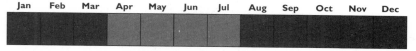

| Jan | Feb | Mar | Apr | May | Jun | Jul | Aug | Sep | Oct | Nov | Dec |
|-----|-----|-----|-----|-----|-----|-----|-----|-----|-----|-----|-----|

**Winter visitor and recently established breeding resident**                    *

Numbers have increased since 1985 and two small breeding colonies were established in 1994 – the first successful breeding this century. Over one hundred roost around the north coast, with counts of 300+ now being recorded at Elmley and in the estuaries of the Medway and Thames.

# Shag

*Phalacrocorax aristotelis*

| Jan | Feb | Mar | Apr | May | Jun | Jul | Aug | Sep | Oct | Nov | Dec |
|-----|-----|-----|-----|-----|-----|-----|-----|-----|-----|-----|-----|

**Passage migrant and winter visitor, becoming increasingly regular in summer**

The status of this species has changed during the ten years, with a few almost resident in the Swale, opposite Elmley Hills, since 1991. Occasionally seen on inland waters.

Common Bittern

# Common Bittern

*Botaurus stellaris*

| Jan | Feb | Mar | Apr | May | Jun | Jul | Aug | Sep | Oct | Nov | Dec |
|-----|-----|-----|-----|-----|-----|-----|-----|-----|-----|-----|-----|

**Annual winter visitor**

The number of birds wintering varies from 4–15 annually, with an average of seven. Improved habitat on the Stodmarsh NNR may encourage this species to breed again, but it remains a winter visitor at present. In severe winters, Common Bitterns may turn up anywhere in localities with reed-fringed open water, but they are frustratingly difficult to see.

Find out where one is roosting and be there towards dusk.

# Night Heron

*Nycticorax nycticorax*

| Jan | Feb | Mar | Apr | May | Jun | Jul | Aug | Sep | Oct | Nov | Dec |
|-----|-----|-----|-----|-----|-----|-----|-----|-----|-----|-----|-----|

**Rare vagrant**

The Dungeness area attracted seven individuals, with two each at Stodmarsh and the Sevenoaks Wildfowl Reserve, and singles at Ham Fen, Foreness and Bough Beech Reservoir.

## Squacco Heron                                   *Ardeola ralloides*

**Very rare vagrant**

An adult was present on Elmley RSPB Reserve in May 1990. The only other county record this century concerns one on the Thames marshes in July 1979.

## Cattle Egret                                      *Bubulcus ibis*

**Very rare vagrant**

The first county record concerns one at Stodmarsh in May 1992, with the second in May 1993, first seen flying NE at Dungeness then NW at Sandwich Bay.

## Little Egret                                     *Egretta garzetta*

| Jan | Feb | Mar | Apr | May | Jun | Jul | Aug | Sep | Oct | Nov | Dec |

**Now almost resident**

The status of this species has changed markedly since 1985. Although there were five singles in 1989, just one occurred in 1990, with the first multiple records four years later, when up to nine were seen in the Swale. A flock of 22 was present in 1995.

## Great White Egret                                 *Egretta alba*

**Very rare vagrant**

The second and third county records concern singles at Dungeness in August 1988 and in the Stour Valley from late August to mid-October 1990. Presumably this was the same bird seen earlier in August that year at Dungeness. The first county record was in May 1977.

## Grey Heron                                         *Ardea cinerea*

| Jan | Feb | Mar | Apr | May | Jun | Jul | Aug | Sep | Oct | Nov | Dec |

**Resident**                                                   \*\*\*

At least eight heronries are occupied in the county, including the largest in Britain at Northward Hill RSPB Reserve, where around 200 pairs nest annually.

## Purple Heron                                      *Ardea purpurea*

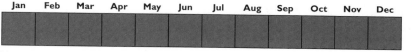

| Jan | Feb | Mar | Apr | May | Jun | Jul | Aug | Sep | Oct | Nov | Dec |

**Rare passage migrant**

A total of 25, ranging from none in 1993 to seven in 1987. A good spread of sightings, from Dartford Marsh and Hayesden, to Capel Fleet, Reculver, Sandwich Bay and Folkestone, with 10 in the Dungeness area and five in the Stour Valley.

# Black Stork
*Ciconia nigra*

| Jan | Feb | Mar | Apr | May | Jun | Jul | Aug | Sep | Oct | Nov | Dec |
|-----|-----|-----|-----|-----|-----|-----|-----|-----|-----|-----|-----|

**Very rare vagrant**

The six records, all of single birds between 1988 and 1993, were at Cliffe, Murston (twice), Elmley, Sandwich, and Dungeness.

# White Stork
*Ciconia ciconia*

| Jan | Feb | Mar | Apr | May | Jun | Jul | Aug | Sep | Oct | Nov | Dec |
|-----|-----|-----|-----|-----|-----|-----|-----|-----|-----|-----|-----|

**Rare passage migrant**

Widely scattered sightings, with none in four years and just 1–4 in the other six.

# Glossy Ibis
*Plegadis falcinellus*

**Very rare vagrant**

One commenced wintering at Stodmarsh in December 1975, and was joined by a second in October 1979. They both remained in the county until February 1985, when one disappeared. The other, which summered on Sheppey and continued to winter in the Stour Valley, was last seen in January 1993.

In addition, one flew over Dungeness in October 1986, two were seen at Seaton in April 1987 and another was seen on Walland Marsh in May 1990.

# Spoonbill
*Platalea leucorodia*

**Almost annual visitor in small numbers**

Two birds summered on the North Kent Marshes during 1988, 1989 and 1990. Usually seen in ones and twos, but up to four were seen in 1989. The three most favoured sites are Elmley, Dungeness and Stodmarsh.

# Mute Swan
*Cygnus olor*

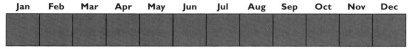

**Widespread resident**     \*\*\*

Flocks of moulting and non-breeding birds may occasionally exceed 100, with a total of 300+ in the Stour Valley. Flocks of 100+ gather in the winter months on coastal lowlands, where they sometimes graze on cereal crops. Across the Walland Marsh a total of 300+ is not unusual.

Mute Swan

## Bewick's Swan
*Cygnus columbianus*

| Jan | Feb | Mar | Apr | May | Jun | Jul | Aug | Sep | Oct | Nov | Dec |
|-----|-----|-----|-----|-----|-----|-----|-----|-----|-----|-----|-----|

**Annual winter visitor and passage migrant**

Most regular on Walland Marsh, sometimes in fields near the Woolpack Inn, where wintering numbers may exceed 300. Smaller numbers winter intermittently on Sheppey, the Thames marshes, the Wantsum marshes, or in the Stour Valley. In some winters the Walland flock flies to the Dungeness RSPB Reserve to roost.

## Whooper Swan
*Cygnus cygnus*

| Jan | Feb | Mar | Apr | May | Jun | Jul | Aug | Sep | Oct | Nov | Dec |
|-----|-----|-----|-----|-----|-----|-----|-----|-----|-----|-----|-----|

**Irregular winter visitor and passage migrant**

Relatively scarce since the cold winter of 1987, but a few records of 1–4 occur in most winters, often in association with the previous two species.

## Bean Goose
*Anser fabalis*

| Jan | Feb | Mar | Apr | May | Jun | Jul | Aug | Sep | Oct | Nov | Dec |
|-----|-----|-----|-----|-----|-----|-----|-----|-----|-----|-----|-----|

**Almost annual winter visitor**

Records generally involve just 1–10 birds, but flocks of 19 and 22 visited Sheppey in January 1985 and Reculver in November 1993, while flocks of 58 and 87 flying SW and W at Sandwich Bay in late October 1991 are the largest ever seen in Kent. Most likely to be seen on the Thames or Sheppey marshes, but becoming more regular and occurring in the Stour Valley and on Dengemarsh.

# Pink-footed Goose

*Anser brachyrhynchus*

| Jan | Feb | Mar | Apr | May | Jun | Jul | Aug | Sep | Oct | Nov | Dec |
|-----|-----|-----|-----|-----|-----|-----|-----|-----|-----|-----|-----|

**Annual winter visitor or passage migrant in small numbers**

Individuals or small flocks of up to 20 occur occasionally on the North Kent Marshes, in the Stour Valley, or in the Dungeness area. Larger flocks are more often seen on passage: 52 flew W at Minnis Bay on 30 January 1991 and 46 flew S at Sandwich Bay on 1 December 1993. Feral individuals may be seen in widespread localities at any time of the year.

# White-fronted Goose

*Anser albifrons*

| Jan | Feb | Mar | Apr | May | Jun | Jul | Aug | Sep | Oct | Nov | Dec |
|-----|-----|-----|-----|-----|-----|-----|-----|-----|-----|-----|-----|

**Regular winter visitor**

The main wintering area is on Sheppey, with smaller numbers on the Thames marshes and occasionally on Chetney. Sheppey may attract up to 2,000 birds, the peak numbers often not occurring until late January or early February. The Sheppey flock often roosts at Elmley and sometimes visits the Swale NNR during the day.

# Lesser White-fronted Goose

*Anser erythropus*

**Very rare winter visitor**

The only record that suggests genuine vagrancy involves an adult and an immature which were present with the wintering White-fronted Geese on Sheppey between January and March 1994.

This species, like other wildfowl, escapes from collections and up to four have been seen occasionally at various times of the year, frequently at inland localities such as Bough Beech, Sevenoaks and the Stour Valley.

# Greylag Goose

*Anser anser*

| Jan | Feb | Mar | Apr | May | Jun | Jul | Aug | Sep | Oct | Nov | Dec |
|-----|-----|-----|-----|-----|-----|-----|-----|-----|-----|-----|-----|

**Resident, and occasional winter visitor**                     ***

Feral populations are thriving on the Thames, Medway and Sheppey marshes, in the Stour Valley, at Dungeness and inland at Sevenoaks and Bough Beech. Peak totals in each of these areas, except Stodmarsh, exceed 300. Occasionally, immigrants from the east, with pink bills, may be seen in winter on Sheppey or at Sandwich Bay.

# Canada Goose

*Branta canadensis*

| Jan | Feb | Mar | Apr | May | Jun | Jul | Aug | Sep | Oct | Nov | Dec |
|-----|-----|-----|-----|-----|-----|-----|-----|-----|-----|-----|-----|

**Resident**                     ***

An extremely successful introduced species, now breeding throughout the county. Flocks of 500+ may be seen at Bough Beech or Sevenoaks, with 300+ at Dungeness, and on the Medway and Sheppey marshes.

# Barnacle Goose

*Branta leucopsis*

| Jan | Feb | Mar | Apr | May | Jun | Jul | Aug | Sep | Oct | Nov | Dec |
|-----|-----|-----|-----|-----|-----|-----|-----|-----|-----|-----|-----|

**Scarce winter visitor**

Genuine winter visitors are most often seen with the wintering flocks of grey geese, or occasionally with the Brent Geese. Up to ten or so may occur in these situations, but confidence in genuine vagrancy increases when flocks of 20+ are involved, as in early 1991, 1992 and 1993. The peak count in this period was 45 at Stodmarsh on 29 January 1992.

Confusion with feral birds is inevitable, as free-flying birds breed in the county and are increasing nationally.

# Brent Goose

*Branta bernicla*

| Jan | Feb | Mar | Apr | May | Jun | Jul | Aug | Sep | Oct | Nov | Dec |
|-----|-----|-----|-----|-----|-----|-----|-----|-----|-----|-----|-----|

**Winter visitor and passage migrant**

Numbers have increased and wintering flocks totalling 1,900 occur in the Thames estuary, with 4,000 in the south Medway and 2,000 in the Swale. In March and early April a heavy up-Channel passage involving day totals of several thousands occurs off Dungeness, while in late October and early November a marked passage can be witnessed along the north Kent coast. Some flocks also fly overland to the Sussex coast. A few birds summer in the Medway.

Birds of the pale-bellied race *B. b. horta* occur rarely, while a Black Brant *B. b. nigricans* has been seen in three winters, usually in the Swale.

# Red-breasted Goose

*Branta ruficollis*

**Very rare winter visitor**

In 1985 singles were present at Shellness from January to February and on Chetney between January and March, often feeding with Brent Goose flocks. One returned in November, remaining until January 1986. Another was seen at Shellness in December 1993. These are the first Kent records of genuine vagrants.

# Egyptian Goose

*Alopochen aegyptiacus*

| Jan | Feb | Mar | Apr | May | Jun | Jul | Aug | Sep | Oct | Nov | Dec |
|-----|-----|-----|-----|-----|-----|-----|-----|-----|-----|-----|-----|

**Rare visitor**

A feral species, which can occur anywhere.

# Ruddy Shelduck

*Tadorna ferruginea*

**Possible vagrant**

In 1994 three were seen at Dungeness in August and on Sheppey in September. The origins of this species remain open to speculation. There is a small feral population in The Netherlands, but vagrancy from Turkey is not impossible.

95

# Common Shelduck

*Tadorna tadorna*

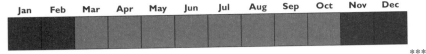

**Resident**

***

Each of the three estuaries in north Kent regularly attract 1,000-3,000 birds in winter, with peaks of up to 6,000 in the Medway. Post-breeding creches may hold up to 250 ducklings on Elmley. Also seen commonly inland at Bough Beech, where several pairs breed.

# Mandarin Duck

*Aix galericulata*

**Resident**

***

Small feral populations are widely scattered, but most often seen in C and W Kent, at sites such as Hayesden, Bough Beech, Mote and Eastwell Parks, and along the River Len near Leeds Castle.

# Eurasian Wigeon

*Anas penelope*

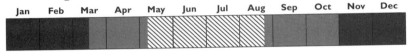

**Winter visitor**

*

5,000-10,000 winter in both the Medway and Swale estuaries, with rare peaks of 20,000+ on Elmley. Up to 3,000 may also be seen on the Dungeness RSPB Reserve. A few remain throughout the summer and one pair bred in 1985.

# American Wigeon

*Anas americana*

**Very rare vagrant**

The four records in the period all involve singles. A duck at Sandwich Bay in February 1987 was the seventh Kent record, followed by drakes on Elmley in April 1990, again in April–May 1991 and in December 1992, with presumably the same bird at Minnis Bay in January 1993.

# Gadwall

*Anas strepera*

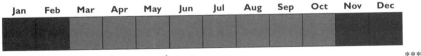

**Resident, winter visitor and passage migrant**

***

The population is increasing. Almost 300 at Seaton in December 1993 is a county record for one site. Close to 200 may now be seen at Cliffe and over 150 at Dungeness in winter. Gadwall can be seen occasionally on most inland waters and coastal marshes.

# Common Teal

*Anas crecca*

**Resident and winter visitor**

**

Widespread during the winter months, with peak numbers occasionally reaching 5,000 in the Swale estuary. Declining as a breeding species.

## Green-winged Teal

*Anas crecca carolinensis*

Single drakes of this very rare American race of Common Teal were seen at the Sevenoaks Wildfowl Reserve in February–March 1990 and on the Dungeness RSPB Reserve in June 1993.

## Mallard

*Anas platyrhynchos*

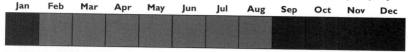

| Jan | Feb | Mar | Apr | May | Jun | Jul | Aug | Sep | Oct | Nov | Dec |

**Resident and winter visitor** ***

Early autumn and winter peaks of 1,000+ occur on the estuaries of the Medway and Swale, in the Stour Valley and occasionally at Dungeness.

## Pintail

*Anas acuta*

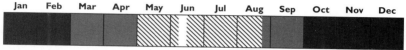

| Jan | Feb | Mar | Apr | May | Jun | Jul | Aug | Sep | Oct | Nov | Dec |

**Winter visitor and passage migrant**

Increased numbers noted in recent winters, with over 1,000 in the Medway and 1,600 on Elmley. One or two occasionally summer on the North Kent Marshes. Rarely seen on inland waters.
Visit Funton Creek on the south Medway, or Elmley for good views of this elegant duck.

## Garganey

*Anas querquedula*

| Jan | Feb | Mar | Apr | May | Jun | Jul | Aug | Sep | Oct | Nov | Dec |

**Summer visitor** **

Although fairly widespread on passage, occasionally visiting inland waters, relatively few birds are involved. Autumn flocks rarely reach double figures.
Try the Dungeness or Elmley RSPB Reserves in early spring for views of the splendid drake.

Garganey

# Blue-winged Teal

*Anas discors*

**Very rare vagrant**

The third county record concerns a duck present on Stoke Lagoon in May 1994. The first two were both in the Stour Valley, in April 1970 and May–June 1978.

# Shoveler

*Anas clypeata*

**Resident, winter visitor and passage migrant**                                    \*\*\*

Breeds on freshwater marshes. The highest winter concentrations of 500+ usually occur on Elmley or at Dungeness. Migrants swell the numbers in both March and September. Small numbers also visit inland waters.

# Red-crested Pochard

*Netta rufina*

| Jan | Feb | Mar | Apr | May | Jun | Jul | Aug | Sep | Oct | Nov | Dec |
|-----|-----|-----|-----|-----|-----|-----|-----|-----|-----|-----|-----|

**Scarce visitor**

The situation is confused by the presence of escaped birds, but mid-summer and autumn arrivals probably include some genuine vagrants from the Continent.

# Common Pochard

*Aythya ferina*

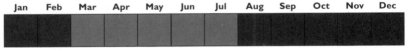

**Resident, passage migrant and winter visitor**                                    \*\*\*

Breeds regularly on the North Kent Marshes, in the Stour Valley and at Dungeness, where autumn peaks exceed 750. Winter flocks of 500+ also occur at Cliffe and New Hythe.

# Ring-necked Duck

*Aythya collaris*

**Very rare vagrant**

A drake on the Dungeness RSPB Reserve in May 1992 was the sixth record for Kent, and the first since 1979.

# Ferruginous Duck

*Aythya nyroca*

**Very rare vagrant**

A drake on the Dungeness RSPB Reserve in July–August 1987.

Beware the possibility of confusion with *Aythya* hybrids. It is essential to make detailed field notes at the time. Note the bill colour, including the extent of black on the 'nail'.

# Tufted Duck

*Aythya fuligula*

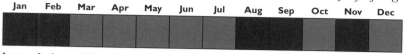

| Jan | Feb | Mar | Apr | May | Jun | Jul | Aug | Sep | Oct | Nov | Dec |

**Resident and winter visitor**                                             \*\*\*

A widespread breeding species. Autumn numbers may increase to 500+ at Dungeness and totals occasionally reach 800 at Cliffe and 600 at New Hythe in winter.

# Scaup

*Aythya marila*

| Jan | Feb | Mar | Apr | May | Jun | Jul | Aug | Sep | Oct | Nov | Dec |

**Winter visitor and passage migrant**

May be seen on passage around the coast, particularly with the onset of severe weather, when three-figure numbers may occur. Although a small flock of 20-30 Scaup usually winters in the Medway estuary, other small flocks show a preference for coastal freshwater pits and lakes. When these freeze over, they gather on the sea. There were up to 190 in St. Mary's Bay, Dymchurch in late February 1985.

Try the quarry at Cliffe, or Scotney Pit at Dungeness, but they may be over the border in Sussex!

# Common Eider

*Somateria mollissima*

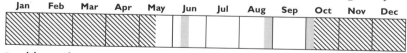

| Jan | Feb | Mar | Apr | May | Jun | Jul | Aug | Sep | Oct | Nov | Dec |

**Regular visitor and passage migrant**

A sea duck only very rarely seen on freshwater. Flocks of non-breeding birds may favour one locality throughout the year. They may total 40-80 birds, occasionally 150+, and can usually be found along the north coast between the Swale and Thanet, or in Pegwell Bay. A smaller flock may be present off Dungeness, where passage birds are also recorded in both spring and autumn. Late autumn passage off Thanet and around the coast may occasionally involve several hundred birds.

# Long-tailed Duck

*Clangula hyemalis*

| Jan | Feb | Mar | Apr | May | Jun | Jul | Aug | Sep | Oct | Nov | Dec |

**Winter visitor and passage migrant**

Ones and twos usually winter on various coastal pits, those at Dungeness and Cliffe being the most favoured. In 1990 one remained throughout the summer on Elmley, with another there from mid-June to early July 1992. On passage, records are almost annual off Dungeness in spring, and off Thanet and in the Thames estuary in autumn. Six inland at Bough Beech in December 1990 was exceptional.

## Common Scoter

*Melanitta nigra*

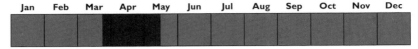

**Regular passage migrant**

A marked up-Channel spring passage may be witnessed off Dungeness between late March and early May, when day totals sometimes exceed 5,000. Fewer are seen on autumn passage, and small flocks may be seen offshore at any time of the year. Overland passage is confirmed by annual records at Bough Beech reservoir.

## Surf Scoter

*Melanitta perspicillata*

**Very rare vagrant**

The second Kent record was a drake flying W at Minnis Bay in October 1988. The first involved a drake off the South Brooks in April 1984.

## Velvet Scoter

*Melanitta fusca*

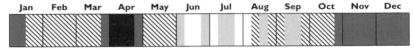

**Passage migrant and winter visitor**

Spring passage off Dungeness may occasionally produce day totals of 50+. In late autumn, small numbers can be seen on passage off Thanet and in the Thames estuary.

Scanning through wintering flocks of Common Scoter along the north coast, or off Dungeness, may produce a few Velvet Scoter.

## Goldeneye

*Bucephala clangula*

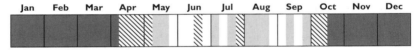

**Winter visitor and passage migrant**

Flocks of about 50 may occasionally be seen in the south Medway, from Motney Hill, and similar numbers winter at Dungeness. Others regularly winter on inland waters and gravel pits throughout the county. Summering birds occasionally occur at Dungeness.

Look for the drakes displaying on the pits at Dungeness in spring.

## Smew

*Mergus albellus*

**Regular winter visitor**

Small numbers are most frequently seen on the Dungeness RSPB Reserve, but in severe winters Smew may occur on any sizeable inland waters that remain open. During severe spells in 1985-87 over 100 Smew were recorded, with 140 in February 1991, but more usually 20-30 winter.

The magnificent adult drake is relatively scarce, but the ducks and immature drakes are also most attractive.

## Red-breasted Merganser

*Mergus serrator*

**Winter visitor and passage migrant**

Small flocks totalling 50+ winter regularly in the estuaries of both the Swale and Medway. Off Dungeness this species features frequently up-Channel spring passage, with peak day totals of 100+. Rare on inland waters.

Various sites along the south Medway will usually provide good views of this species.

## Goosander

*Mergus merganser*

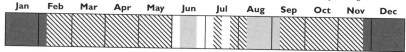

**Winter visitor and passage migrant**

The Dungeness RSPB Reserve, the Sevenoaks Wildfowl Reserve and Bough Beech reservoir regularly attract small wintering groups of up to a dozen or so. Like Smew this species only appears in three-figure numbers in Kent in severe winters. An influx in mid-January 1985 produced an exceptional total of 230.

## Ruddy Duck

*Oxyura jamaicensis*

| Jan | Feb | Mar | Apr | May | Jun | Jul | Aug | Sep | Oct | Nov | Dec |
|-----|-----|-----|-----|-----|-----|-----|-----|-----|-----|-----|-----|

**Uncommon visitor, but increasing**

Most regular on the Dungeness RSPB Reserve, where up to 14 have occurred, but 1–4 may be seen throughout the county on suitable open waters. Becomes extremely secretive during spring and summer, and increasing records during this period may presage breeding.

An attractive addition to the county list, though not welcome in southern Europe, where it competes with the rare White-headed Duck *O. leucocephala*. Successful breeding was confirmed in 1995.

## Honey Buzzard

*Pernis apivorus*

| Jan | Feb | Mar | Apr | May | Jun | Jul | Aug | Sep | Oct | Nov | Dec |
|-----|-----|-----|-----|-----|-----|-----|-----|-----|-----|-----|-----|

**Increasingly regular passage migrant**

During the first eight years, seven produced totals of 1–8, followed by 40 during 1993-94 giving a grand total of 80. Invariably seen in flight, with the majority of records along the south and east coasts.

Fine weather in late June or easterly winds in September may produce a number of migrants. Try viewing from a high point along the North Downs Way anywhere between St. Margaret's and Capel-le-Ferne.

# Black Kite
## *Milvus migrans*

| Jan | Feb | Mar | Apr | May | Jun | Jul | Aug | Sep | Oct | Nov | Dec |
|-----|-----|-----|-----|-----|-----|-----|-----|-----|-----|-----|-----|

**Rare vagrant**

A total of 24, with one or two almost annually and six in both 1993 and 1994. The distribution is widespread, though mainly coastal, with six at Dungeness, nine between Dover and Broadstairs, three between Reculver and Grain, and six inland, at Hamstreet, Lyminge, Wingham, Stodmarsh and Bough Beech.

# Red Kite
## *Milvus milvus*

| Jan | Feb | Mar | Apr | May | Jun | Jul | Aug | Sep | Oct | Nov | Dec |
|-----|-----|-----|-----|-----|-----|-----|-----|-----|-----|-----|-----|

**Scarce vagrant**

3–5 annually, with a marked peak of 12 in 1988. Reports come from localities throughout the county. Over half the records were in spring and late autumn, between 16 March–20 April and 24 October–6 December.

Although I have sought at least half-a-dozen, even an overwintering bird, I still have not added it to my Kent list! However, my chances must be improving, with the reintroduction schemes proving to be extremely successful!

# White-tailed Eagle
## *Haliaeetus albicilla*

**Very rare vagrant**

One on Sheppey from November 1988 to January 1989 and another N over St. Margaret's Bay in October 1990 are the first Kent records since 1932.

# Marsh Harrier
## *Circus aeruginosus*

| Jan | Feb | Mar | Apr | May | Jun | Jul | Aug | Sep | Oct | Nov | Dec |
|-----|-----|-----|-----|-----|-----|-----|-----|-----|-----|-----|-----|

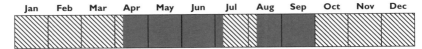

**Passage migrant and winter visitor, now breeding annually**                    **

Status has changed markedly during the ten years. The males can be polygamous so the number of pairs breeding is misleading, but at least 40 young were fledged from 11 nests in 1994.

There has been a population explosion during the last five years and up to ten now winter on Sheppey, often roosting with the Hen Harriers. Watch from the Capel Fleet road.

# Hen Harrier
## *Circus cyaneus*

| Jan | Feb | Mar | Apr | May | Jun | Jul | Aug | Sep | Oct | Nov | Dec |
|-----|-----|-----|-----|-----|-----|-----|-----|-----|-----|-----|-----|

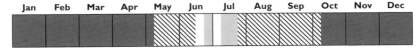

**Annual winter visitor and passage migrant**

Totals of 35–50 now winter regularly in the county, with roosts of up to ten or so on Walland Marsh, in the Stour Valley and on the North Kent Marshes.

Visit Stodmarsh, the reedbed near the Woolpack Inn on Walland Marsh, or the eastern end of Capel Fleet towards dusk, when they often gather before dropping in to roost.

Hen Harriers

## Montagu's Harrier *Circus pygargus*

| Jan | Feb | Mar | Apr | May | Jun | Jul | Aug | Sep | Oct | Nov | Dec |
|-----|-----|-----|-----|-----|-----|-----|-----|-----|-----|-----|-----|

**Annual passage migrant and summer visitor** ✱✱

An average of about 15 birds each year. A good number are passage migrants, but some make prolonged stays. One pair bred successfully in 1986 and another bred but failed in 1994. One overwintered in 1991-92.

## Goshawk *Accipiter gentilis*

| Jan | Feb | Mar | Apr | May | Jun | Jul | Aug | Sep | Oct | Nov | Dec |
|-----|-----|-----|-----|-----|-----|-----|-----|-----|-----|-----|-----|

**Rare visitor**

A total of 20 birds in just five years (the bar chart suggests more, but probably includes the same birds on several dates).

The status is confused by falconers' birds, several of which escaped after the great storm in October 1987. A few passage migrants can be anticipated and coastal sightings in spring and autumn are likely to be genuine vagrants. A pair was observed displaying during 1994, but breeding has yet to be confirmed.

## Sparrowhawk *Accipiter nisus*

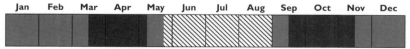

| Jan | Feb | Mar | Apr | May | Jun | Jul | Aug | Sep | Oct | Nov | Dec |
|-----|-----|-----|-----|-----|-----|-----|-----|-----|-----|-----|-----|

**Resident, winter visitor and passage migrant** ✱✱✱

Spring and autumn passage migrants can be seen around the coast, while the breeding and wintering populations continue to increase.

# Common Buzzard

*Buteo buteo*

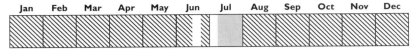

| Jan | Feb | Mar | Apr | May | Jun | Jul | Aug | Sep | Oct | Nov | Dec |
|-----|-----|-----|-----|-----|-----|-----|-----|-----|-----|-----|-----|

**Annual visitor and passage migrant**

An average of 20 per year, but 50+ were seen in both 1993 and 1994. There was an exceptional autumn passage in 1993 and an unprecedented flock of ten was seen flying S at Folkestone in 1994. An average of 13 for the first eight years still represents a marked increase and a few are wintering more regularly. The few summer records suggest that nesting may yet be proven.

# Rough-legged Buzzard

*Buteo lagopus*

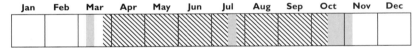

| Jan | Feb | Mar | Apr | May | Jun | Jul | Aug | Sep | Oct | Nov | Dec |
|-----|-----|-----|-----|-----|-----|-----|-----|-----|-----|-----|-----|

**Irregular winter visitor and passage migrant**

The only overwintering involved three birds on Sheppey and one at Reculver in 1994-95. These birds were part of the second biggest autumn influx into Britain and 17 were observed in Kent. None stayed to winter after two smaller influxes in 1985 and 1988. Otherwise one or two birds are usually recorded each autumn, but records in the first quarter are rare.

# Osprey

*Pandion haliaetus*

| Jan | Feb | Mar | Apr | May | Jun | Jul | Aug | Sep | Oct | Nov | Dec |
|-----|-----|-----|-----|-----|-----|-----|-----|-----|-----|-----|-----|

**Annual passage migrant**

The average number of birds for 1985-89 was 14, increasing to 32 for 1990-94. Birds occur at widely scattered localities, but Bough Beech is often the most favoured and four were seen there in May 1994. Autumn migrants occasionally make more prolonged stays.

Can the Osprey be attracted to nest on the platforms provided for this purpose at Bough Beech?

# Lesser Kestrel

*Falco naumanni*

**Very rare vagrant**

The second Kent record, the first this century, concerns one found dead in the grounds of Dover Castle on 20th April 1989.

# Common Kestrel

*Falco tinnunculus*

| Jan | Feb | Mar | Apr | May | Jun | Jul | Aug | Sep | Oct | Nov | Dec |
|-----|-----|-----|-----|-----|-----|-----|-----|-----|-----|-----|-----|

**Resident and passage migrant**       \*\*\*

A widespread breeding species. In autumn, numbers are supplemented by coastal migrants. The motorway verges provide good hunting grounds for this attractive falcon.

# Red-footed Falcon

*Falco vespertinus*

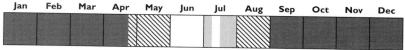

**Rare vagrant**

A total of 40 records. Excluding the unprecedented influx in spring 1992, when there were an estimated 22, this species is a less than annual vagrant. The influx included at least seven at Stodmarsh, a site which has attracted another four. There were also four at Dungeness, with three at St. Margaret's and singles at seven other widespread localities.

# Merlin

*Falco columbarius*

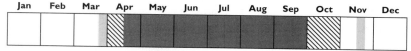

**Winter visitor and passage migrant**

20-30 regularly winter on the coastal marshes from north Kent to Dungeness and passage migrants occasionally occur inland.

    Merlins sometimes hunt with Hen Harriers, but careful scanning of the fields near the Swale NNR, where waders come in to roost, may be more profitable, as they often perch there on sods of earth.

# Hobby

*Falco subbuteo*

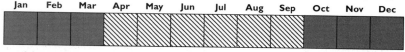

**Summer visitor and passage migrant**         ***

With 50+ passage migrants reported each spring and autumn, the Hobby may occur anywhere. A small breeding population, using widespread localities, is well established.

    To observe this species hunting Sand Martins or Common Swifts is a magnificent spectacle. Visit Stodmarsh in late May and early June, where ten or more have been seen in recent springs.

# Peregrine

*Falco peregrinus*

**Winter visitor and passage migrant, now breeding**        **

Regularly seen during the winter on the North Kent Marshes and around the coast at Sandwich Bay and Dungeness. Scarce inland. Since 1989 one pair has bred annually, increasing to three pairs in 1994.

    The Elmley RSPB Reserve and Capel Fleet are regular winter haunts for this magnificent falcon.

# Red-legged Partridge

*Alectoris rufa*

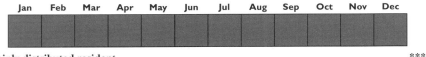

| Jan | Feb | Mar | Apr | May | Jun | Jul | Aug | Sep | Oct | Nov | Dec |

**Thinly distributed resident**                                       \*\*\*

Scarce on Sheppey and Thanet, but common on the Thames marshes. Regularly seen at Dungeness and on Walland and Romney Marshes.

# Grey Partridge

*Perdix perdix*

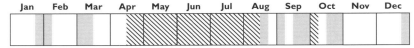

| Jan | Feb | Mar | Apr | May | Jun | Jul | Aug | Sep | Oct | Nov | Dec |

**Declining resident**                                       \*\*\*

Although numbers have declined considerably, there are still healthy populations on the coastal marshes. In winter family parties form large coveys.

# Quail

*Coturnix coturnix*

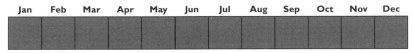

| Jan | Feb | Mar | Apr | May | Jun | Jul | Aug | Sep | Oct | Nov | Dec |

**Annual summer visitor**

Occasional 'Quail years' may produce 20-40 reports, as in 1987, 1989 and 1994, but less than ten is more usual. An extremely elusive species, so sight records are rare. Proof of breeding is difficult to establish, but is likely in 'Quail years'.

Listen for the distinctive 'wet-my-lips' call-note from cereal crops, particularly towards dusk, although they do call at all times of the day and night.

# Common Pheasant

*Phasianus colchichus*

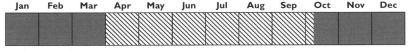

| Jan | Feb | Mar | Apr | May | Jun | Jul | Aug | Sep | Oct | Nov | Dec |

**Widespread resident**                                       \*\*\*

The population is artificially stocked by those with shooting interests.

# Water Rail

*Rallus aquaticus*

| Jan | Feb | Mar | Apr | May | Jun | Jul | Aug | Sep | Oct | Nov | Dec |

**Resident and winter visitor**                                       \*\*\*

Widespread during the winter months, but its breeding range is more restricted, the Stour Valley being a major stronghold.

Another species whose presence is more easily established by hearing its various calls, or its song.

Common Pheasant

## Spotted Crake
*Porzana porzana*

| Jan | Feb | Mar | Apr | May | Jun | Jul | Aug | Sep | Oct | Nov | Dec |
|-----|-----|-----|-----|-----|-----|-----|-----|-----|-----|-----|-----|
|     |     |     |     |     |     |     |     |     |     |     |     |

**Very rare vagrant**

The eight records concern singles at Newington cress beds, Kingsgate, Dungeness and Denton, with two each at Broomfield and Stodmarsh.

## Corncrake
*Crex crex*

| Jan | Feb | Mar | Apr | May | Jun | Jul | Aug | Sep | Oct | Nov | Dec |
|-----|-----|-----|-----|-----|-----|-----|-----|-----|-----|-----|-----|
|     |     |     |     |     |     |     |     |     |     |     |     |

**Rare passage migrant**

The 12 records in the last ten years include one which walked into a classroom at Broadstairs, another found dead at High Halstow and further singles at localities as widespread as Headcorn, Foreness and St. Margaret's.

## Moorhen
*Gallinula chloropus*

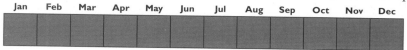

| Jan | Feb | Mar | Apr | May | Jun | Jul | Aug | Sep | Oct | Nov | Dec |
|-----|-----|-----|-----|-----|-----|-----|-----|-----|-----|-----|-----|

**Resident**   ***

Extremely widespread, found on even the smallest of ponds.

# Coot

*Fulica atra*

| Jan | Feb | Mar | Apr | May | Jun | Jul | Aug | Sep | Oct | Nov | Dec |

**Resident and winter visitor**     ***

Widespread, with large flocks occurring in the winter months, occasionally exceeding 1,000 at Cliffe, New Hythe and Dungeness.

# Common Crane

*Grus grus*

| Jan | Feb | Mar | Apr | May | Jun | Jul | Aug | Sep | Oct | Nov | Dec |

**Rare vagrant**

Less than annual occurrences have produced eight records of one or two birds, two of three birds and one of four birds. Exceptionally, a flock of 71 flew S over Cheriton and out to sea at Dungeness in October 1985. One on the Halstow marshes in October 1988 remained for 17 days and another stayed for six days at Dungeness in May 1985.

# Oystercatcher

*Haematopus ostralegus*

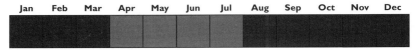

| Jan | Feb | Mar | Apr | May | Jun | Jul | Aug | Sep | Oct | Nov | Dec |

**Resident, passage migrant and winter visitor**     ***

The largest breeding population is on the Medway islands. Peak numbers in the Swale occasionally reach 5,000 in winter. Smaller numbers occur all round the coast. Passage migrants are occasionally seen on inland waters.

Be at Shellness before high tide to witness an impressive spectacle, as flocks of Oystercatchers fly in to roost, either on the point, or at Harty.

# Black-winged Stilt

*Himantopus himantopus*

**Very rare vagrant**

Four singles only, at Cliffe in May 1987 and May 1990, and at Dungeness in June 1993 and August 1994.

# Avocet

*Recurvirostra avosetta*

| Jan | Feb | Mar | Apr | May | Jun | Jul | Aug | Sep | Oct | Nov | Dec |

**Breeding summer visitor, passage migrant and winter visitor**     ***

Regular on spring passage at Dungeness and Sandwich Bay. The breeding population has increased from two to over 100 pairs in the ten years. Post breeding flocks build up during the autumn, one frequenting Higham Bight and another Funton Creek. Nearly 600 were present at the latter site in October 1992, a combination of the two flocks. Wintering numbers have increased to 400+.

Avocets

## Stone-curlew

*Burhinus oedicnemus*

**Very rare vagrant**

The six records concern singles on Dungeness RSPB Reserve and Stoke Ooze in 1987, inland at Hawden and Sandwich Bay in 1988, at Cliffe in 1990 and finally at Capel Fleet in 1991. The Stoke Ooze bird was present for five days.

## Collared Pratincole

*Glareola pratincola*

**Very rare vagrant**

The third and fourth county records concern singles present at Dungeness in June 1986 and in the Minster/Pegwell area in May 1987. The first two were at Worth in September–October 1976 and at Pegwell Bay in November 1977.

## Oriental Pratincole

*Glareola maldivarum*

**Very rare vagrant**

The only Kent record concerns one on Sheppey between June and October 1988.

## Black-winged Pratincole

*Glareola nordmanni*

**Very rare vagrant**

The second county record was one on Sheppey in June 1988, remarkably, at the same time as the Oriental Pratincole. The first was at Sandwich Bay in August–September 1969.

## Little Ringed Plover

*Charadrius dubius*

| Jan | Feb | Mar | Apr | May | Jun | Jul | Aug | Sep | Oct | Nov | Dec |
|-----|-----|-----|-----|-----|-----|-----|-----|-----|-----|-----|-----|

**Summer visitor and passage migrant**     ✳✳✳

The number of breeding pairs has declined from about 16 in 1985 to only six in recent years. Most easily seen from the causeway at Bough Beech, but small numbers pass through the county from late July, when they can be seen regularly at other sites, such as Cliffe Pools and Dungeness RSPB Reserve.

## Ringed Plover · *Charadrius hiaticula*

| Jan | Feb | Mar | Apr | May | Jun | Jul | Aug | Sep | Oct | Nov | Dec |
|-----|-----|-----|-----|-----|-----|-----|-----|-----|-----|-----|-----|

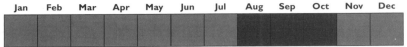

**Passage migrant, winter visitor and summer resident**                    \*\*\*

Peak counts during August and September usually involve over 1,000 in the Medway estuary, while flocks of 500+ may be seen at Cliffe Pools, Elmley and Sandwich Bay. Smaller numbers are present all round the coast, with occasional records inland.

## Kentish Plover · *Charadrius alexandrinus*

| Jan | Feb | Mar | Apr | May | Jun | Jul | Aug | Sep | Oct | Nov | Dec |
|-----|-----|-----|-----|-----|-----|-----|-----|-----|-----|-----|-----|

**Passage migrant**

An annual average of ten birds, with over half occurring at Dungeness and Sandwich Bay. Most records involve ones and twos, but on 22 September 1992 there were six at Greatstone and three in Pegwell Bay. With so many just across the Channel, why doesn't this happen more often?

## Greater Sand Plover · *Charadrius leschenaultii*

**Very rare vagrant**

The first county record was one at Cliffe in August 1992.

## Dotterel · *Charadrius morinellus*

| Jan | Feb | Mar | Apr | May | Jun | Jul | Aug | Sep | Oct | Nov | Dec |
|-----|-----|-----|-----|-----|-----|-----|-----|-----|-----|-----|-----|

**Scarce passage migrant**

Well over half the records involved 1–3 birds, often on single dates. There were also five records of 4–5 birds and one of seven. In 1992 at St. Margaret's flocks of 3-12 were seen daily between the 21–26 August, with two more on 29 August, while an unprecedented flock of 19 visited Elmley in September 1985.

Try scanning the cliff-top fields near St. Margaret's during the last week of August. In recent years almost annual sightings of this attractive wader have been noted there.

## American Golden Plover · *Pluvialis dominica*

**Very rare vagrant**

The fourth county record concerns one present on Dungeness RSPB Reserve in May 1987.

## Pacific Golden Plover · *Pluvialis fulva*

**Very rare vagrant**

The first county record occurred at Sandwich Bay in June 1990. Another was seen at Elmley in August 1995.

# Golden Plover
*Pluvialis apricaria*

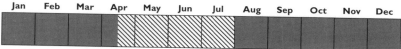

**Winter visitor and passage migrant**

Flocks totalling several thousands regularly winter on the coastal lowlands, feeding on the pasture and arable fields of the North Kent Marshes, the Wantsum, the lower Stour Valley and Sandwich, and the Romney and Walland Marshes. One or two inland localities south of Wye and Ashford, and south of Sutton Valence, regularly attract smaller numbers, with up to 900+ occasionally, but this species is rare in the west of the county.

The birds of the northern race *P. a. altifrons* can be seen in breeding plumage, while on passage in late spring.

# Grey Plover
*Pluvialis squatarola*

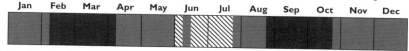

**Winter visitor and passage migrant**

Favours estuarine mudflats and may be seen all round the coast, but is rare inland. Numbers have shown a recent increase and the estuaries of both the Medway and Swale may hold 2,000+ in winter, with combined autumn totals of 6,000-7,500.

Look for this species in its fine breeding plumage in May.

# Sociable Plover
*Chettusia gregaria*

**Very rare vagrant**

The fourth Kent record concerns one on Dartford Marsh during March–April 1985.

# Lapwing
*Vanellus vanellus*

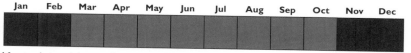

**Resident, winter visitor and passage migrant**        ***

Becoming less widespread as a breeding species, but large wintering flocks of several thousands feed on the coastal lowlands. From early June post-breeding flocks disperse to the southwest, while severe weather in winter can cause spectacular southerly movements.

# Knot
*Calidris canutus*

**Winter visitor and passage migrant**

An estuarine species, rarely seen inland. Most numerous in the Thames and Swale estuaries, where respective wintering totals may reach 12,000 and 6,500.

Watch the Shellness roost for a magnificent spectacle. In late spring some birds may be in their beautiful 'red' breeding plumage.

# Sanderling
## *Calidris alba*

**Winter visitor and passage migrant**

This species favours the sandy shores at Lade, Sandwich Bay and around Thanet to Minnis Bay, with comparatively small numbers further west in north Kent. Rarely occurs inland. Winter counts of 400+ are regular at Minnis Bay and Foreness, and occasional at Lade. The total number wintering around Thanet may exceed 1,000, which makes the site of international importance for this species.

# Little Stint
## *Calidris minuta*

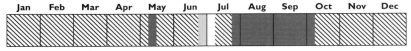

**Regular passage migrant**

Spring passage is usually light, with peaks of less than ten. In autumn, small flocks of 15-30 are regular. During larger influxes flocks of 80+ may occur, as in September 1993 at Cliffe. A few overwinter, most often on Elmley. Favours the muddy fringes of freshwater marshes or sandy gravel pits. Occasionally seen inland and on estuarine mud.

# Temminck's Stint
## *Calidris temminckii*

| Jan | Feb | Mar | Apr | May | Jun | Jul | Aug | Sep | Oct | Nov | Dec |
|-----|-----|-----|-----|-----|-----|-----|-----|-----|-----|-----|-----|

**Passage migrant**

Numbers have increased to an average of twelve records per year, with 67% in spring. Most involve singles, though two or three are occasionally seen together, with four at Elmley in May 1989. Favours freshwater margins, often disappearing into vegetation while feeding.

# White-rumped Sandpiper
## *Calidris fuscicollis*

**Very rare vagrant**

One at Sandwich Bay in April 1986 was the first spring record for the county. Another was present at Cliffe in August 1994.

# Baird's Sandpiper
## *Calidris bairdii*

**Very rare vagrant**

The third to fifth Kent records were singles at Dungeness in September 1987 and 1988, possibly the same bird, with another at Elmley RSPB Reserve in September–October 1989.

# Pectoral Sandpiper
*Calidris melanotos*

| Jan | Feb | Mar | Apr | May | Jun | Jul | Aug | Sep | Oct | Nov | Dec |
|-----|-----|-----|-----|-----|-----|-----|-----|-----|-----|-----|-----|

**Very rare vagrant**

After two in 1985 there was a gap of five years before two more were seen in 1991, with 1–3 annually since. The distribution of records comprises three at Cliffe and two each at Elmley, Sandwich Bay and Dungeness, with one on the Thames at Dartford.

# Sharp-tailed Sandpiper
*Calidris acuminata*

**Very rare vagrant**

One on Elmley RSPB Reserve in July 1985 was the first county record. Another was present on Worth Marshes in September 1987.

# Curlew Sandpiper
*Calidris ferruginea*

| Jan | Feb | Mar | Apr | May | Jun | Jul | Aug | Sep | Oct | Nov | Dec |
|-----|-----|-----|-----|-----|-----|-----|-----|-----|-----|-----|-----|

**Regular passage migrant**

Essentially a freshwater wader favouring muddy pools around the coastal marshes, although feeding on the muddy foreshore is not unusual. As with Little Stints, the autumn passage of adults precedes that of the juveniles, often forming two distinct waves. Numbers vary considerably from year to year, but spring passage is almost insignificant. Autumn flocks of 40 occur most years, with 125 at Cliffe in July–August 1990 being the largest. In 1985 the combined total of 512 adults and juveniles formed the heaviest autumn passage recorded in Kent.

# Purple Sandpiper
*Calidris maritima*

| Jan | Feb | Mar | Apr | May | Jun | Jul | Aug | Sep | Oct | Nov | Dec |
|-----|-----|-----|-----|-----|-----|-----|-----|-----|-----|-----|-----|

**Winter visitor and passage migrant**

50-100 winter regularly on Thanet and can best be seen when roosting at high tide in the sheltered bays between Foreness and North Foreland. At other times scan the rocky foreshore. Smaller numbers winter westwards towards Swalecliffe and southwards to Dover and Folkestone. Elsewhere it is relatively scarce.

# Dunlin
*Calidris alpina*

| Jan | Feb | Mar | Apr | May | Jun | Jul | Aug | Sep | Oct | Nov | Dec |
|-----|-----|-----|-----|-----|-----|-----|-----|-----|-----|-----|-----|

**Winter visitor and passage migrant**

A common wader all round the coast, and regularly occurs at Bough Beech reservoir and occasionally on other inland waters. Up to 60,000 winter in the three north Kent estuaries, where a few non-breeding birds may remain throughout the summer.

# Broad-billed Sandpiper
## *Limicola falcinellus*

| Jan | Feb | Mar | Apr | May | Jun | Jul | Aug | Sep | Oct | Nov | Dec |
|-----|-----|-----|-----|-----|-----|-----|-----|-----|-----|-----|-----|

**Very rare vagrant**

There were five Kent records before this period, during which seven more occurred, including an exceptional group of three at Cliffe in May 1988. The other records, involving singles, were all on Sheppey.


# Stilt Sandpiper
## *Micropalama himantopus*

**Very rare vagrant**

One at Dungeness in August 1985 was the first county record, with further singles at Cliffe in August 1987 and July 1990.


# Buff-breasted Sandpiper
## *Tryngites subruficollis*

**Very rare vagrant**

Singles at Sandwich Bay in August 1986 and at Cliffe in August 1994 bring the county total to nine.


# Ruff
## *Philomachus pugnax*

| Jan | Feb | Mar | Apr | May | Jun | Jul | Aug | Sep | Oct | Nov | Dec |
|-----|-----|-----|-----|-----|-----|-----|-----|-----|-----|-----|-----|

**Regular passage migrant and winter visitor**

A bird essentially of freshwater marshes, although it often feeds on pasture, such as at Dengemarsh where up to 80 winter. Passage migrants swell the numbers and 179 were at Elmley in April 1994. A few are seen at inland localities almost annually.

Individual males in fine breeding plumage are worth looking for on the Elmley RSPB Reserve in early May.


# Jack Snipe
## *Lymnocryptes minimus*

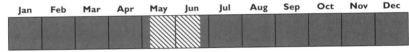

| Jan | Feb | Mar | Apr | May | Jun | Jul | Aug | Sep | Oct | Nov | Dec |
|-----|-----|-----|-----|-----|-----|-----|-----|-----|-----|-----|-----|

**Winter visitor and passage migrant**

A species that seems to favour the same marshy tracts year after year, throughout the county. Small flocks of up to ten may occasionally winter or migrate together, but it is more usual to flush just one or two birds – provided that you practically tread on them!

# Common Snipe

*Gallinago gallinago*

**Resident, winter visitor and passage migrant** ✳✳✳

A widespread species in the winter months, favouring freshwater habitats. Estimates of 1,000 at Dartford in January 1985 and Stodmarsh in October–November 1992 are the highest counts, but gatherings of 100+ are common, and not only on the coastal marshes.

In the breeding season the curious 'drumming' display can be witnessed at Stodmarsh, where several pairs breed annually.

# Long-billed Dowitcher

*Limnodromus scolopaceus*

**Very rare vagrant**

The fourth Kent record to be specifically assigned to this species, rather than Short-billed, concerns one present on Dengemarsh during December 1990–February 1991.

# Woodcock

*Scolopax rusticola*

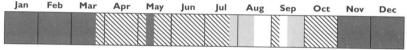

**Resident, passage migrant and winter visitor** ✳✳✳

Usually found in ones and twos in various types of woodland, but one has practically to tread on one before it rises. In the breeding season, coppiced areas are favoured. In October–November migrants may be seen at coastal sites.

Evening visits in May–June are a must if you want to witness the curious 'roding' display flights. Try Mereworth Woods or Bedgebury Forest.

# Black-tailed Godwit

*Limosa limosa*

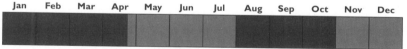

**Winter visitor, passage migrant and summer visitor** ✳✳✳

Numbers have increased and 1,000+ may be present in winter, while spring and autumn peaks may exceed 2,000 on the North Kent Marshes. This species is relatively scarce elsewhere in the county and inland records are unusual.

Visit either of the Sheppey reserves in May or June.

# Bar-tailed Godwit

*Limosa lapponica*

**Winter visitor and passage migrant**

The largest numbers winter in the Swale, where 500-600 may be present, but smaller numbers can be seen all round the coast. A marked up-Channel passage can be observed off Dungeness, where day totals of 2,000 have been recorded during late April and early May. Small flocks occasionally migrate overland.

# Whimbrel
## Numenius phaeopus

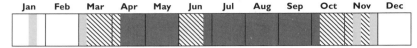

**Passage migrant**

A bird essentially of the coastal marshes, where roosting flocks of 60+ may be seen in early May, or from late July to August. The up-Channel passage at Dungeness peaks in late April and early May.

# Curlew
## Numenius arquata

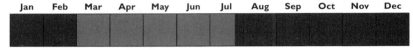

**Winter visitor and passage migrant**

All three north Kent estuaries regularly hold 1,000-2,000 during the winter, or at times of peak passage from late July–September. Smaller numbers can be seen all round the coast, often feeding on mudflats at low tide. The few inland records usually concern birds flying over.

# Spotted Redshank
## Tringa erythropus

**Passage migrant**

The North Kent Marshes provide this species' favoured habitat, the brackish waters of Elmley and the Medway islands attracting the highest numbers, with roosts of 100-150 from early July and a peak of 188 in August 1988. Up to 20 or so winter regularly in the Medway. Comparatively few are seen elsewhere in the county, although a few migrants do occur inland.

An early May visit to Elmley should provide the memorable sight of this species in its fine, dusky breeding plumage.

# Common Redshank
## Tringa totanus

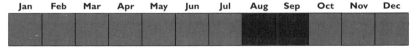

**Resident, passage migrant and winter visitor**                                    ***

Commonly seen all round the coast and on adjacent marshland, with rather fewer now occurring on damp inland localities. The Medway is a particularly important estuary for this species, often holding 5,000+ in the autumn. Since the early 1980s the breeding population has declined.

# Marsh Sandpiper
## Tringa stagnatilis

**Very rare vagrant**

Nine previous Kent records, and another seven singles in this period. Three were on the Thames marshes, two at Dungeness RSPB Reserve and one each at Elmley and Grove Ferry.

Greenshank

# Greenshank

*Tringa nebularia*

| Jan | Feb | Mar | Apr | May | Jun | Jul | Aug | Sep | Oct | Nov | Dec |

**Passage migrant**

The three north Kent estuaries attract the largest flocks in autumn, when 50+ may gather to roost, while 40+ occur at Sandwich. Up to ten or more winter regularly in the Medway. Tidal creeks and coastal freshwater marshes are favoured.

# Lesser Yellowlegs

*Tringa flavipes*

**Very rare vagrant**

One on Worth Marshes in November 1987. Six previous records and two more in 1995, in May and August.

# Green Sandpiper

*Tringa ochropus*

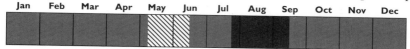

| Jan | Feb | Mar | Apr | May | Jun | Jul | Aug | Sep | Oct | Nov | Dec |

**Passage migrant and winter visitor**

Ones and twos may occur at any wetland habitat, even small ponds and streams, throughout the county. On autumn passage small flocks of up to 20 may gather at favoured sites such as Elmley, the Swale NNR and Sandwich Bay, with a peak of 46 at Elmley in August 1994.

# Wood Sandpiper

*Tringa glareola*

| Jan | Feb | Mar | Apr | May | Jun | Jul | Aug | Sep | Oct | Nov | Dec |

**Passage migrant**

A relatively scarce migrant, particularly in spring. 15-40+ occur each autumn, with peak counts of only single figures. Favours coastal freshwater marshes and gravel pits, occasionally inland.

# Terek Sandpiper

*Xenus cinereus*

**Very rare vagrant**

One at Cliffe in June 1989 was the third Kent record. The first two were at Sandwich Bay in May 1973 and Dungeness in August 1982.

## Common Sandpiper
*Actitis hypoleucos*

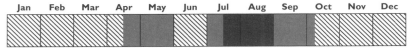

| Jan | Feb | Mar | Apr | May | Jun | Jul | Aug | Sep | Oct | Nov | Dec |
|-----|-----|-----|-----|-----|-----|-----|-----|-----|-----|-----|-----|

**Passage migrant**

Influxes in mid-May occasionally produce counts of 20+, with an exceptional count of 45 at Reculver in 1991. Peak autumn numbers of 70+ may occur at Sandwich Bay, with 20-30 more usual at other localities, such as Elmley, Dungeness or Bough Beech.

## Spotted Sandpiper
*Actitis macularia*

**Very rare vagrant**

The fourth county record was an adult in summer plumage at Aldington in June 1994.

## Turnstone
*Arenaria interpres*

| Jan | Feb | Mar | Apr | May | Jun | Jul | Aug | Sep | Oct | Nov | Dec |
|-----|-----|-----|-----|-----|-----|-----|-----|-----|-----|-----|-----|

**Winter visitor and passage migrant**

Although present all round the Kent coast, this species has a preference for rocky shores. The largest flocks are seen between Swalecliffe and Sandwich Bay, which is a site of international importance for this species, as is the Medway in autumn. The roost at Minnis Bay often attracts 500+ during the winter, with increased numbers in spring and autumn, while counts of 1,000+ are recorded in the Medway.

## Wilson's Phalarope
*Phalaropus tricolor*

**Very rare vagrant**

One on Elmley RSPB Reserve in September–October 1988 was the fourth county record.

## Red-necked Phalarope
*Phalaropus lobatus*

| Jan | Feb | Mar | Apr | May | Jun | Jul | Aug | Sep | Oct | Nov | Dec |
|-----|-----|-----|-----|-----|-----|-----|-----|-----|-----|-----|-----|

**Rare passage migrant**

Twenty-one records, with two together at Elmley in October 1985. Elmley has also hosted five singles, with five at Cliffe, two each at Dungeness, Stodmarsh and Bough Beech, and four elsewhere.

## Grey Phalarope
*Phalaropus fulicaria*

| Jan | Feb | Mar | Apr | May | Jun | Jul | Aug | Sep | Oct | Nov | Dec |
|-----|-----|-----|-----|-----|-----|-----|-----|-----|-----|-----|-----|

**Scarce passage migrant**

Its almost annual occurrences are often associated with stormy weather. Apart from one at Wouldham in September 1994, all have been on the coast. One wintering in Ramsgate Harbour remained for three months, while Elmley has hosted two for 11 and 28 days in the autumn.

# Pomarine Skua

*Stercorarius pomarinus*

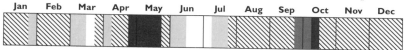

**Passage migrant**

A short, but annual spring passage off Dungeness in early May, when small flocks fly up-Channel. The spring of 1994 was the best on record, when 238 flew E, with a peak day total of 88. The peak day totals vary from 14 to 92 annually. In autumn, with strong winds in the northerly quarter, small flocks can be anticipated in the Thames estuary, where a few occasionally over-winter.

Be at Dungeness in early May – in fine weather with southeasterly winds.

# Arctic Skua

*Stercorarius parasiticus*

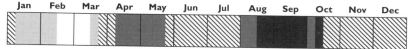

**Passage migrant**

Spring passage at Dungeness may produce day totals of 40+, but the largest numbers are most likely to occur in the Thames Estuary during northerly winds in autumn, when 100-150 may be counted in a day. Exceptionally, day totals of 195 and 263 flew W off Dungeness in August 1990 and September 1987 respectively, while the county record is 318 W at Reculver on 7 September 1991.

Look for one chasing the terns over the Patch at Dungeness, or for groups gathering in the mouth of the Swale in autumn.

# Long-tailed Skua

*Stercorarius longicaudus*

**Passage migrant**

One or two occur almost annually off Dungeness in spring. In autumn this species has become increasingly regular, averaging 16 per year. In each of the years 1988, 1993 and 1994 over 20 were identified, while over 60 occurred in 1991.

Long-tailed Skua

# Great Skua

*Catharacta skua*

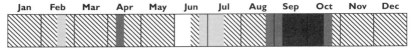

**Passage migrant, occasionally present in winter**

Off Dungeness spring passage is relatively light, but autumn passage is more prolonged, with day totals in double figures. However, the Thames estuary offers the best opportunites in autumn. In northerly winds they tend to gather in small flocks in the mouth of the Swale, before circling high and continuing their migration, possibly overland. Peak movements involve 100+ in a day, while a record total of 260 occurred at Shellness on 14 October 1993.

When the wind veers into the northerly quarter in autumn, be at Shellness to witness these impressive movements.

# Mediterranean Gull

*Larus melanocephalus*

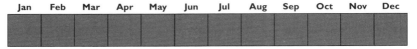

**Regular visitor, now breeding** ***

Essentially a coastal species, but with the increase in numbers, one or two occasionally occur inland. Up to ten pairs may breed in the county, while a small flock of up to 50 birds is present for most of the year at Copt Point, Folkestone.

# Laughing Gull

*Larus atricilla*

**Very rare vagrant**

The second Kent record concerns one at Dungeness on 8 August 1986.

The first was also at Dungeness on 11 May 1966. A third was present, also at Dungeness, for three weeks in July 1995.

# Little Gull

*Larus minutus*

**Passage migrant, occasional in summer and winter**

Essentially a coastal species, but occasionally recorded on inland waters. The most marked passage occurs off Dungeness, with day totals of 100+ occasionally in spring and 400+ just twice in autumn. Regular also off Thanet and in the Thames estuary in autumn. There was a record north Kent movement past Minnis Bay of 384 E on 23 October 1990.

# Sabine's Gull

*Larus sabini*

**Passage migrant**

Annual since 1986, with a record 25 in 1987 and 15 in 1993, increasing the average to eight per year. Over 30% have been seen off Dungeness, with around 22% in the mouth of the Swale and 16% off Thanet.

# Bonaparte's Gull

*Larus philadelphia*

**Very rare vagrant**

The first county record concerns one at Dungeness in April 1989.

# Black-headed Gull

*Larus ridibundus*

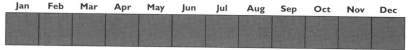

| Jan | Feb | Mar | Apr | May | Jun | Jul | Aug | Sep | Oct | Nov | Dec |
|-----|-----|-----|-----|-----|-----|-----|-----|-----|-----|-----|-----|

**Resident and winter visitor** ***

There are large breeding colonies on the North Kent Marshes, particularly on the Medway islands and in the Swale, with smaller numbers at Dungeness. Extremely widespread in the winter months, when flights to and from roosts at dawn and dusk are part of the everyday scene.

# Ring-billed Gull

*Larus delawarensis*

**Very rare vagrant**

The first county record concerns one at Sandwich Bay in April–May 1986. Since then singles have been found at Pegwell Bay in February 1992 and at Dungeness in January 1994. All have been in immature plumage.

# Common Gull

*Larus canus*

| Jan | Feb | Mar | Apr | May | Jun | Jul | Aug | Sep | Oct | Nov | Dec |
|-----|-----|-----|-----|-----|-----|-----|-----|-----|-----|-----|-----|

**Resident and winter visitor** ***

A widespread species in the winter months, though less common inland than Black-headed Gull. A few pairs breed at Dungeness.

# Lesser Black-backed Gull

*Larus fuscus*

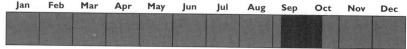

| Jan | Feb | Mar | Apr | May | Jun | Jul | Aug | Sep | Oct | Nov | Dec |
|-----|-----|-----|-----|-----|-----|-----|-----|-----|-----|-----|-----|

**Passage migrant, winter and occasional summer visitor** **

Like other gulls, often frequents rubbish tips. Passage birds fly overland. The darker backed Scandinavian race *L. f. fuscus* is often the commoner subspecies around the coast. Only a few pairs of the British race *L. f. graellsii* breed and some, like the next species, nest on roofs of inland industrial estates.

# Herring Gull

*Larus argentatus*

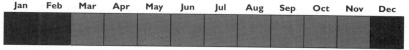

| Jan | Feb | Mar | Apr | May | Jun | Jul | Aug | Sep | Oct | Nov | Dec |
|-----|-----|-----|-----|-----|-----|-----|-----|-----|-----|-----|-----|

**Resident, passage migrant and winter visitor** ***

Breeds commonly on the east Kent cliffs and at Dungeness, and increasingly they are spreading from coastal roof tops to inland localities. Large numbers are attracted to rubbish tips.

# Yellow-legged Gull
## *Larus argentatus cachinnans*

Some authorities consider this form a separate species from Herring Gull. It is now being seen with increasing regularity and counts of 100+ are being recorded in the Thames, between Dartford and Higham Bight. Peak numbers occur from July to September, when up to 30 have been noted at Dungeness. Smaller numbers occur all year round.

# Iceland Gull
## *Larus glaucoides*

| Jan | Feb | Mar | Apr | May | Jun | Jul | Aug | Sep | Oct | Nov | Dec |
|-----|-----|-----|-----|-----|-----|-----|-----|-----|-----|-----|-----|

**Winter visitor and passage migrant**

An average of six per year, but only one in 1988 and 18 in 1993, which included an unprecedented 16 at Dungeness. As the plumages of different aged birds vary so much, it is possible to separate individuals of this and the next species more easily. Essentially coastal, but singles have been seen inland at Tunbridge Wells (it is worth checking rubbish tips), Bough Beech and New Hythe.

# Glaucous Gull
## *Larus hyperboreus*

| Jan | Feb | Mar | Apr | May | Jun | Jul | Aug | Sep | Oct | Nov | Dec |
|-----|-----|-----|-----|-----|-----|-----|-----|-----|-----|-----|-----|

**Winter visitor and passage migrant**

An average of 20 per year hides the fact that only eight occurred in 1993, with 20+ in five years and 35 in 1985. One summered at Sandwich Bay in 1986. As numbers fluctuate, so do the favoured sites; Sandwich Bay and Richborough rubbish tip may attract more than Dungeness in some years, or vice versa, but this species can occur all round the coast and occasionally inland.

# Great Black-backed Gull
## *Larus marinus*

| Jan | Feb | Mar | Apr | May | Jun | Jul | Aug | Sep | Oct | Nov | Dec |
|-----|-----|-----|-----|-----|-----|-----|-----|-----|-----|-----|-----|

**Winter visitor**

Essentially a coastal species, though attracted to inland rubbish tips, like other gulls. Non-breeding birds remain throughout the summer.

# Kittiwake
## *Rissa tridactyla*

| Jan | Feb | Mar | Apr | May | Jun | Jul | Aug | Sep | Oct | Nov | Dec |
|-----|-----|-----|-----|-----|-----|-----|-----|-----|-----|-----|-----|

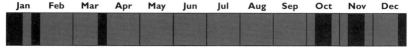

**Summer visitor and passage migrant**     ***

A pelagic species, though a few occur inland occasionally. About 2,500 pairs breed on the Dover cliffs. In late autumn and in the winter, northerly gales may produce big movements of 2,000+ around the north coast and off Dungeness. An exceptional count of 10,500 E off Minnis Bay was noted on 24 January 1986.

The evocative sound of breeding birds makes a visit to Langdon Cliffs in June most rewarding.

# Gull-billed Tern                                    *Gelochelidon nilotica*

**Very rare vagrant**

One at Sandwich Bay in July 1986. A surprisingly rare species on the Kent coast, yet it is known to migrate regularly along the continental coast.

# Caspian Tern                                        *Sterna caspia*

**Very rare vagrant**

Singles off Dover in August 1985, off Folkestone and at Dungeness in June 1988 and at Dungeness again in July 1990.

# Lesser Crested Tern                                 *Sterna bengalensis*

**Very rare vagrant**

The first accepted county record was one flying E at Dungeness in May 1989. This bird was presumed to be the one that returned to the Farne Islands annually between 1988 and 1994.

# Sandwich Tern                                       *Sterna sandvicensis*

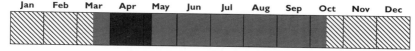

| Jan | Feb | Mar | Apr | May | Jun | Jul | Aug | Sep | Oct | Nov | Dec |

**Summer visitor and passage migrant**                              **\*\***

Up to 350 pairs breed regularly on Dungeness RSPB Reserve, although the colony mysteriously transferred to Rye Harbour in both 1987 and 1994. Recorded all round the coast, but is relatively rare on inland waters. In spring there is a marked up-Channel passage off Dungeness, with day totals of several hundreds.

# Roseate Tern                                        *Sterna dougallii*

| Jan | Feb | Mar | Apr | May | Jun | Jul | Aug | Sep | Oct | Nov | Dec |

**Passage migrant and occasional summer visitor**                   **\*\***

Regular at Dungeness, but scarce elsewhere around the coast. Attempted to breed in two years, but failed to raise any young.

# Common Tern                                         *Sterna hirundo*

| Jan | Feb | Mar | Apr | May | Jun | Jul | Aug | Sep | Oct | Nov | Dec |

**Summer visitor and passage migrant**                              **\*\*\***

The 'sea' tern most likely to occur on inland waters. In spring a marked up-Channel passage occurs off Dungeness, with peak day totals of 1,500+ annually. The largest breeding colonies are also at Dungeness, with several smaller colonies on the North Kent Marshes.

# Arctic Tern

*Sterna paradisaea*

| Jan | Feb | Mar | Apr | May | Jun | Jul | Aug | Sep | Oct | Nov | Dec |
|-----|-----|-----|-----|-----|-----|-----|-----|-----|-----|-----|-----|

**Passage migrant**

A regular spring passage off Dungeness may occasionally involve day totals of 300+. Small numbers also occur regularly in the Thames estuary in late autumn. Only occasionally seen inland.

# Forster's Tern

*Sterna forsteri*

**Very rare vagrant**

One at Margate in October 1986 was the first county record.

# Bridled Tern

*Sterna anaethetus*

**Very rare vagrant**

One on the Thames at Swanscombe in June 1991 was the first record of a live bird in Kent.

Little Terns

# Little Tern

*Sterna albifrons*

| Jan | Feb | Mar | Apr | May | Jun | Jul | Aug | Sep | Oct | Nov | Dec |
|-----|-----|-----|-----|-----|-----|-----|-----|-----|-----|-----|-----|

**Summer visitor and passage migrant**                                                    ***

Spring passage off Dungeness usually involves day totals of up to 100 birds, and very rarely 200+. Small numbers breed at several colonies, usually on shingle around the coast, where they are vulnerable to disturbance. In early autumn peak numbers involve post-breeding flocks of 100-200, usually at Yantlet Creek, Shellness and Reculver, with an exceptional peak of 340 at Shellness in July 1988.

# Whiskered Tern

*Chlidonias hybridus*

**Very rare vagrant**

The third to fifth county records involved singles at Stodmarsh in June 1987, at Dungeness in May 1988 and on Dungeness RSPB Reserve in May 1994.

# Black Tern

*Chlidonias niger*

| Jan | Feb | Mar | Apr | May | Jun | Jul | Aug | Sep | Oct | Nov | Dec |
|-----|-----|-----|-----|-----|-----|-----|-----|-----|-----|-----|-----|

**Passage migrant**

A marsh tern which often favours inland waters, though peak numbers invariably occur off-shore at Dungeness. Spring passage there varies from day totals of just 15 up to 175, but there was a record movement in May 1989 when 950 were seen in three days, with day totals of 240 on the pits and a similar number E over the sea. Autumn passage also varies considerably from year to year. Movements of small numbers can be witnessed in north Kent off Sheppey and Reculver. A flock of 439 was seen at Elmley on 5 September 1987. On 1 September 1994, between Reculver and Lower Hope Point, there were four counts of 300+ and one of 550, probably involving 875 birds, but these highs were all eclipsed by an exceptional count of 10,125 flying W off Dungeness on 6 September 1992.

Visit the power station outflow at Dungeness to get good views of this most attractive tern.

# White-winged Black Tern

*Chlidonias leucopterus*

| Jan | Feb | Mar | Apr | May | Jun | Jul | Aug | Sep | Oct | Nov | Dec |
|-----|-----|-----|-----|-----|-----|-----|-----|-----|-----|-----|-----|

**Rare passage migrant**

1–4 records almost annually, with nine at Dungeness and seven at localities along the north coast between Minnis Bay and Dartford.

# Common Guillemot
# Razorbill

*Uria aalge*
*Alca torda*

| Jan | Feb | Mar | Apr | May | Jun | Jul | Aug | Sep | Oct | Nov | Dec |
|-----|-----|-----|-----|-----|-----|-----|-----|-----|-----|-----|-----|

**Winter visitors and passage migrants**

The offshore movements of distant large auks inevitably restrict specific identification, though both species can be seen on the sea, close to the shore on occasions, particularly in winter. When separation is possible it seems that only 7% are Razorbills. Day totals of 2,000+ have been noted off Thanet in winter, with counts of 5,000+ off Dungeness.

# Black Guillemot

*Cepphus grylle*

**Very rare vagrant**

Singles near the Goodwin Sands in November 1987 and off Reculver in September 1989. There are only seven earlier records this century. Another was present off Reculver in December 1995.

# Little Auk

*Alle alle*

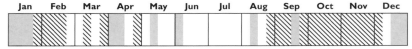

**Passsage migrant**

An oceanic species, most often appearing during severe northerly gales, which occasionally produce autumn totals of 100+ or even 200+, as in 1991. In other years only 4-5 may be seen. In the severest conditions storm-blown individuals may be found inland. There was an exceptional movement of 105 W at Dungeness on 28 December 1990. A massive influx occurred in November 1995.

Try any one of the seawatching points along the north coast, when the weather looks suitable.

# Puffin

*Fratercula arctica*

**Passage migrant**

An average annual occurrence of 15 and, like the other auks, may appear in the Thames estuary and off Thanet during northerly gales in late autumn. Regular seawatching at Dungeness may also produce occasional sightings.

# Stock Dove

*Columba oenas*

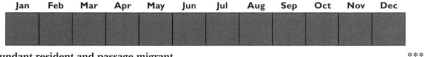

**Widespread resident** *** 

A woodland species that frequently feeds on open farmland. Flocks of several hundreds may be seen on the drained marshes of north and east Kent.

# Woodpigeon

*Columba palumbus*

**Abundant resident and passage migrant** *** 

Large flocks form in winter and in some autumns impressive movements may be observed.

# Collared Dove

*Streptopelia decaocto*

| Jan | Feb | Mar | Apr | May | Jun | Jul | Aug | Sep | Oct | Nov | Dec |
|-----|-----|-----|-----|-----|-----|-----|-----|-----|-----|-----|-----|

**Widespread resident** *** 

Flocks of 100+ form, often in association with grain stores. The highest count of 360 was at Minnis Bay in October 1992.

# Turtle Dove
*Streptopelia turtur*

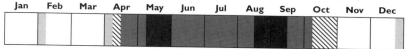

**Widespread summer visitor** \*\*\*

Visible migration in spring, involving day totals of 100+, may be witnessed along the north coast. In late August and early September flocks may build up to 100+. The highest count of 300 was at Elmley on 9 September 1985. One was seen at Ditton in late January–early February 1987, with another at St. Mary's Hoo in December 1991.

# Ring-necked Parakeet
*Psittacula krameri*

**Local resident** \*\*\*

The main population is still centred on Thanet, with roost counts of 100+ in Ramsgate cemetery. Occasionally seen at other localites throughout the county.

# Great Spotted Cuckoo
*Clamator glandarius*

**Very rare vagrant**

The second and third county records involved singles at Dungeness in July 1989 and at Sandwich Bay in March 1990. The first was at Dungeness in August 1970.

# Common Cuckoo
*Cuculus canorus*

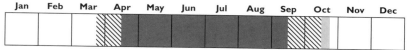

**Common summer visitor** \*\*\*

Widespread as a breeding species, using a variety of hosts. The adults usually depart in early July, when peak numbers of migrants at Dungeness may reach 15+. Singles on 24 March 1991 and 19 October 1992 are new record arrival and departure dates for Kent.

# Barn Owl
*Tyto alba*

**Resident** \*\*\*

Thinly distributed throughout the county. Most obvious when hunting towards dusk. Try the Harty Road at Capel Fleet, or the Woolpack Inn area on Walland Marsh late on a winter's afternoon.

# Little Owl

*Athene noctua*

**Resident** ***

The most widespread owl species in Kent, favouring agricultural countryside, but by no means restricted to it.

Often seen by day perched in the open, but on the edge of woodland the persistent calls of mobbing passerines may well locate this species.

# Tawny Owl

*Strix aluco*

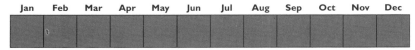

**Resident** ***

Favours mature woodland, but may frequently be heard calling in suburban districts and parkland, particularly towards dawn and at dusk.

Long-eared Owl

# Long-eared Owl

*Asio otus*

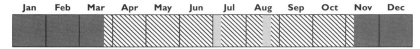

**Uncommon resident and winter visitor** ***

Thinly distributed and difficult to locate, due to its nocturnal habits. It roosts in small flocks during the winter and, once established, the same roost site may be used year after year.

Listen for its calls at dusk or towards dawn in February, from copses with a few conifers along the Downs.

# Short-eared Owl

*Asio flammeus*

**Winter visitor, occasional in summer** **

Favours the coastal marshes around the county, comparatively rare inland. A few pairs bred almost annually from 1989-94. In late autumn it is fascinating to watch migrants arriving off the North Sea. In good winters groups of up to 10 can sometimes be seen hunting together on Sheppey.

# Nightjar

*Caprimulgus europaeus*

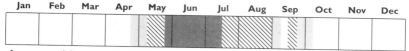

**Local summer visitor** ***

Survey work in 1992 revealed a healthy population of 85 males churring at 19 different sites. The majority were in chestnut coppice, though young conifer plantations, planted as a result of the great storm in October 1987 were also favoured.

Try Mereworth Woods, King's Wood, Challock Forest or Bedgebury towards dusk in June.

# White-throated Needletail

*Hirundapus caudacutus*

**Very rare vagrant**

One at Wierton Hill, Maidstone in May 1991 is the only county record.

# Common Swift

*Apus apus*

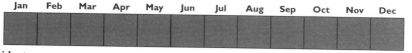

**Abundant summer visitor** ***

Peak numbers show weeks when counts of 2,000+ have been noted in three or more years. Spectacular gatherings associated with thundery weather may occasionally be witnessed, when they are attracted by insects that have become concentrated in localised air currents.

# Alpine Swift

*Apus melba*

**Scarce vagrant**

On three occasions two were seen together, but the majority of the almost annual records were of single birds. All were coastal, with 12 between Dungeness and St. Margaret's, and 16 between Sandwich Bay and Whitstable.

# Common Kingfisher

*Alcedo atthis*

**Resident** ***

Well distributed along the major river valleys and their tributaries. The dispersal of young birds in autumn produces a few coastal records, with some remaining to winter.

# Blue-cheeked Bee-eater

*Merops superciliosus*

**Very rare vagrant**

One at Church Hougham, Dover in July 1989 is the only county record.

## European Bee-eater

*Merops apiaster*

| Jan | Feb | Mar | Apr | May | Jun | Jul | Aug | Sep | Oct | Nov | Dec |
|---|---|---|---|---|---|---|---|---|---|---|---|

**Rare vagrant**

Singles at Dungeness in 1986 were the first since 1981. There were then 1–3 records annually until 1993, with 10 in 1991 which may have included the same flock of 4–5 on several dates between 14 and 27 July. A flock of six at Deal in June 1987 was the largest group, but over 60% of the 25 records involved singles. Apart from five at Cliffe and four at Walderslade in July and August 1991, all sightings were along the coast, between Dungeness and Thanet.

## Roller

*Coracias garrulus*

**Very rare vagrant**

The fifth county record this century was one at Monkton, Thanet in June 1992; this was the first since 1980.

## Hoopoe

*Upupa epops*

| Jan | Feb | Mar | Apr | May | Jun | Jul | Aug | Sep | Oct | Nov | Dec |
|---|---|---|---|---|---|---|---|---|---|---|---|

**Annual passage migrant**

An average of six per year, recorded in widespread localities. One overwintered in 1984-85, but was killed by a cat in early March!

## Wryneck

*Jynx torquilla*

| Jan | Feb | Mar | Apr | May | Jun | Jul | Aug | Sep | Oct | Nov | Dec |
|---|---|---|---|---|---|---|---|---|---|---|---|

**Annual passage migrant**

An average of 17 per year, with 25% in spring. The majority of records are coastal, but inland records are well distributed across the county.

To see this fascinating bird, visit coastal sites around Thanet, or the bird observatories, when conditions are suitable for falls of Scandinavian autumn migrants – a northeasterly air flow is a vital component.

## Green Woodpecker

*Picus viridis*

| Jan | Feb | Mar | Apr | May | Jun | Jul | Aug | Sep | Oct | Nov | Dec |
|---|---|---|---|---|---|---|---|---|---|---|---|

**Widespread resident**     ***

A bird of mature, deciduous woodland and parks, with areas of short grass where it can feed on ants.

# Great Spotted Woodpecker

*Dendrocopos major*

| Jan | Feb | Mar | Apr | May | Jun | Jul | Aug | Sep | Oct | Nov | Dec |
|-----|-----|-----|-----|-----|-----|-----|-----|-----|-----|-----|-----|

**Widespread resident**      ***

Commonly associated with mature trees, it is generally absent as a breeding species from the county's lowland marshes. In winter it can be attracted to bird feeders. Occasionally, in autumn, continental migrants may occur on the coast, but the dispersal of Kentish bred birds probably accounts for most isolated sightings.

# Lesser Spotted Woodpecker

*Dendrocopos minor*

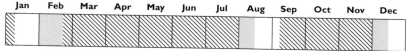

| Jan | Feb | Mar | Apr | May | Jun | Jul | Aug | Sep | Oct | Nov | Dec |
|-----|-----|-----|-----|-----|-----|-----|-----|-----|-----|-----|-----|

**Resident**      ***

The least common of the three woodpeckers, but widespread in mature woodland. Often associated with old alders and birches.

# Short-toed Lark

*Calandrella brachydactyla*

**Very rare vagrant**

The second to fifth county records involved singles at Sandwich Bay in September 1986, Foreness in May 1987, Dungeness in May 1993 and Cliffe in November 1994. The first Kent record was at Dungeness in July 1984.

# Woodlark

*Lullula arborea*

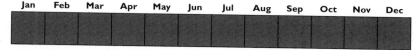

| Jan | Feb | Mar | Apr | May | Jun | Jul | Aug | Sep | Oct | Nov | Dec |
|-----|-----|-----|-----|-----|-----|-----|-----|-----|-----|-----|-----|

**Passage migrant and summer visitor**      **

The great storm of 1987 brought a welcome change to this species' status by effectively creating suitable breeding habitat. Several pairs bred annually at one site between 1992 and 94. The numbers on autumn passage have increased to around 15 per year, with occasional parties of 3–7. Try Dungeness in October.

# Skylark

*Alauda arvensis*

| Jan | Feb | Mar | Apr | May | Jun | Jul | Aug | Sep | Oct | Nov | Dec |
|-----|-----|-----|-----|-----|-----|-----|-----|-----|-----|-----|-----|

**Resident, passage migrant and winter visitor**      ***

Large diurnal movements may be witnessed at coastal sites, particularly during October. Severe weather may also cause southwesterly cold weather movements. Large feeding flocks form in the winter months.

## Shore Lark
*Eremophila alpestris*

| Jan | Feb | Mar | Apr | May | Jun | Jul | Aug | Sep | Oct | Nov | Dec |
|-----|-----|-----|-----|-----|-----|-----|-----|-----|-----|-----|-----|

**Almost annual passage migrant and winter visitor**

Numbers fluctuated from none to 20 birds in any one year, with the majority of records involving just 1–2 birds, mostly on passage. Up to eight were present at Shellness in December 1986, with seven at both Shellness and Minnis Bay the previous December. There was an exceptional record of one at Tunbridge Wells rubbish tip in February 1991.

## Sand Martin
*Riparia riparia*

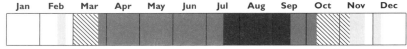

| Jan | Feb | Mar | Apr | May | Jun | Jul | Aug | Sep | Oct | Nov | Dec |
|-----|-----|-----|-----|-----|-----|-----|-----|-----|-----|-----|-----|

**Summer visitor and passage migrant** \*\*\*

Breeding colonies are mainly associated with sand and gravel workings along the greensand belt. From late July large roosts of several thousands may be seen frequenting reedbeds, for example at Stodmarsh or Cliffe. There was a peak count of 15,000 going to roost on Grain in mid-September 1993. Migration day totals sometimes involve several thousands, with 10,000 at Dungeness in late August 1989.

## Barn Swallow
*Hirundo rustica*

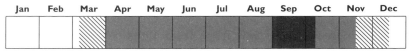

| Jan | Feb | Mar | Apr | May | Jun | Jul | Aug | Sep | Oct | Nov | Dec |
|-----|-----|-----|-----|-----|-----|-----|-----|-----|-----|-----|-----|

**Widespread summer visitor and passage migrant** \*\*\*

In autumn large diurnal movements may be observed, particularly around the coast, involving day totals of up to 20,000-30,000, with an exceptional 48,000 W at Reculver in mid-September 1991. Reedbed roosts may also involve several thousands.

## Red-rumped Swallow
*Hirundo daurica*

| Jan | Feb | Mar | Apr | May | Jun | Jul | Aug | Sep | Oct | Nov | Dec |
|-----|-----|-----|-----|-----|-----|-----|-----|-----|-----|-----|-----|

**Rare vagrant**

Sixteen records in seven years, all singles apart from two at Dungeness in April 1990. The favoured sites are the Stour Valley, with four records, and Dungeness and Thanet, both with three. There was also one at Bough Beech in April 1988. The rest were all coastal sightings from Abbot's Cliff round to Grain.

# House Martin

*Delichon urbica*

**Widespread summer visitor and passage migrant** ***

Large diurnal movements involving 20,000+ birds in a day are almost annual, but in 1988 there were exceptional estimates of 100,000 W at Foreness on 11 September and 127,000 W at Reculver the next day – a county record.

# Richard's Pipit

*Anthus novaeseelandiae*

**Scarce annual passage migrant**

Of 41 records just two were in spring and almost 60% were at Sandwich Bay and Thanet. The rest were around the coast from Dungeness to Swalecliffe, across to Elmley and Kingsnorth in the Medway, and along the Thames to Higham and Dartford.

# Blyth's Pipit

*Anthus godlewskii*

**Very rare vagrant**

One at the South Swale Reserve in November–December 1994 is the only Kent record.

# Tawny Pipit

*Anthus campestris*

**Scarce annual passage migrant**

In contrast to Richard's Pipit, 30% of the records were in spring, between Folkestone and Sheppey. In autumn 40% were at Dungeness, with the rest around the coast as far as the Medway.

# Olive-backed Pipit

*Anthus hodgsoni*

**Very rare vagrant**

Four Kent records, with the first at Lydd in October 1986 and another at Sandwich Bay in October 1988. An injured bird, seen caged in 1991, was apparently found on the Hoo Peninsula, possibly in late autumn 1987. Another was present at Capel-le-Ferne in October 1992.

# Tree Pipit

*Anthus trivialis*

**Summer visitor and passage migrant** ***

A thinly spread breeding species, favouring coppiced woodland which provides suitable open areas for nesting and scattered, solitary trees as song posts.

## Meadow Pipit

Anthus pratensis

**Resident and passage migrant**　　　　　　　　　　　　　　　　　***

Widespread in a variety of habitats during the winter. Favours coastal marshlands during the breeding season, although a few pairs breed inland.

## Red-throated Pipit

Anthus cervinus

**Very rare vagrant**

Singles at St. Margaret's Bay in June and Dungeness in October 1985, at St. Margaret's again in October 1987, at Foreness in May 1992 and at Elmley in October 1994.

## Rock Pipit

Anthus petrosus

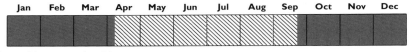

**Winter visitor, occasional in summer**　　　　　　　　　　　　　　　**

Essentially a coastal species, commonly frequenting the muddy creeks and rocky shores around north and east Kent, but relatively scarce south of Folkestone. Breeds on chalk cliffs.

Separating spring migrants of the Scandinavian race *A. p. littoralis* is difficult.

## Water Pipit

Anthus spinoletta

| Jan | Feb | Mar | Apr | May | Jun | Jul | Aug | Sep | Oct | Nov | Dec |
|-----|-----|-----|-----|-----|-----|-----|-----|-----|-----|-----|-----|

**Winter visitor and passage migrant**

Thinly distributed, with the majority of winter records from the Stour and Little Stour valleys. Spring migrants tend to be more widespread.

## Yellow Wagtail

Motacilla flava

| Jan | Feb | Mar | Apr | May | Jun | Jul | Aug | Sep | Oct | Nov | Dec |
|-----|-----|-----|-----|-----|-----|-----|-----|-----|-----|-----|-----|

**Summer visitor and passage migrant**　　　　　　　　　　　　　　　***

The breeding race, *M. f. flavissima*, is commonly seen on the coastal lowlands, but a few pairs breed at inland localities, along river valleys, or at gravel pits. More widespread on autumn passage when roosts of 300+ may be found in reedbeds.

Various other races can be distinguished, but the problem of hybrids causes considerable identification hazards. The Blue-headed Wagtail *M. f. flava* occurs annually on spring migration and does interbreed with the Yellow. A few birds showing the characteristics of Grey-headed Wagtail *M. f. thunbergi* also occur each spring. The taxonomy of Yellow Wagtails is a complex, but fascinating subject .

Yellow Wagtail

# Grey Wagtail
*Motacilla cinerea*

| Jan | Feb | Mar | Apr | May | Jun | Jul | Aug | Sep | Oct | Nov | Dec |
|-----|-----|-----|-----|-----|-----|-----|-----|-----|-----|-----|-----|
|     |     |     |     |     |     |     |     |     |     |     |     |

**Resident**                                                                    ***

Prefers fast flowing waterways, but is attracted to weirs and waterfalls on slower streams. In autumn, migrants occur on the coast, while in winter this species can be expected in more widespread localities, including sewage farms and gravel pits.

# Pied Wagtail
*Motacilla alba*

| Jan | Feb | Mar | Apr | May | Jun | Jul | Aug | Sep | Oct | Nov | Dec |
|-----|-----|-----|-----|-----|-----|-----|-----|-----|-----|-----|-----|
|     |     |     |     |     |     |     |     |     |     |     |     |

**Widespread resident**                                                         ***

Frequently forms roosts of 300+ birds, often in reedbeds, but sometimes favouring warmer zones created by man, such as greenhouses or industrial estates.

The Continental race, the White Wagtail *M. a. alba*, occurs regularly in spring, but is often more difficult to identify in autumn.

# Waxwing
*Bombycilla garrulus*

| Jan | Feb | Mar | Apr | May | Jun | Jul | Aug | Sep | Oct | Nov | Dec |
|-----|-----|-----|-----|-----|-----|-----|-----|-----|-----|-----|-----|
|     |     |     |     |     |     |     |     |     |     |     |     |

**Occasional winter visitor and passage migrant**

Ones and twos occur almost annually. A sizeable influx occurred in October–November 1988, when about 100 birds arrived, but only a few overwintered.

There was a large irruption in early 1996.

# Dipper
*Cinclus cinclus*

**Very rare vagrant**

In 1988 one was present along the Loose stream, Maidstone in March, with a second near Chilham between March and May. One wintered in Brockhill Park, Hythe during January – March 1989. In November 1993, one seen briefly along the River Stour at Sandwich may possibly have been the same bird that wintered near Kearsney Abbey, Dover from late December 1993 to March 1994.

All those seen well were of the Continental 'Black-bellied' race *C. c. cinclus*. The British race has never been recorded in Kent.

# Wren

*Troglodytes troglodytes*

**Abundant resident**                                                          ***

A widespread and extremely vocal species.

# Dunnock

*Prunella modularis*

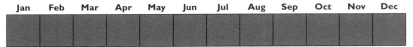

**Abundant resident**                                                          ***

Increased coastal records in autumn indicate arrivals of continental migrants from farther north, but our Kentish birds are fairly sedentary.

# Robin

*Erithacus rubecula*

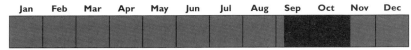

**Abundant resident and winter visitor**                                       ***

Marked falls of this species may be evident along the coast in autumn, when optimum weather conditions bring Scandinavian migrants across the North Sea.

# Thrush Nightingale

*Luscinia luscinia*

**Very rare spring vagrant**

The second and third Kent records concern singles heard singing and seen at Dungeness and Sandwich Bay in May 1988. The fourth was trapped at Dungeness in May 1989, with two more there in May and June 1994.

The first was trapped at Sandwich Bay in August 1968.

# Common Nightingale

*Luscinia megarhynchos*

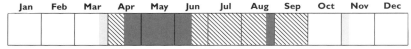

**Summer visitor and passage migrant**                                         ***

The largest concentrations of breeding birds are in the lower Medway valley and on the Hoo Peninsula, in the southern Weald and in the Canterbury 'ring-woods'. The Common Nightingale favours coppice woodland and other broad-leaved woodland supporting dense undergrowth. When not singing they are difficult to locate, hence the paucity of late summer and autumn records. Exceptionally, two were seen on 23 October 1990, one remaining until 1 November and found dead the next day, the latest record.

# Bluethroat

*Luscinia svecica*

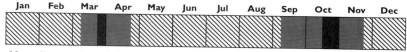

**Rare passage migrant**

There were 15 records between 1985 and 1989, but only three between 1990 and 1994. A skulking species that is easily overlooked and in the past most records have been at the two bird observatories. In this period there were eight at Foreness, and only three at Sandwich Bay and two at Dungeness, with two at Reculver and singles at Dover, Cliffe and Sevenoaks.

# Black Redstart

*Phoenicurus ochruros*

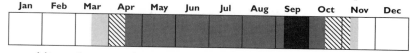

**Local breeding species, winter visitor and passage migrant**     ***

A predominantly coastal species in Kent, although it may be seen in widespread localities on migration. The majority of breeding records are associated with old buildings or industrial sites, such as power stations.

Visit Dungeness during migration peaks, preferably in spring.

# Common Redstart

*Phoenicurus phoenicurus*

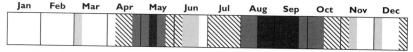

**Summer visitor and passage migrant**     ***

The small breeding population is found in two main localities, which may hold a total of up to five pairs. Spring passage is generally light, but in autumn it can be more widespread and heavy, particularly when falls of Scandinavian migrants are involved.

Common Redstarts favour old timber for nesting, and prefer open, mixed woodland. Try Knole Park in May–June, when the males are still in good plumage.

# Whinchat

*Saxicola rubetra*

**Passage migrant**

Autumn passage is generally more marked than spring, with falls around the coast and regular sightings at inland localities. One overwintered at Seasalter in 1989-90 and another remained through December 1994.

Stonechat

# Stonechat                                      *Saxicola torquata*

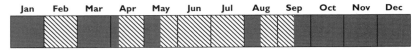

| Jan | Feb | Mar | Apr | May | Jun | Jul | Aug | Sep | Oct | Nov | Dec |

**Local breeding species and winter visitor**                    **

A few pairs breed around the coast in most years. Since the great storm of 1987, which created some open, almost heathland-like habitat, a few pairs have bred at inland localities.

The first Kentish Siberian Stonechat *S. t. maura/stejnegeri* was identified at Dungeness in November 1986. Since then five more have been seen, twice at both Dungeness and Foreness, and once at St. Margaret's.

# Northern Wheatear                              *Oenanthe oenanthe*

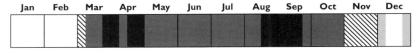

| Jan | Feb | Mar | Apr | May | Jun | Jul | Aug | Sep | Oct | Nov | Dec |

**Summer visitor and passage migrant**                           ***

Up to 20 pairs breed regularly at Dungeness, with just one or two pairs occasionally at other sites. On migration may be expected in widespread localities, with large falls around the coast, occasionally reaching 100+ at one site in both spring and autumn. Exceptionally there were 200 at Foreness on 26 August 1987.

Look for larger birds of the Greenland race *O. o. leucorhoa* in May.

# Pied Wheatear                                  *Oenanthe pleschanka*

**Very rare autumn vagrant**

The first county record was one at Reculver in October 1986, with further singles at Foreness in November 1987 and at Sheerness, Sheppey in October 1994.

# Black-eared Wheatear                           *Oenanthe hispanica*

**Very rare vagrant**

The second and third Kent records involved singles at Bewl Water in May 1988 and at Dungeness in May 1992.

The first record was of two on Dengemarsh in May 1974.

# Desert Wheatear

*Oenanthe deserti*

**Very rare vagrant**

The first county record was one at St. Margaret's in April 1989, with a second at nearby Langdon Bay in November 1991.

# Ring Ouzel

*Turdus torquatus*

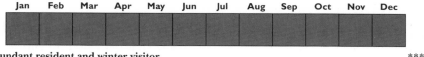

**Annual passage migrant**

Occasionally seen in widespread localities across the county, but most often concentrated around the coast. The highest spring falls involved 53 and 55 birds at Foreness on 16 April 1988 and 23 April 1989 respectively. However, the largest numbers usually occur in October. One of the heaviest falls was on 7 October 1992, when 50+ were seen at Aycliffe, 66 at St. Margaret's and 80 at Dungeness. In some years the spring passage may be heavier than the autumn.

# Blackbird

*Turdus merula*

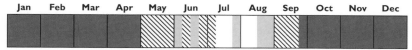

**Abundant resident and winter visitor**                                                ***

Winter numbers are increased by the arrival of continental migrants from late September to November.

# Black-throated Thrush

*Turdus ruficollis*

**Very rare vagrant**

One on Dengemarsh in May 1993 is the only county record.

# Fieldfare

*Turdus pilaris*

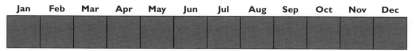

**Widespread winter visitor and passage migrant**

The main arrival normally takes place in October, but large movements, involving several thousand birds, may also be witnessed in November. Numbers increase again on the return passage during March and early April. Daily roost movements may be a feature of the winter months.

# Song Thrush

*Turdus philomelos*

| Jan | Feb | Mar | Apr | May | Jun | Jul | Aug | Sep | Oct | Nov | Dec |
|-----|-----|-----|-----|-----|-----|-----|-----|-----|-----|-----|-----|

**Abundant resident and winter visitor**                                                ***

Winter numbers are increased with the arrival of continental migrants from late September to November.

# Redwing
## *Turdus iliacus*

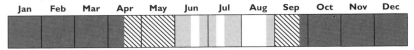

**Widespread winter visitor and passage migrant**

Large diurnal movements, involving day totals of up to 9,000 birds, may be witnessed in October–November, but listen for the long *tseeep* call-note from nocturnal migrants. In mild winters, roost counts may involve up to 3,000 birds, but at other times spectacular cold-weather movements may be witnessed. On 4 January 1985, at Dungeness, 20,000 flew W. Numbers increase again on return migration in March, when day totals of up to 8,000 have been recorded. Breeding was recorded in several years just before 1985.


# Mistle Thrush
## *Turdus viscivorus*

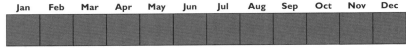

**Abundant resident**                                                                ***

In the summer months, family parties may occasionally form post-breeding flocks of 50+.


# Cetti's Warbler
## *Cettia cetti*

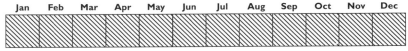

**Local resident and passage migrant**                                               **

The severe winter of 1984/85 wiped out the Stour Valley breeding population and that of 1986/87 did the same in the Medway Valley. Numbers have built up slowly since, with a wide scattering of records, particularly in 1994, when there were reports from at least nine localities; breeding is not yet well established again.

Listen for its explosive, unmistakable song from suitably wet habitat. A walk round the Abbey Mead gravel pit at New Hythe might be rewarding.


# Grasshopper Warbler
## *Locustella naevia*

**Summer visitor and passage migrant**                                               **

Numbers declined during the ten years, with the majority of records in east Kent. A skulking species, often located by its reeling song, hence the paucity of late summer and autumn records.

# Savi's Warbler
### *Locustella luscinioides*

| Jan | Feb | Mar | Apr | May | Jun | Jul | Aug | Sep | Oct | Nov | Dec |
|-----|-----|-----|-----|-----|-----|-----|-----|-----|-----|-----|-----|

**Very local summer visitor** **

The Savi's Warbler is barely maintaining its breeding status in Kent, but the Stour Valley is the favoured locality. Listen for the reeling song from the reedbeds or sallows, but beware of confusion with the very similar, though higher pitched, more mechanical and often more prolonged reeling of the previous species – which may also sing from sallows.

# Aquatic Warbler
### *Acrocephalus paludicola*

| Jan | Feb | Mar | Apr | May | Jun | Jul | Aug | Sep | Oct | Nov | Dec |
|-----|-----|-----|-----|-----|-----|-----|-----|-----|-----|-----|-----|

**Very rare vagrant**

Seven records from six different sites. Regular bird ringing has produced two at Stodmarsh.

# Sedge Warbler
### *Acrocephalus schoenobaenus*

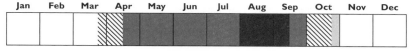

**Locally numerous summer visitor and passage migrant** ***

Breeds commonly on the coastal marshlands and in the Stour Valley reedbeds, with smaller numbers at other suitable inland localities. More widespread on autumn passage.

# Marsh Warbler
### *Acrocephalus palustris*

| Jan | Feb | Mar | Apr | May | Jun | Jul | Aug | Sep | Oct | Nov | Dec |
|-----|-----|-----|-----|-----|-----|-----|-----|-----|-----|-----|-----|

**Local summer visitor and passage migrant** ***

An important British breeding population is present in east Kent, favouring sites with willowherb. Most easily located by its mimetic song.

# Reed Warbler
### *Acrocephalus scirpaceus*

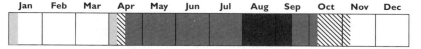

**Locally numerous summer visitor and passage migrant** ***

Wherever *Phragmites* reedbeds occur, this species can be expected. Where a large population exists, it may move into nearby, drier vegetation to breed. One trapped at Sturry on 1 January 1987 was the first winter record for Kent.

On migration this species is not restricted to reedbeds. When seen in bushes well away from water, it frequently causes identification problems.

# Great Reed Warbler
## *Acrocephalus arundinaceus*

**Very rare spring visitor**

One at St. Mary's Marsh, Hoo in May 1992 was followed the next spring by one near the Dungeness RSPB Reserve in early May and another on Elmley RSPB Reserve in May–June. In 1994 there was a similar pattern, with one at Dungeness in May and another at Elmley in June. These are the first since May 1982.


# Booted Warbler
## *Hippolais caligata*

**Very rare autumn vagrant**

The second to fifth Kent records involved singles at Dungeness in September 1987, at Pegwell village in September 1988, at North Foreland and on the Isle of Grain in September 1993 and at Minnis Bay in September 1994. The first was at Foreness in October 1984.


# Icterine Warbler
## *Hippolais icterina*

| Jan | Feb | Mar | Apr | May | Jun | Jul | Aug | Sep | Oct | Nov | Dec |
|---|---|---|---|---|---|---|---|---|---|---|---|

**Scarce passage migrant**

Nearly 80% of the records were at three sites – Dungeness, Sandwich Bay and Thanet. Apart from one at Stodmarsh, the rest were also coastal, including five between Warden Point and Allhallows.


# Melodious Warbler
## *Hippolais polyglotta*

| Jan | Feb | Mar | Apr | May | Jun | Jul | Aug | Sep | Oct | Nov | Dec |
|---|---|---|---|---|---|---|---|---|---|---|---|

**Rare passage migrant**

The 17 records comprised nine at Dungeness, three each at Sandwich Bay and on Thanet, and singles at St. Margaret's and Brenzett.


# Dartford Warbler
## *Sylvia undata*

| Jan | Feb | Mar | Apr | May | Jun | Jul | Aug | Sep | Oct | Nov | Dec |
|---|---|---|---|---|---|---|---|---|---|---|---|

**Scarce winter visitor and passage migrant**

Over half of the 50 or so records were in the Dungeness area, with 15 between Folkestone and Thanet, and eight between Minnis Bay and Grain.

The mild winters and subsequent increase in records, particularly at Dungeness, may presage breeding in the county; it is over 100 years since this species last bred. Breeding was, in fact, confirmed in 1995.

# Subalpine Warbler

*Sylvia cantillans*

**Very rare vagrant**

In May 1986 single males were seen and heard singing in Margate and at Dungeness, with another male at New Romney in April 1987, while in 1988 there were females at Dungeness in April and Reculver in May. Two more singles followed, both on 30 April on Dengemarsh, in 1993 and 1994, bringing the county total to ten.

# Sardinian Warbler

*Sylvia melanocephala*

**Very rare spring vagrant**

The second and third county records concern singles at Sandwich Bay in June 1988 and at Dungeness in May 1993. The first was at Dungeness in April 1973.

# Desert Warbler

*Sylvia nana*

**Very rare vagrant**

One near Seasalter in November 1991 is the only county record.

# Barred Warbler

*Sylvia nisoria*

| Jan | Feb | Mar | Apr | May | Jun | Jul | Aug | Sep | Oct | Nov | Dec |
|-----|-----|-----|-----|-----|-----|-----|-----|-----|-----|-----|-----|

**Rare passage migrant**

The 26 records comprised ten at Dungeness, five between Minnis Bay and Bishopstone and three at both Sandwich Bay and on Thanet. It was not recorded every year during the period.

# Lesser Whitethroat

*Sylvia curruca*

| Jan | Feb | Mar | Apr | May | Jun | Jul | Aug | Sep | Oct | Nov | Dec |
|-----|-----|-----|-----|-----|-----|-----|-----|-----|-----|-----|-----|

**Summer visitor and passage migrant**                                    \*\*\*

One at Sandwich Bay on 3 April 1985 was the earliest county record, while another overwintered at Sevenoaks Weald in 1992-93. Autumn day totals of 50-100 are noted almost annually at regularly watched coastal sites.

Common Whitethroat
DAB

## Common Whitethroat

*Sylvia communis*

| Jan | Feb | Mar | Apr | May | Jun | Jul | Aug | Sep | Oct | Nov | Dec |
|-----|-----|-----|-----|-----|-----|-----|-----|-----|-----|-----|-----|

**Summer visitor and passage migrant** ***

Following the population collapse in 1969, the Whitethroat is again well distributed in Kent, favouring more open habitat than the previous species. Good falls of migrants occur more often in autumn than in spring, although on 29 April 1989 a widespread fall included 98 at Minnis Bay, 60 at St. Margaret's, 30 at Dungeness and 22 at Sandwich Bay. The highest autumn counts were in 1992, with 100 at St. Margaret's on 9 August and 150 at Dungeness on 14 September.

## Garden Warbler

*Sylvia borin*

| Jan | Feb | Mar | Apr | May | Jun | Jul | Aug | Sep | Oct | Nov | Dec |
|-----|-----|-----|-----|-----|-----|-----|-----|-----|-----|-----|-----|

**Summer visitor and passage migrant** ***

Widespread, but less common than the next species. Its English name is misleading, as it favours coppice, or open woodland, with dense scrub. Coastal falls rarely exceed 25 at any one locality, though there were 60 at Dungeness on 15 May 1985.

## Blackcap

*Sylvia atricapilla*

| Jan | Feb | Mar | Apr | May | Jun | Jul | Aug | Sep | Oct | Nov | Dec |
|-----|-----|-----|-----|-----|-----|-----|-----|-----|-----|-----|-----|

**Summer visitor, passage migrant, regular in winter** ***

Widespread and, compared with the previous species, more commonly found in parks and suburbs where enough tall trees with undergrowth occur. The increasing numbers that are overwintering are primarily continental breeding birds and they may occasionally be seen feeding at bird tables. Spring falls rarely exceed 30, but autumn numbers can be impressive with 290 at Sandwich Bay in September 1991 and exceptional counts of 500 at St. Margaret's in September 1992 and 600 there the following September.

## Greenish Warbler

*Phylloscopus trochiloides*

| Jan | Feb | Mar | Apr | May | Jun | Jul | Aug | Sep | Oct | Nov | Dec |
|-----|-----|-----|-----|-----|-----|-----|-----|-----|-----|-----|-----|

**Very rare vagrant**

Almost annual since 1989. Two were present during the latter half of June 1993 near Capel-le-Ferne and three singles occurred at St. Margaret's, with two at Dungeness and others at Kingsgate, Reculver and Bishopstone.

# Pallas's Warbler
*Phylloscopus proregulus*

| Jan | Feb | Mar | Apr | May | Jun | Jul | Aug | Sep | Oct | Nov | Dec |
|-----|-----|-----|-----|-----|-----|-----|-----|-----|-----|-----|-----|

**Scarce autumn vagrant**

Six in 1985 followed by none the next year, then annual records of 1–5 until a remarkable 18 in 1994, which increased the annual average to four. Of the 42 birds, in a short six-week period of autumn, 15 were at Dungeness (10 in 1994), eight each at Sandwich Bay and Thanet, and five at St. Margaret's. One at Stodmarsh was the only inland record, and there were three between Minnis Bay and Bishopstone and two on Sheppey.

# Yellow-browed Warbler
*Phylloscopus inornatus*

| Jan | Feb | Mar | Apr | May | Jun | Jul | Aug | Sep | Oct | Nov | Dec |
|-----|-----|-----|-----|-----|-----|-----|-----|-----|-----|-----|-----|

**Annual autumn vagrant**

Up to 1984 there had been 83 in Kent in total. In 1985 there were 61 in a single season, with subsequent totals ranging from just eight in 1993 to 97 in 1988, averaging 35 a year. The vast majority are coastal, with a few in the Stour Valley and one well inland at Goose Green, Tonbridge.

# Radde's Warbler
*Phylloscopus schwarzi*

| Jan | Feb | Mar | Apr | May | Jun | Jul | Aug | Sep | Oct | Nov | Dec |
|-----|-----|-----|-----|-----|-----|-----|-----|-----|-----|-----|-----|

**Very rare autumn vagrant**

The third county record, one at Dungeness in October 1989, was followed by further singles at Sandwich Bay, Dungeness and Kingsgate, with two at St. Margaret's, bringing the Kent total to eight.

# Dusky Warbler
*Phylloscopus fuscatus*

| Jan | Feb | Mar | Apr | May | Jun | Jul | Aug | Sep | Oct | Nov | Dec |
|-----|-----|-----|-----|-----|-----|-----|-----|-----|-----|-----|-----|

**Very rare autumn vagrant**

An exceptional five in 1987, with singles in five other years, brings the county total to 16. The distribution of the recent ten records involved two each at Dungeness, Sandwich Bay, Thanet and Minnis Bay, with singles at St. Margaret's and Bishopstone.

# Bonelli's Warbler
*Phylloscopus bonelli*

**Very rare vagrant**

Five singles, at St. Margaret's in April 1987, Reculver in October 1988, Dungeness in September 1989, Grain in August 1990 and Minnis Bay in October–November 1991, bring the Kent total to 11.

## Wood Warbler                    *Phylloscopus sibilatrix*

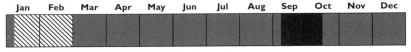

| Jan | Feb | Mar | Apr | May | Jun | Jul | Aug | Sep | Oct | Nov | Dec |

**Passage migrant and summer visitor**                    **\*\***

Regular on spring and autumn passage, but this species is now a rare breeding species in Kent. Mature oak woods, with open glades and birch are favoured. Try Church Wood RSPB Reserve in May.

## Chiffchaff                    *Phylloscopus collybita*

| Jan | Feb | Mar | Apr | May | Jun | Jul | Aug | Sep | Oct | Nov | Dec |

**Summer visitor, passage migrant, regular in winter**                    **\*\*\***

At least 50 may overwinter, often associated with damp habitats. Falls of migrants, most noticeable at coastal sites, are larger and more freqent in autumn, though there were 100+ at Minnis Bay on 2 April 1985. Autumn falls of 100+ are almost annual, but a heavy passage in 1988 included 300 at Dungeness on 18 September, with 410 at Minnis Bay on 2 October.

## Willow Warbler                    *Phylloscopus trochilus*

| Jan | Feb | Mar | Apr | May | Jun | Jul | Aug | Sep | Oct | Nov | Dec |

**Summer visitor and passage migrant**                    **\*\*\***

Marked falls of migrants may occur at coastal localities in both spring and autumn, while sudden increases inland may also be noticeable. Spring falls of 100+ are almost annual, with peaks of 400 at Dungeness in three years. Autumn falls of 100-150 are regular, but in 1985 autumn passage peaked at 1,500 at Dungeness on 18 August, and 300 at St. Margaret's.

## Goldcrest                    *Regulus regulus*

| Jan | Feb | Mar | Apr | May | Jun | Jul | Aug | Sep | Oct | Nov | Dec |

**Widespread resident and passage migrant**                    **\*\*\***

Autumn passage may involve marked falls of several hundred birds, most obvious on the coast. The relatively sparse vegetation at sites such as Shellness can come alive with these tiny migrants. Increases are sometimes noticeable inland, too. Numbers plummeted following the severe weather of February 1986 and none bred that year.

## Firecrest                    *Regulus ignicapillus*

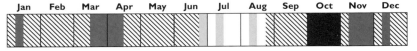

| Jan | Feb | Mar | Apr | May | Jun | Jul | Aug | Sep | Oct | Nov | Dec |

**Passage migrant, small numbers in summer and winter**                    **\*\***

In 1989, 20 wintered and nine singing males were located in summer, but there has been a decline since. Try Dungeness in October, and also for wintering birds.

# Spotted Flycatcher

*Muscicapa striata*

| Jan | Feb | Mar | Apr | May | Jun | Jul | Aug | Sep | Oct | Nov | Dec |
|-----|-----|-----|-----|-----|-----|-----|-----|-----|-----|-----|-----|

**Widespread summer visitor and passage migrant** ***

The largest falls of around 30 migrants usually occur in spring, but an exceptional fall on 13 May 1992 involved 50+ at Minnis Bay, 47 at Foreness and 33 at Sandwich Bay. One at Darenth on 17 March 1990 is the earliest record in Kent.

# Red-breasted Flycatcher

*Ficedula parva*

| Jan | Feb | Mar | Apr | May | Jun | Jul | Aug | Sep | Oct | Nov | Dec |
|-----|-----|-----|-----|-----|-----|-----|-----|-----|-----|-----|-----|

**Scarce passage migrant**

2–6 in all years but 1990, with a remarkable fall of four at Foreness on 30 September 1987. In autumn 12 occurred on Thanet, six at Sandwich Bay, four between Minnis Bay and Bishopstone, three on Sheppey and two at Dungeness. The one spring record was at Sandwich Bay in May 1989.

# Pied Flycatcher

*Ficedula hypoleuca*

| Jan | Feb | Mar | Apr | May | Jun | Jul | Aug | Sep | Oct | Nov | Dec |
|-----|-----|-----|-----|-----|-----|-----|-----|-----|-----|-----|-----|

**Passage migrant**

Comparatively few are seen on spring passage, but in autumn it may appear in widespread localities. Coastal falls of 40 occur on average every other year. Exceptionally there were 70 at Minnis Bay on 11 September 1989. One in Hartley Woods on 27 March 1986 is the earliest Kent record.

# Bearded Tit

*Panurus biarmicus*

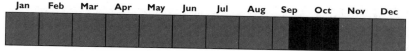

| Jan | Feb | Mar | Apr | May | Jun | Jul | Aug | Sep | Oct | Nov | Dec |
|-----|-----|-----|-----|-----|-----|-----|-----|-----|-----|-----|-----|

**Local resident and irruptive migrant** ***

Stodmarsh holds a large breeding population, but other colonies exist in smaller beds of *Phragmites*. In autumn our own birds disperse and the numbers are supplemented by the arrival of migrants which may turn up in widespread localities, some remaining to winter.

Bearded Tits

## Long-tailed Tit
### *Aegithalos caudatus*

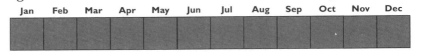

**Common resident**     ***

Forms loose flocks from late summer through the winter.


## Marsh Tit
### *Parus palustris*

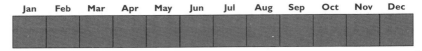

**Resident**     ***

Commonly found along the wooded North Downs.


## Willow Tit
### *Parus montanus*

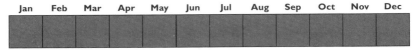

**Local resident**     ***

Thinly distributed, possibly declining. Favours damp areas, along river valleys with alder and birch, around reservoirs, or overgrown flooded gravel pits. Requires rotting timber in which to excavate its nest hole. May wander into drier areas in winter.


## Coal Tit
### *Parus ater*

**Widespread resident**     ***

This species shows a marked preference for conifers. Continental birds, with whiter head markings and greyer mantles, may be seen along the east coast in autumn.


## Blue Tit
### *Parus caeruleus*

| Jan | Feb | Mar | Apr | May | Jun | Jul | Aug | Sep | Oct | Nov | Dec |
|-----|-----|-----|-----|-----|-----|-----|-----|-----|-----|-----|-----|

**Common resident**     ***

Autumn flocks may be augmented by migrants from the Continent and small falls may be witnessed around the coast from late September to October.

# Great Tit

*Parus major*

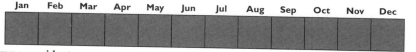

| Jan | Feb | Mar | Apr | May | Jun | Jul | Aug | Sep | Oct | Nov | Dec |

**Common resident**          ***

Small groups of continental migrants may be seen around the coast in late autumn.

# Nuthatch

*Sitta europaea*

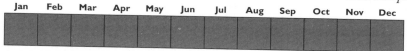

| Jan | Feb | Mar | Apr | May | Jun | Jul | Aug | Sep | Oct | Nov | Dec |

**Locally common resident**       ***

Favours suitably mature deciduous woodland and parkland, particularly with beeches. Most easily located by its distinctive calls and song.

# Common Treecreeper

*Certhia familiaris*

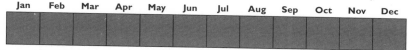

| Jan | Feb | Mar | Apr | May | Jun | Jul | Aug | Sep | Oct | Nov | Dec |

**Widespread resident**       ***

Familiarity with the thin call-note and high-pitched song is important in locating this inconspicuous bird.

# Short-toed Treecreeper

*Certhia brachydactyla*

| Jan | Feb | Mar | Apr | May | Jun | Jul | Aug | Sep | Oct | Nov | Dec |

**Very rare vagrant**

The eight records between 1988 and 1994 comprised four at Dungeness, two at Sandwich Bay and one each at St. Margaret's and Reculver.

The majority of British records have been in Kent, since the first in September 1969, but it is still a very rare vagrant.

# Penduline Tit

*Remiz pendulinus*

| Jan | Feb | Mar | Apr | May | Jun | Jul | Aug | Sep | Oct | Nov | Dec |

**Rare vagrant**

The 15 records in seven years comprised ten at Dungeness, three in the Stour Valleys and two at Sandwich Bay. All were singles, apart from two at Sandwich Bay in October 1991 and three at Dungeness in November 1993.

Only five other records since the first in Kent in 1980, but could this species soon colonise Kent?

# Golden Oriole

*Oriolus oriolus*

| Jan | Feb | Mar | Apr | May | Jun | Jul | Aug | Sep | Oct | Nov | Dec |
|-----|-----|-----|-----|-----|-----|-----|-----|-----|-----|-----|-----|

**Passage migrant and annual visitor in very small numbers** *

An average of 17 per year. Most often seen on migration at coastal sites such as Dungeness and Sandwich Bay, but occurs in widespread localities throughout the county.

# Isabelline Shrike

*Lanius isabellinus*

**Very rare autumn vagrant**

Four records in Kent, with the first at Sandwich Bay in October 1988. Remarkably, a second individual was at Stodmarsh in November 1988. Singles were also at North Foreland in October 1991 and at Worth in October–November 1993.

# Red-backed Shrike

*Lanius collurio*

| Jan | Feb | Mar | Apr | May | Jun | Jul | Aug | Sep | Oct | Nov | Dec |
|-----|-----|-----|-----|-----|-----|-----|-----|-----|-----|-----|-----|

**Annual passage migrant**

An average of ten records per year, with 30% in spring. The majority of spring and autumn migrants occur at Dungeness and around the coast from Abbot's Cliff to Bishopstone, although a few occasionally appear inland, more often in spring.

# Lesser Grey Shrike

*Lanius minor*

**Very rare vagrant**

One at Sandwich Bay in August 1994. There are just five previous Kent records, the most recent being in 1980. There was another record in August 1995, at St. Margarets.

# Great Grey Shrike

*Lanius excubitor*

| Jan | Feb | Mar | Apr | May | Jun | Jul | Aug | Sep | Oct | Nov | Dec |
|-----|-----|-----|-----|-----|-----|-----|-----|-----|-----|-----|-----|

**Winter visitor and passage migrant**

An average of six birds per year. Autumn migrants may be expected around the east coast. However, wintering birds may turn up in widespread localities, often returning to the same site year after year, although their winter territories may be extensive.

# Woodchat Shrike

*Lanius senator*

**Very rare passage migrant**

Singles at Cliffe in May 1986, Lydd in April 1987, Brockhill Park in May 1991 and at Dungeness in June and August 1993.

Woodchat Shrike

# Jay

*Garrulus glandarius*

| Jan | Feb | Mar | Apr | May | Jun | Jul | Aug | Sep | Oct | Nov | Dec |
|-----|-----|-----|-----|-----|-----|-----|-----|-----|-----|-----|-----|

**Resident and passage migrant**        ***

A few coastal migrants are seen almost annually. One irruptive movement, along the north and east coast in October 1993, included peaks of 135 SW at St. Margaret's and 40 W at Foreness.

# Magpie

*Pica pica*

| Jan | Feb | Mar | Apr | May | Jun | Jul | Aug | Sep | Oct | Nov | Dec |
|-----|-----|-----|-----|-----|-----|-----|-----|-----|-----|-----|-----|

**Increasingly common resident**        ***

May form sizeable flocks in the winter. There were 120 on Whitstable Downs in December 1993.

# Nutcracker

*Nucifraga caryocatactes*

**Very rare vagrant**

One at Northward Hill in October 1985. Apart from the unprecedented influx of 1968, there have been very few records.

# Jackdaw

*Corvus monedula*

| Jan | Feb | Mar | Apr | May | Jun | Jul | Aug | Sep | Oct | Nov | Dec |
|-----|-----|-----|-----|-----|-----|-----|-----|-----|-----|-----|-----|
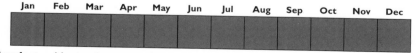

**Abundant resident and passage migrant**        ***

Flocks of several hundreds form during the winter and may often be seen in mixed corvid flocks. Westerly movements along the coast in autumn may involve continental birds.

# Rook

*Corvus frugilegus*

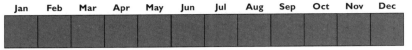

**Widespread resident**      \*\*\*

Large flocks gather for feeding and roosting. Some rookeries may contain as many as 200 nests.

# Carrion Crow

*Corvus corone*

**Widespread resident**      \*\*\*

Although generally more solitary than the Rook, flocks of 100-200 may gather to feed at rubbish dumps, and estimates of 300+ may roost together.

# Hooded Crow

*Corvus corone cornix*

**Occasional winter visitor and passage migrant**

An average of ten per year during 1985-89, with five per year from 1990-95. The vast majority of sightings were around the coast, with a few individuals remaining for several weeks.

# Raven

*Corvus corax*

**Possible vagrant**

Singles at Dungeness in May 1987 and May 1990, Minnis Bay in September 1991, North Foreland in April 1994 and Herne in June 1994.

The origins of these birds remain a mystery, as the Raven in northern Europe is essentially a sedentary bird. There have been reintroductions in Belgium and The Netherlands in recent years.

# Common Starling

*Sturnus vulgaris*

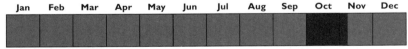

**Abundant resident, passage migrant and winter visitor**      \*\*\*

In autumn, westerly movements of 10,000-20,000 may be witnessed at coastal sites, particularly in the north and east. Winter roosts can also provide spectacular sights, akthough numbers are decreasing.

# Rose-coloured Starling

*Sturnus roseus*

**Very rare vagrant**

Single adults at Biddenden in May 1990 and at Aylesford in March–April 1994.

# House Sparrow

*Passer domesticus*

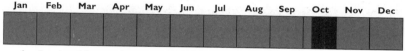

**Abundant resident** ***

An adaptable, opportunist feeder and flocks of 1,000+ may be seen, particularly among cereal crops, both before and after harvest. Similar numbers may be seen roosting in dense hedgerows.

# Tree Sparrow

*Passer montanus*

**Decreasing local resident and passage migrant** ***

There has been a decline in the breeding population, with a complete absence from localities where formerly common. Diurnal passage involves day totals of 100-200 along the coast most autumns. Similar numbers form winter flocks, wherever food is readily available.

# Red-eyed Vireo

*Vireo olivaceus*

**Very rare vagrant**

The second Kent record concerns one at Dungeness on 7 October 1986. The first was also at Dungeness between 3 and 10 October 1984.

# Chaffinch

*Fringilla coelebs*

**Widespread resident, passage migrant and winter visitor** ***

Winter flocks may be augmented by continental migrants. Diurnal passage in autumn may involve day totals of 4,000-5,000, with 1,000+ occasionally in spring.

# Brambling

*Fringilla montifringilla*

**Winter visitor and passage migrant**

Numbers vary considerably from year to year, but winter flocks rarely exceed 150. Diurnal autumn movements frequently involve 100+ birds, with rare peaks of 400+. In spring 100+ is relatively unusual. Although beech mast is one of the favoured foods, Bramblings may frequently join mixed finch flocks in stubble and other seedy habitats. Get to know the distinctive call-notes to locate them among migrant Chaffinch flocks, or flying to roost – for example at Bedgebury.

# Serin                                                    *Serinus serinus*

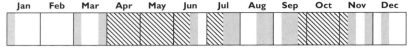

| Jan | Feb | Mar | Apr | May | Jun | Jul | Aug | Sep | Oct | Nov | Dec |

**Annual passage migrant**

An average of 15 per year, but an exceptional total of 30+ in 1993 and 20+ in 1994. One wintered in Ramsgate from January to April 1994. Virtually all records were coastal, with nearly 50% at Dungeness and 27% on Thanet.

# Greenfinch                                               *Carduelis chloris*

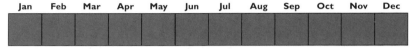

| Jan | Feb | Mar | Apr | May | Jun | Jul | Aug | Sep | Oct | Nov | Dec |

**Widespread resident and passage migrant**                          ***

The availability of food determines the size and distribution of winter flocks, which may occasionally involve 500+. Post-breeding flocks sometimes build up to 1,000. Day totals on diurnal passage in autumn may exceed 500 in mid-October, but only rarely reach 1,000.

# Goldfinch                                                *Carduelis carduelis*

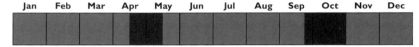

| Jan | Feb | Mar | Apr | May | Jun | Jul | Aug | Sep | Oct | Nov | Dec |

**Widespread resident**                                              ***

Spring passage occasionally involves day totals of 1,000+ flying W along the north coast. Flocks feeding on thistles are typical in autumn, when diurnal movements of 1,000+ are almost annual, but there was a peak of 5,000 at Dungeness on 19 October 1988. In hard winters very few remain, but those that do may often be found feeding in alders.

# Siskin                                                   *Carduelis spinus*

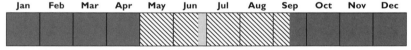

| Jan | Feb | Mar | Apr | May | Jun | Jul | Aug | Sep | Oct | Nov | Dec |

**Winter visitor and passage migrant, occasional in summer**         **

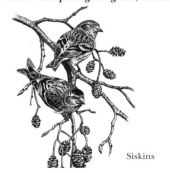

Wintering flocks of 100+ occur most years, with 250+ being unusual. Spring passage is usually light. One or two pairs bred in three years. The autumn passage of 1993 set new records, with bird/day totals at Dungeness and St. Margaret's exceeding 4,500 and 4,000 and a peak of 700+. An earlier heavy autumn passage in 1991 produced peaks of 1,000+ at Dungeness and nearly 900 at St. Margaret's on successive days. In winter, check any damp habitat with alders.

Siskins

# Linnet
## *Carduelis cannabina*

| Jan | Feb | Mar | Apr | May | Jun | Jul | Aug | Sep | Oct | Nov | Dec |

**Widespread resident and passage migrant**                    \*\*\*

Post breeding flocks of 1,000+ may be seen feeding on grass seeds, but winter flocks usually number a few hundred, most often around the coast. In hard winters Linnets may be scarce, even absent from inland localities. Day totals on autumn passage regularly exceed 1,000.

# Twite
## *Carduelis flavirostris*

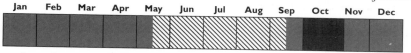

| Jan | Feb | Mar | Apr | May | Jun | Jul | Aug | Sep | Oct | Nov | Dec |

**Decreasing winter visitor**

Favours the coastal marshes in north Kent and Sandwich Bay, often feeding on the saltings with Linnets. Very rarely seen inland. Flocks of 50 are scarce, but Stoke Ooze remains a favoured locality.

# Common Redpoll
## *Carduelis flammea*

| Jan | Feb | Mar | Apr | May | Jun | Jul | Aug | Sep | Oct | Nov | Dec |

**Decreasing resident and passage migrant**                    \*\*\*

Up to 300 wintered in Church Wood, Blean in 1990/91, but winter flocks of 100+ are more usual. The breeding population is declining and recent autumn passages have rarely produced day totals of 100+.

The larger, greyer Mealy Redpoll *C. f. flammea* occurs most years, usually in late autumn and early spring.

# Arctic Redpoll
## *Carduelis hornemanni*

**Very rare vagrant**

The third county record concerns four different individuals that were identified among some 300 Redpolls in Church Wood, Blean during February–March 1991.

# Two-barred Crossbill
## *Loxia leucoptera*

**Very rare vagrant**

In October–November 1990 two in Bedgebury Pinetum were the first to be recorded in Kent. Another, or one of the two from Bedgebury, was present at nearby Round Green in March–April 1991.

# Common Crossbill

*Loxia curvirostra*

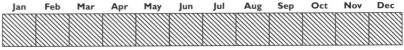

| Jan | Feb | Mar | Apr | May | Jun | Jul | Aug | Sep | Oct | Nov | Dec |

**An irruptive species**                                                                     *

In a typical invasion year, numbers build up from July onwards, with a few remaining to breed the following spring. Irruptive influxes were noted in 1985, 1990 and 1993. Flocks of up to 30 were noted intermittently throughout 1986 and early 1987, when one pair bred. In other years there may only be occasional reports of 1–4. Check conifer plantations, particularly larch, and listen for their distinctive call-notes.

# Parrot Crossbill

*Loxia pytyopsittacus*

**Very rare vagrant**

One at Sandwich Bay in October 1990 is the only county record.

# Common Rosefinch

*Carpodacus erythrinus*

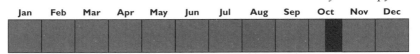

| Jan | Feb | Mar | Apr | May | Jun | Jul | Aug | Sep | Oct | Nov | Dec |

**Rare vagrant**

Singles annually in 1987-90 and 2–3 in 1992-94. Apart from an adult male in song at Lullingstone in June 1992 and another at Stodmarsh the following June, the nine birds were all coastal, with four at Dungeness and singles at Folkestone, Port Regis, Minnis Bay, Swalecliffe and Shellness.

# Bullfinch

*Pyrrhula pyrrhula*

| Jan | Feb | Mar | Apr | May | Jun | Jul | Aug | Sep | Oct | Nov | Dec |

**Widespread resident**                                                                 ***

Small flocks may be seen in winter. A small coastal movement is noted most years, with an exceptional total of 107 NE at St. Margaret's in October 1987. A few days earlier 32 flew S at Foreness.

# Hawfinch

*Coccothraustes coccothraustes*

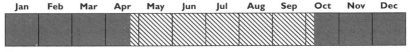

| Jan | Feb | Mar | Apr | May | Jun | Jul | Aug | Sep | Oct | Nov | Dec |

**Resident**                                                                            ***

Forms regular winter roosts, the best known of which is in Bedgebury Pinetum, where they use cypress trees. Counts there have fallen from 140 in 1985 to 30+ in 1994. Breeding populations have disappeared from other localities, which also indicates that this species is declining in Kent.

## Golden-winged Warbler

*Vermivora chrysoptera*

**Very rare vagrant**

One at Larkfield during January–April 1989 is the only county record. To have two American passerines (see next species) wintering in Kent at the same time is quite extraordinary.

## Common Yellowthroat

*Geothlypis trichas*

**Very rare vagrant**

One at Murston during January–April 1989 is the only county record.

## Lapland Bunting

*Calcarius lapponicus*

| Jan | Feb | Mar | Apr | May | Jun | Jul | Aug | Sep | Oct | Nov | Dec |
|-----|-----|-----|-----|-----|-----|-----|-----|-----|-----|-----|-----|

**Winter visitor and passage migrant**

Numbers vary considerably from year to year, but occasionally small flocks overwinter. Very rare inland. Exceptional numbers arrived in late autumn 1985, when 220 were present, including a flock of 123 at Allhallows. A flock of 50+ returned there annually until November 1990. Since then smaller flocks have wintered at Reculver or Elmley. In 1993 few wintered, but there was a marked increase in autumn passage.

## Snow Bunting

*Plectrophenax nivalis*

| Jan | Feb | Mar | Apr | May | Jun | Jul | Aug | Sep | Oct | Nov | Dec |
|-----|-----|-----|-----|-----|-----|-----|-----|-----|-----|-----|-----|

**Winter visitor**

This species favours the shingle beaches along the Thames and Swale, round to Sandwich Bay. Very rare inland and numbers vary considerably. In November–December 1987 and 1988 there were five flocks of 30-60, but this spread of good numbers has not been noted since. However, the largest flocks of 100-130 were present at Sandwich Bay early in 1991 and 1992.

## Yellowhammer

*Emberiza citrinella*

| Jan | Feb | Mar | Apr | May | Jun | Jul | Aug | Sep | Oct | Nov | Dec |
|-----|-----|-----|-----|-----|-----|-----|-----|-----|-----|-----|-----|

**Widespread resident**                                                    \*\*\*

Like other seed-eaters, this species gathers in flocks of 100-200 in winter.

## Ortolan Bunting

*Emberiza hortulana*

| Jan | Feb | Mar | Apr | May | Jun | Jul | Aug | Sep | Oct | Nov | Dec |
|-----|-----|-----|-----|-----|-----|-----|-----|-----|-----|-----|-----|

**Rare passage migrant**

A total of 23, with 1–5 almost annually. Apart from one inland at Wierton Hill, Maidstone in August 1991, all were coastal. Five of the seven spring birds occurred at Foreness, the other two at Dungeness. The autumn coastal distribution comprises five at Dungeness, four between Minnis Bay and Bishopstone, and three each at St. Margaret's and on Thanet.

# Rustic Bunting

*Emberiza rustica*

**Very rare vagrant**

The fifth and sixth county records concern singles at Port Regis in October 1990 and the first inland Kent record at Wierton Hill, Maidstone in March 1993.

# Little Bunting

*Emberiza pusilla*

**Very rare vagrant**

The third to fifth county records concern singles at Dungeness in April 1990, Sandwich Bay in October 1991 and St. Margaret's in September 1993. These are the first since October 1956.

Reed Bunting

# Reed Bunting

*Emberiza schoeniclus*

| Jan | Feb | Mar | Apr | May | Jun | Jul | Aug | Sep | Oct | Nov | Dec |
|-----|-----|-----|-----|-----|-----|-----|-----|-----|-----|-----|-----|

**Abundant breeding species and passage migrant**          \*\*\*

Widespread in suitably damp, waterside localities, though occasionally found breeding in drier habitats. Day totals of 100+ occasionally noted on autumn passage. Similar numbers gather in winter when they may associate with other buntings and finches in mixed feeding flocks.

# Black-headed Bunting

*Emberiza melanocephala*

**Very rare vagrant**

The fourth county record was one at Dungeness in June 1987 and the fifth was in May 1993.

# Corn Bunting

*Miliaria calandra*

| Jan | Feb | Mar | Apr | May | Jun | Jul | Aug | Sep | Oct | Nov | Dec |
|-----|-----|-----|-----|-----|-----|-----|-----|-----|-----|-----|-----|

**Resident**          \*\*\*

Widespread, particularly on the coastal marshlands, but virtually absent from the Weald. In winter, the distribution is almost entirely coastal, though still well distributed across Walland and Romney Marshes, with a high roost count at Stodmarsh. In these areas roosts of up to 200 are regular, and occasionally higher.

# Appendix I

## Species on the Kent List not seen during 1985-94

* single records since 1900
** no records since 1900

Little Bittern
Snow Goose
* Black Duck
* King Eider
* Golden Eagle
* Gyr Falcon
* Baillon's Crake
Little Bustard
Great Bustard
* Cream-coloured Courser
* Semipalmated Sandpiper
Least Sandpiper
Great Snipe
Greater Yellowlegs
* Slender-billed Gull
Ivory Gull
* Royal Tern
* Sooty Tern
* Pallas's Sandgrouse

* Scops Owl
Snowy Owl
** Tengmalm's Owl
Pallid Swift
* Crested Lark
Alpine Accentor
* Rufous Bush Chat
* Red-flanked Bluetail
Rock Thrush
* Swainson's Thrush
* Moustached Warbler
* Arctic Warbler
* Collared Flycatcher
** Chough
Pine Grosbeak
* Dark-eyed Junco
Cirl Bunting
* Rock Bunting
* Yellow-breasted Bunting

# Appendix II

## Status of species recorded at Boughton Park and Wierton Hill Farm during 1985-94

| | | | |
|---|---|---|---|
| *a* | Annual | *ab* | Annual breeder |
| *o* | Occasional | *ob* | Occasional breeder |
| | (recorded in 6-9 years) | | (bred in 1-9 years) |
| *s* | Scarce – recorded in less than six years | | |
| *r* | Rare – less than five records | | |
| *v* | Very rare – one record only | | |

Little Grebe *ab*
Great Crested Grebe *sb*
Fulmar *v*
Cormorant *a*
Grey Heron *a*
Mute Swan *a*
Bewick's Swan *v*
Whooper Swan *v*
Bean Goose *v*
White-fronted Goose *r*
Greylag Goose *o*
Canada Goose *a ob*
Brent Goose *o*
Common Shelduck *s*
Mandarin *r*
Eurasian Wigeon *o*
Gadwall *o*
Common Teal *o*
Mallard *ab*
Pintail *r*
Garganey *v*
Shoveler *o*
Red-crested Pochard *v*
Common Pochard *a*
Tufted Duck *a ob*
Scaup *v*
Goldeneye *r*
Goosander *r*
Honey Buzzard *v*
Marsh Harrier *r*
Hen Harrier *r*
Montagu's Harrier *v*
Sparrowhawk *a ob*
Common Buzzard *r*
Osprey *v*
Common Kestrel *ab*
Red-footed Falcon *v*
Merlin *r*
Hobby *a*
Peregrine *r*
Red-legged Partridge *o ob*
Grey Partridge *o ob*
Quail *v*
Common Pheasant *a ob*
Water Rail *o*
Corncrake *v*

Moorhen *ab*
Coot *ab*
Oystercatcher *r*
Avocet *v*
Little Ringed Plover *aa ob*
Ringed Plover *s*
Golden Plover *a*
Grey Plover *r*
Lapwing *ob*
Little Stint *v*
Dunlin *r*
Jack Snipe *r*
Common Snipe *a*
Woodcock *o*
Bar-tailed Godwit *v*
Whimbrel *a*
Curlew *o*
Spotted Redshank *v*
Common Redshank *o*
Greenshank *a*
Green Sandpiper *a*
Common Sandpiper *a*
Turnstone *v*
Arctic Skua *v*
Mediterranean Gull *v*
Black-headed Gull *a*
Common Gull *a*
Lesser Black-backed Gull *a*
Herring Gull *a*
Great Black-backed Gull *a*
Sandwich Tern *v*
Common Tern *s*
Arctic Tern *r*
Black Tern *r*
Stock Dove *ab*
Woodpigeon *ab*
Collared Dove *a ob*
Turtle Dove *ab*
Ring-necked Parakeet *r*
Common Cuckoo *a ob*
Barn Owl *o ob*
Little Owl *ab*
Tawny Owl *a ob*
Short-eared Owl *v*
Long-eared Owl *v*
White-throated Needletail *v*

Common Swift *a ob*
Common Kingfisher *a*
Green Woodpecker *ab*
Great Spotted Woodpecker *ab*
Lesser Spotted Woodpecker *a ob*
Woodlark *r*
Skylark *ab*
Sand Martin *a*
Barn Swallow *ab*
House Martin *a*
Tree Pipit *a*
Meadow Pipit *a*
Yellow Wagtail *a*
Grey Wagtail *a*
Pied Wagtail *a ob*
Wren *ab*
Dunnock *ab*
Robin *ab*
Common Nightingale *o*
Black Redstart *o*
Common Redstart *s*
Whinchat *o*
Stonechat *o*
Northern Wheatear *o*
Ring Ouzel *r*
Blackbird *ab*
Fieldfare *a*
Song Thrush *ab*
Redwing *a*
Mistle Thrush *ab*
Grasshopper Warbler *r*
Sedge Warbler *o*
Marsh Warbler *v*
Reed Warbler *a ob*
Lesser Whitethroat *ab*
Common Whitethroat *a ob*
Garden Warbler *a ob*
Blackcap *ab*
Wood Warbler *o*
Chiffchaff *ab*
Willow Warbler *a ob*
Goldcrest *a ob*
Firecrest *s*
Spotted Flycatcher *ab*
Pied Flycatcher *o*
Long-tailed Tit *ab*

Marsh Tit *o ob*
Willow Tit *o ob*
Coal Tit *ab*
Blue Tit *ab*
Great Tit *ab*
Nuthatch *ab*
Common Treecreeper *ab*
Golden Oriole *s*
Great Grey Shrike *v*
Jay *a ob*
Magpie *a ob*

Jackdaw *ab*
Rook *a*
Carrion Crow *ab*
Common Starling *ab*
House Sparrow *ab*
Tree Sparrow *ab*
Chaffinch *ab*
Brambling *a*
Greenfinch *ab*
Goldfinch *ab*
Siskin *a*

Linnet *ab*
Common Redpoll *a ob*
Common Crossbill *s*
Bullfinch *ab*
Hawfinch *o*
Lapland Bunting *r*
Yellowhammer *ab*
Ortolan Bunting *v*
Rustic Bunting *v*
Reed Bunting *a ob*

# Appendix III

## Gazetteer of place names mentioned in the text

Ordnance Survey maps are essential to enable you to locate the place names mentioned in the text. Where a large area is referred to, the four-figure map reference, which pinpoints a 1 kilometre square, is usually towards the centre of that area, where the name is printed on the 1:50,000 map. Alternatively it may show the square in which the entrance lies or where the site referred to is, rather than the nearby village of the same name.

The first two figures of the grid reference show the west edge of the 1 kilometre square in which the locality lies – the figures in the north and south margins of the map. The second two figures show the south edge of the 1 kilometre square – the figures in the west and east margins of the map.

Four Landranger maps cover the vast majority of Kent: 178 – The Thames Estuary; 179 – Canterbury; 188 – Maidstone and 189 – Ashford, while 177 – East London is required for the extreme north-west of the county. These map numbers prefix the four-figure grid references.

| | | | |
|---|---|---|---|
| Abbey Mead | 178 & 188/7160 | Denge Wood | 179 & 189/0951 |
| Abbot's Cliff | 179/2738 | Detling | 188/7858 |
| Allhallows | 178/8378 | Dover | 179/3241 |
| Aylesford | 178 & 188/7259 | Dungeness Airport Pits | 189/0620 |
| Bagham | 179 & 189/0753 | Dungeness ARC Pit | 189/0619 |
| Barksore | 178/8768 | Dungeness Bird Observatory | 189/0817 |
| Bartlett Creek | 178/8269 | Dungeness Hooker's Pits | 189/0518 |
| Bedgebury Pinetum | 188/7133 | Dungeness Long Pits | 179/0818 |
| Bedgebury Forest | 188/7433 | Dungeness New Diggings | 189/0619 |
| Bewl Water | 188/6733 | Dungeness RSPB Reserve | 189/0618 |
| Birchington | 179/3069 | Eastborough Farm | 178/7776 |
| Blean Wood | 179/0860 | Eastchurch | 178/9871 |
| Botany Bay | 179/3971 | East Sutton | 188/8348 |
| Botolph's Dyke | 189/1233 | Eastwell Park | 189/0148 |
| Bough Beech Reservoir | 188/4948 | Egypt Bay | 178/7779 |
| Boughton Monchelsea | 188/7650 | Elhampark Wood | 179 & 189/1646 |
| Boughton Park | 188/7749 | Elmley Hills | 178/9267 |
| Bridge | 179/1754 | Elmley RSPB Reserve | 178/9567 |
| Broadstairs | 179/3967 | Fagg's Wood | 189/9834 |
| Brockhill Country Park | 189/1435 | Fairfield | 189/9626 |
| Brooks | 189/0217 | Ferry House Inn, Harty | 178/0165 |
| Broomfield | 188/8452 | Folkestone Harbour | 179 & 189/2335 |
| Burham Marsh | 178 & 188/7162 | Folkestone Warren | 179 & 189/2437 |
| Canterbury | 179/1457 | Fordwich | 179/1859 |
| Capel Fleet | 178/0168 | Foreness Point | 179/3871 |
| Capel Hill | 178/0069 | Funton Creek | 178/8868 |
| Capel-le-Ferne | 179/2538 | Grain | 178/8976 |
| Challock Forest | 189/0250 | Grain Refinery | 178/8774 |
| Chartham | 179/1055 | Graveney Marshes | 178 & 179/0664 |
| Chetney Marshes | 178/8969 | Gravesend | 177 & 178/6474 |
| Chilham | 179 & 189/0662 | Great Heron Wood | 189/9531 |
| Chislet Marshes | 179/2366 | Greatstone | 189/0822 |
| Church Wood RSPB Reserve | 179/1059 | Greatstone Sewage Farm | 189/0723 |
| Cliffe Pools | 178/7277 | Grove Ferry | 179/2362 |
| Cliffe Quarry | 178/7275 | Half Acre | 178/8369 |
| Conningbrook Gravel Pit | 189/0343 | Halstow Marshes | 178/7778 |
| Cooling Marshes | 178/7577 | Ham Green | 178/8469 |
| Copt Point | 179 & 189/2436 | Hamstreet Woods | 189/0033 |
| Deal | 179/3752 | Harrietsham | 189/8753 |
| Dengemarsh | 189/0518 | Harty Ferry | 178/0165 |

# Appendix IV

## Addresses of Organisations and Reserves

**British Trust for Ornithology**
National Centre for Ornithology, The Nunnery, Thetford, Norfolk IP24 2PU          01842 750050

**Church Wood RSPB Reserve**
Warden: Michael Walter, 11 Garden Close, Rough Common, Canterbury CT2 9BP          01227 462491

**Dungeness Bird Observatory**
Warden: Dave Walker, DBO, 11 RNSSS Cottages, Dungeness, Romney Marsh
TN29 9NA          01797 321309

**Dungeness RSPB Reserve**
Warden: Simon Busuttil, Boulderwall Farm, Dungeness Road, Lydd, Romney Marsh
TN29 9PN

**Elmley RSPB Reserve**
Warden: Bob Gomes, Kingshill Farm, Elmley, Sheerness, Isle of Sheppey
ME12 3RW          01795 665969

**English Nature**
South-East Region: Countryside Management Centre, Coldharbour Farm, Wye,
Ashford TN25 5DB          01233 812525

**Kent County Council**
Kent Countryside and Coast Information: Judith Roberts, Planning Department,
KCC, Springfield, Maidstone ME14 2LX          01622 696411

**Kent Ornithological Society**
Secretary: Keith Derrett, 14 Chestnut Avenue, Staplehurst TN24 9PS          01580 892220
Membership Secretary: Steve Davies, 13 Crown Lane, Bromley BR2 9PG          0181 289 0378
Recorder: Ian Hodgson, Whitgift House, Hardy Close, Canterbury CT2 8JJ          01227 784303

**Kent Trust for Nature Conservation**
Tyland Barn, Sandling, Maidstone ME14 3BD          01622 662012

**Northward Hill RSPB Reserve**
Warden: Alan Parker, RSPB office, Northward Hill Reserve, Bronhey Farm,
Eastborough, Cooling, Kent ME3 8DS          01634 222480

**Royal Society for the Protection of Birds**
The Lodge, Sandy, Bedfordshire SG19 2DL          01767 680551

**RSPB Local Members' Groups**
Canterbury: Alan Prior, 1 Lower Road, Faversham ME13 7NB          01795 534720
Gravesend: David Arnold, Painswick, Norwood Lane, Meopham DA13 0YB          01474 812582
Maidstone: Denise Morgan, 1 Somerfield Close, Maidstone ME16 8JL          01622 757340
Medway: Linda Sweeney, 30A Chalfont Drive, Rainham, Gillingham ME8 9DN          01634 372604
Sevenoaks: Julie Childs, Quornden Farm, Emmetts Lane, Ide Hill,
Sevenoaks, TN14 6BD          01732 750698
South-east Kent: Keith Shepherd, 15 Effingham Crescent, Dover CT17 9RH          01304 225757
Thanet: Stephen Blaskett, Flat 2, 36 Connaught Road, Margate CT9 5TW          01834 299212
Tonbridge: Dennis Potter, 16 Leybank, Hildenborough, Tonbridge, TN119EH          01732 833367

**Sandwich Bay Bird Observatory**
Warden: Rab Morton, SBBO, Guilford Road, Sandwich Bay, Sandwich CT13 9PF          01304 617341

**Sevenoaks Wildfowl Reserve**
Warden: John Tyler, Tadorna, Bradbourne Vale Road, Sevenoaks TN13 3DH          01732 456407

# References

Cramp, S. *et al.* 1977. *The Birds of the Western Palearctic* Vol.1. Oxford University Press, Oxford.

— 1980. *The Birds of the Western Palearctic* Vol.2. Oxford University Press, Oxford.

Davenport, D. L. 1989. Seabird Movements in Kent: Autumn 1987. *Kent Bird Report* 36: 93-97.

Gooders, J. (ed). 1974. Big Day in East Suffolk, in *The Birdwatchers' Book*. David & Charles, Newton Abbot.

Grant, P. J. & Mullarney K. 1989. *The New Approach to Identification*. Ashford.

Harris, A., Tucker, L., & Vinicombe, K .1989. *The Macmillan Field Guide to Bird Identification*. Macmillan, London and Basingstoke.

Hume, R. 1990. *Birds by Character: the Fieldguide to Jizz Identification*. Macmillan, London.

Marchant, J. H. *et al.* 1990. *Population Trends in British Breeding Birds*. BTO, Tring.

Marchant, J. H. & Balmer, D. 1994. Common Birds Census: 1992-93 index report. *BTO News* No.193.

Marchant, J. H. & Wilson, A. 1995. Common Birds Census: 1993-94 index report. *BTO News* No.198.

Oddie, B. & Tomlinson, D. 1983. *The Big Bird Race*. Collins, London.

Ogilvie, M. & Winter, S. 1989. 1st January 1982 – Kent by Don Taylor, in *Best Days with British Birds*. British Birds, Blunham.

Peach, W., Crick, H., & Marchant, J. 1995. The decline of the Willow Warbler in southern Britain. *BTO News* No.197.

Taylor, D. W. 1985. *Birdwatching in Kent*. Meresborough Books, Gillingham.

Taylor, D. W. 1992. Aggressive Blackbird grounding Little Owl. *British Birds* 85: 617-618.

Taylor, D. W. 1992. My Local Patch. *Birdwatch* 1: 18-19.

Taylor, D. W. 1994. House Sparrow x Tree Sparrow hybrids in Kent. *Dutch Birding* 16: 122-123.

Taylor, D. W. 1994a. Water Rail feeding in overhanging alder. *British Birds* 87: 624.

# Index to Systematic List

## (including Appendix I)